159

Scotch Reviewers

SCOTCH REVIEWERS

The *Edinburgh Review*, 1802-1815

JOHN CLIVE

FABER AND FABER LTD
24 Russell Square
London

First published in mcmlvii
by Faber and Faber Limited
24 Russell Square London W.C.1
Printed in Great Britain by
Western Printing Services Limited, Bristol

To My Parents *34254*

Acknowledgements

I owe special thanks to David Owen under whose direction this book, in somewhat different form, was first written as a doctoral dissertation; and to Oscar Handlin and Mark Howe for their interest and encouragement. My friends Bernard Bailyn, John T. Bethell, Charles Breunig, and Valerie Lynn provided aid and counsel at various crucial stages. Walter Jackson Bate was kind enough to read and criticize Chapter VI. For suggestions, offered in writing or in person, I am grateful to the following: J. Raymond Derby, Frank W. Fetter, Henry W. Meikle, Chester W. New, Elisabeth Schneider, and A. L. Strout. It goes without saying that any errors are mine alone.

I received every co-operation from library staffs at Harvard and Yale, as well as from those at the British Museum, the British Library of Political and Economic Science at the London School of Economics, the Birmingham Reference Library, the National Library of Scotland, and the Library of the Writers to the Signet in Edinburgh. Lady Eleanor Langman gave me her kind permission to make use of the Horner Papers. And Cyprian Blagden, permitted me to examine the business ledgers of Longmans Green and Co.

Last, but by no means least, I should like to thank Andreas F. Lowenfeld for helping with the checking of identifications, and Miss Elma S. Leavis who typed the manuscript with devotion and despatch.

J. C.

Cambridge, Mass.
December 21, 1956

Contents

Preface

John Stuart Mill recalls in his *Autobiography* that before his father launched his formidable attack on the Whig party and its chief literary organ, the *Edinburgh Review*, to appear in the first number of its Benthamite rival, the *Westminster*, he made his son, then seventeen years old, 'read through all the volumes of the Review, or as much of each as seemed of any importance . . . and make notes for him of the articles which I thought he would wish to examine, either on account of their good or their bad qualities'. Writing almost half a century later, Mill adds that in 1823 this was 'not so arduous a task . . . as it would be now'. The author of the present work on the early years of the *Edinburgh Review* (1802–1815) cannot help feeling somewhat sheepish in thus submitting the results of a task so lacking in arduousness; and can only comfort himself with the thought that, unlike his illustrious predecessor, he did not begin the study of Greek at the age of three.

The hazards of writing about periodical literature are many. One tends to take the articles too seriously, forgetting that they were often dashed off in great haste by authors more interested in supplying a manuscript on time than in standing its test. Nothing is simpler than to construct consistent systems of thought and seemingly harmonious lines of development out of the mass of available material. On the other hand, nothing is more dangerous. For almost every assertion a contradiction may be found, if the search be diligent enough. And there is not a great deal to be gained in confronting a quarterly publication with its own contradictions.

Another temptation, difficult to avoid, is that of merely presenting a summary of a few significant articles. Perhaps the best

11

way of guarding against this is to make use, wherever possible, of the correspondence of the principal contributors, of pamphlets, and of historical background material. If the dictum 'there is nothing deader than dead politics' can be applied even more forcefully to dead periodical literature, then any revivalist attempts must seek to surround the dry bones with the flesh and blood of personal context and contemporary setting.

The historian of ideas constantly exposes himself to the accusation that he can never fully demonstrate their relation to action. To the question: 'But did these ideas influence anyone, did they change anyone's mind?' he can safely reply in the affirmative. But when it comes to 'how?' and 'how many?' he becomes less confident. In theory, it should be possible to take an article in the *Edinburgh Review*, to trace the ideas it contains back to their pristine form, perhaps in the mind of some great original thinker, to study the modifications they have undergone by the time they reach the author of the article as well as those imposed by his own situation and the exigencies of periodical writing, and finally to demonstrate the effect of the article on 'public opinion'. It is at this final stage that one opens *The Diary of the Right Honourable William Windham* and finds the following entry:

'Took into room with me "Edinburgh Review": article, "Southey's Madoc". Differ with reviewers and admire it.'[1]

How many diaries and how many entries of this sort are in existence? The question is apt to lead to discouraging reflections.

Even leaving the problem of 'influence' out of consideration, there still remains the question of the extent to which periodical publications are the product of outside forces—social, political, and psychological. To complicate matters further, one finds that the *Edinburgh* reviewers were so inconsiderate of future historians as on occasion consciously to hold back their real views. Thus one of them, Francis Horner, writes to the editor, in reference to an article concerned with religion: 'What I am most anxious about, is, that I may have kept myself in the safe and honest medium, upon those ticklish subjects. I should be

---

[1] Entry for November 20, 1805, *The Diary of the Right Honourable William Windham, 1784–1810*, ed. Mrs. Henry Baring (London, 1866), 454.

sorry to have betrayed any of the scepticism, which is my real sentiment.'[1]

How, then, is one to avoid confusion and error? Perhaps it is really impossible to write about a periodical publication at all without writing a complete history not only of the life and times of its contributors—but of its readers as well! But that is hardly feasible. The *Edinburgh Review* was a sufficiently powerful 'machine' (as its only begetter, Sydney Smith, once called it) to have exerted some influence on opinion and to possess even now some intrinsic interest of its own.[2] If these chapters, based on an intensive analysis of its first fifty numbers, succeed in throwing some light on its origin, its editor and his editorial problems, and its chief contributors and their views on matters political, social and economic, literary, and historical, they will have achieved their object.

[1] Francis Horner to Francis Jeffrey, September 28, 1805, Horner Correspondence, L.S.E., II, 114.

[2] *The Edinburgh Review*, founded in 1802, stopped publication in 1929. For a brief estimate of its entire term of publication, see John Clive, '*The Edinburgh Review*, 150 Years After', *History Today*, II, No. 12 (December, 1952), 844–850.

A Note on Identification and References

Although much scholarly work has been done on the subject of identifying the authors of articles in the *Edinburgh Review*, there are still a great many articles whose authors are unknown, or where authorship is a subject of dispute. In the present work, only the four principal authors of articles during the *Review*'s early years—Jeffrey, Brougham, Horner, and Smith—are regularly identified in the footnotes. The ascriptions are based, for articles in the first twenty-five numbers, on Dr. Leroy H. Buckingham's authoritative Yale Doctoral Dissertation (unpublished): 'The Authorship of the First Twenty-five Numbers of the *Edinburgh Review* (1802–1808)', Yale University, 1938. They were checked, in each instance, against the identifications given in three important articles which appeared after this dissertation: Elisabeth Schneider, Irwin Griggs, and John D. Kern, 'Brougham's Early Contributions to the *Edinburgh Review*: A New List', *Modern Philology*, XLII (1945), 152–73; the same authors' 'Early Edinburgh Reviewers: A New List', *Modern Philology*, XLIII (1946), 192–210; and Frank W. Fetter, 'The Authorship of Economic Articles in the Edinburgh Review, 1802–1847', *The Journal of Political Economy*, LXI (1953), 232–259. For the identification of authorship in Nos. XXV through L of the *Review*, W. A. Copinger, *On the Authorship of the First Hundred Numbers of the Edinburgh Review* (Manchester, 1895), was used to supplement these three articles.[1]

[1] See Frank Whitson Fetter, 'A Probable Source of Copinger's "On the Authorship of the First Hundred Numbers of the *Edinburgh Review*"', *The Library*, Fifth Series, IX, No. 1 (March, 1954), 49–53, for the interesting speculation that a substantial part of Copinger's assignments were taken, either directly or at second hand, from the records of Longmans, Green, or that both records derive from a common source.

A Note on Identification and References

Through the kindness of Professor Elisabeth Schneider of Temple University, I have also been able to consult a copy of the so-called 'Cockburn Manuscript', a list of authors compiled by Lord Cockburn, Jeffrey's first biographer, now in the possession of the Earl of Rosebery. Dr. Buckingham made use of this for his work on the first twenty-five numbers, but I have used it also for numbers twenty-five to fifty of the *Review*.

References to articles in the *Edinburgh Review* have been abbreviated in the following fashion: Jeffrey, *ER*, I (October, 1802), *1* would refer to the fact that Francis Jeffrey was the author of the first review article in the first number of the *Edinburgh Review*. In the event of reasonable doubt about his authorship, his name would appear in parentheses. The decision as to when reasonable doubt exists is my own, based on the sources cited above. The *Edinburgh Review* was eventually published in volumes, each containing two numbers and totalling about 500 pages. But, to prevent confusion, all references in this book are to numbers rather than volumes. The date refers to the original appearance of the number.

The following abbreviations to manuscript references have been used:

Add. MS.: Additional Manuscripts in the British Museum.

Horner Correspondence, L.S.E.: Correspondence of Francis Horner presented by his grand-niece, Lady Eleanor Langman, to the British Library of Political and Economic Science at the London School of Economics. The letters are numbered and bound into volumes. Thus the reference I, 1 would refer to the first letter in Volume One.

[1]

Number One

I like this place extremely and cannot help thinking that for a literary man, by which term I mean a man who is fond of Letters, it is the most eligible situation in the island. It unites good Libraries liberally managed, learned men without any other system than that of pursuing truth, very good general society, large healthy virgins, with mild pleasing countenances and white swelling breasts—shores washed by the Sea—the romantic grandeur of antient and the beautiful regularity of modern, building, and boundless floods of oxygen.[1]

The *Edinburgh Review* first appeared in October, 1802, and must therefore be classified as a nineteenth-century phenomenon. However often it is proclaimed that centuries are artificial dividing lines, and that one must go beyond mere dates in one's search for significant watersheds, all too frequently psychological reflexes still manage to get the better of knowledge. Press the button marked '1799', and though the last two digits speak of Bonaparte and Malthus, the first two conjure up the fountains of Versailles and Mozart at his clavichord. Press the one marked '1800', and there is no keeping out railroads, embattled proletarians, and the awful vision of Victoria and her Consort.

Edinburgh at the beginning of the nineteenth century certainly retained many of those traits and institutions which had come to characterize it in the eighteenth. True, the construction of the New Town and the move there of people of wealth and fashion had, in the words of Cockburn, 'vulgarized our prescriptive gentilities', partly by putting an end to the city's peculiar housing

[1] Sydney Smith to John George Clarke, December 5, 1798, G. C. Heseltine, 'Five Letters of Sydney Smith', *London Mercury*, XXI (1930), 513–514. This is one of the few printed letters unfortunately not included in Mr. Nowell C. Smith's otherwise admirable and definitive edition of Sydney Smith's *Letters*.

arrangements, the tall 'flats' where all ranks and classes could be found living together in amity, albeit on different floors. It was also true that much of Edinburgh's great reputation as a centre of culture and learning, which had earned the city the name of 'Athens of the North' and had made it a logical choice of residence for English students such as Sydney Smith's pupil Michael Hicks-Beach, derived from the dead. The great names of David Hume and Adam Smith had already begun to pass into legend: Kames and Robertson were gone; and so was Burns who not so long ago had first demonstrated his heaven-taught virtues and vices to Edinburgh society. The 'golden age' of the mid-eighteenth century survived to a large degree in legend and reminiscence. Yet the living presence of men like the venerable Adam Ferguson and of Henry Mackenzie, 'The Man of Feeling', constituted a visible reminder of the great past. Now, as then, much of the city's social and intellectual life was given impetus by lawyers, ministers, and university professors. Now, as then, the two principal local pastimes of drinking and dancing helped to soften the rigours of intellectual exertion. Now, as then, visitors were struck by the contrast between the city's congenial society and its abominable sanitary procedures. And now, as then, Edinburgh, for all its reputation as a cultural centre, still retained many of the characteristics resulting from a provincial situation.

This situation was, to some extent, a product of physical removal from London, after the Union no less the arbiter of taste and fashion than of politics. Cockburn recalls that at the time the *Edinburgh Review* was founded, London and Edinburgh were still 2,400 miles apart, according to 'the modern rate of travelling'.[1] But provincialism meant more than mere distance from the capital. It meant, on the one hand, minds conscious of limited awareness, a sense of inferiority increased by the burden of an 'uncouth' accent which, in spite of heroic efforts to rid themselves of it, stuck to all but a few envied ones like a burr. On the other hand, it meant awareness of regional limitations, reinforced by English prejudices and taunts; and led to a compensatory local patriotism, a stress on the real or imagined

---

[1] Henry Thomas Cockburn, Lord Cockburn, *Life of Lord Jeffrey, with a Selection from his Correspondence* (Edinburgh, 1852), I, 159.

purity of native culture and tradition as against cosmopolitan sophistication, and to a justifiably strong sense of pride in Scottish economic advancement and the glories of the Scottish 'Renaissance'.[1]

The *Edinburgh Review* itself was closely bound to the great age. In all likelihood its editor, Francis Jeffrey, had watched the installation of Adam Smith as Lord Rector of Glasgow University. At the age of thirteen he had caught a brief glimpse of Burns and, some time later, had helped carry a drunken Boswell to bed, a literary linkage as dramatic as it must have been tenuous. Henry Brougham, one of the chief *Edinburgh* reviewers, had heard the great historian William Robertson, his great-uncle, deliver a famous centenary sermon on the Glorious Revolution.

In fact, two numbers of an earlier *Edinburgh Review* had appeared in 1755 and 1756, professedly devoted to an account of the books printed by Scottish presses within the six months preceding their publication. Robertson, Adam Smith, and Hugh Blair, the renowned Moderate preacher, were among the editors; and the first number created a sensation. However, it and its successor gave so much offence that 'the authors of the Review did not think themselves bound to hazard their quiet, reputation, and interest, by persevering in their attempt to improve the taste of their countrymen'.[2] Criticism came not only from those who were offended by the tone of some of the reviews of theological works (even though Hume had been excluded as a contributor 'through prudential considerations'), but also from at least one pamphleteer for whom the *Review* constituted a menace to liberty and free inquiry. This critic took exception to the anonymity of the reviewers, their censorious tone, and their presumption in undertaking to 'pronounce the fate of every work and determine the character of every author, who shall continue to appear during their fancied administration'.[3]

[1] For a fuller discussion of the problem of Scottish provincialism in the eighteenth century see John Clive and Bernard Bailyn, 'England's Cultural Provinces: Scotland and America', *The William and Mary Quarterly*, Third Series, XI (April, 1954), 200–213.

[2] Preface to 1818 ed. of *Edinburgh Review* (1755–1756), quoted in Maurice Cross, ed., *Selections from the Edinburgh Review* (Paris, 1835), I, 7.

[3] [Edward Johnston], *A View of the Edinburgh Review Pointing out the Spirit and Tendency of that Paper* (Edinburgh, 1756), 6. Also see Mary E. Craig, *The Scottish Periodical Press, 1750–1789* (Edinburgh and London, 1931), 31–32.

The example of this first *Edinburgh Review* was not lost on the guiding spirits of its namesake, though it is open to question whether it did more to inspire them by the lustre of its famous names than to caution them by the history of its quick failure. It exerted the latter effect on Jeffrey who, as Brougham later recalled, predicted that the second *Edinburgh* was doomed to suffer the fate of the first.[1]

Personal acquaintance and precedent were not the sole forces making for a sense of continuity between past and present. From the earliest days of the Scottish cultural revival after the Union with England when Edinburgh, having lost its pre-eminence as a political capital, still found itself in a unique position as Scotland's legal and ecclesiastical centre, clubs and societies had provided the principal focus not only for the city's social life, but also for the literary, philosophical, and scientific interests of its professional classes. Thus the wigmaker-poet Allan Ramsay (in 1712) had helped to found the Easy Club whose members 'met in a Society By themselves in order that by a Mutual improvement in Conversation they may become more adapted for fellowship with the politer part of mankind and Learn also from one anothers happy observations'.[2] The Rankenian Club, a philosophical society of 'learned and respectable men' (mainly lawyers and ministers) was established four years later, and soon drew the fire of a clergyman of the old Covenanting school who was disturbed by rumours that its members were convinced that 'we're in a way of too narrou [*sic*] thinking in this country'.[3] And in the 1750's the Select Society, established for the dual purpose of philosophical inquiry and improvement in public speaking, included all the Edinburgh literati, as well as many of the nobility and gentry.[4]

[1] Henry Brougham, 1st Baron Brougham and Vaux, *The Life and Times of Henry Lord Brougham, Written by Himself* (Edinburgh and London, 1871), I, 253.

[2] Andrew Gibson, *New Light on Allan Ramsay* (Edinburgh, 1927), 48.

[3] Robert Wodrow, *Analecta* (Edinburgh, 1842–1843), III, 175 (December, 1724); for membership list, undated but probably compiled in the 1720's, see Alexander Tytler, Lord Woodhouselee, *Memoirs of the Life and Writings of the Honourable Henry Home of Kames* (2nd ed., Edinburgh, 1814), III, 75–76.

[4] For membership list, see Dugald Stewart, 'Account of the Life and Writings of William Robertson, D.D.', Sir William Hamilton, ed., *The Collected Works of Dugald Stewart* (Edinburgh, 1854–1860), X, 205–207. Out of 119 members readily identifiable by profession, no fewer than 48 were lawyers or judges.

Number One

Whatever the somewhat disputed sequence of events in the actual founding of the *Edinburgh Review* may have been, it is to clubs and societies founded in this tradition that one must look for the more significant story of its background. For these supplied the essential fertile soil for co-operative literary projects such as the *Review*, social and intellectual camaraderie. Two organizations deserve to be singled out: the Academy of Physics and the Speculative Society. The Academy had come into existence in 1797 as an offshoot of the (University) Literary Society, taking as its object 'the investigation of nature, the laws by which her phenomena are regulated, and the history of opinions concerning these laws'.[1] Brougham, Horner, Jeffrey, Sydney Smith, J. A. Murray, and Thomas Brown—all to be associated with the *Edinburgh Review*—were among the members. Two extracts from its minute book are of particular interest:

Sept. 30, 1797: 'Mr. Brougham was appointed to examine Holcroft's translation of Count Stolberg's Travels, and to report the important notices.' [At the same meeting Brougham and three others were appointed to a committee which was to examine the strata of granite on the banks and in the bed of the 'Water of Leith'.]
Jan. 20, 1798: [Mr. Brougham and Mr. Horner] 'laid before the academy two papers with respect to a reform of the laws.'[2]

Thus, only a short time before the founding of the *Edinburgh Review*, its principal contributors met together in a society concerned with scientific investigations, legal reform, and what amounted to book reviewing. It may be going too far to claim, with Brown's biographer, that the Academy of Physics gave rise to the *Review*; but there is little doubt that it must have played an important part in its genesis.

The role of the Speculative Society, though perhaps less

[1] David Welsh, *Account of the Life and Writings of Thomas Brown*, M.D. (Edinburgh, 1825), 77, where a list of members may be found. Smith's name is spelled 'Smyth'.
[2] *Ibid.*, 503–504. In this connection, it is interesting to note a letter suggesting the establishment in Edinburgh of a periodical paper, 'either by the Academy or elsewhere', sent by John Leyden, another young member of the Academy, to Thomas Brown in March, 1798. Leyden's biographer concludes that Reith must have broached the subject some time in 1796 or 1797. John Reith, *Life of Dr. John Leyden* (Galashiels, 1923), 173.

immediately significant in this process, is nevertheless of special interest, since it has a bearing on the local political background of the *Edinburgh Review*. The 'Spec', as it was familiarly known, had been founded in 1764 by six Edinburgh University students, 'for improvement in Literary Composition and Public Speaking'. By the end of the century it had reached the height of its reputation as an arena for what Cockburn calls 'the exercise of the remarkable young men it excited'.[1] Jeffrey would one day recall the intellectual stimulation afforded by the debates in the Society, where 'free from scholastic restraint, and throwing off the thraldom of a somewhat servile docility, the mind first aspired to reason and question nature for itself—and half wondering at its own temerity, first ventured without a guide into the mazes of speculation, or tried its unaided flight into the regions of intellectual adventure, to revel uncontrolled through the light and boundless realms of literature and science'.[2] But what was even more remarkable about the Society was the fact that, at least for a short while, it was probably the only such organization not dominated by the cohorts of Henry Dundas.

Dundas (Boswell's 'Harry the Ninth'), greatest of all the 'managers' of Scotland, had built up his patronage power by holding in succession the offices of Lord Advocate, Treasurer of the Navy, President of the Board of Control for India, and Secretary of State for War. He reached the height of his power in association with Pitt, from 1783. The Scottish electoral system, damned with faint praise indeed by Charles James Fox who called it 'a state of representation so monstrous and absurd, so ridiculous and so revolting, that it is good for nothing except perhaps to be placed by the side of the English, in order to set off our defective system by the comparison of one still more defective',[3] enabled Dundas to exert almost unlimited power over political life north of the Tweed until the opening years of the

---

[1] Henry Thomas Cockburn, Lord Cockburn, *Memorials of his Time* (Edinburgh and London, 1910), 68.

[2] Jeffrey's speech at the seventieth anniversary of the founding of the Speculative Society. Quoted in William K. Dickson, *The History of the Speculative Society, 1764–1904* (Edinburgh, 1905), 25. Some allowance must naturally be made for a situation which called for nostalgia.

[3] In 1795. Quoted by Edward Porritt, *The Unreformed House of Commons* (London, 1909), II, 5.

nineteenth century and to carry out those machinations which, in the words of Mr. Feiling, 'could make of Scotland almost one large pocket borough'.[1]

The result was that at the turn of the century 'a country gentleman with any public principle except devotion to Henry Dundas was viewed as a wonder, or rather as a monster. This was the breed also of almost all the merchants, all our removable office-holders, and all our public corporations.'[2] The French Revolution was still the principal topic of debate and conversation. 'Everything,' Cockburn recalled, 'not this or that thing, but literally everything, was soaked in this one event.'[3]

Some years before, the war with America and its disastrous outcome had created an unaccustomed general interest in public affairs and had led to demands for county and burgh reform and to the establishment of a 'branch' of the Rockingham Whigs in Scotland under the leadership of Henry Erskine. In this fashion an end had been put to that essentially dynastic alignment of eighteenth-century Scottish parties, for which 'Hanoverian' and 'Jacobite' are terms far more relevant than Whig and Tory. Neither burgh nor county reformers had got very far—and with the coming of the French Revolution they could conveniently be branded and attacked as 'Jacobins', along with all others suspected of supporting political and economic reforms or of holding freethinking religious views. The sequence of agitation and

---

[1] Keith Feiling, *A History of England* (London, 1950), 793. The venality of the Scottish representatives achieved more than a modicum of contemporary notoriety, long before the Whig historians began their mournful chant of 'O tempora, O mores' over the century that knew not the blessedness of middle-class suffrage.

[2] Cockburn, *Memorials*, 78.

[3] *Ibid.*, 73. But Cockburn, good Whig that he was, had some stake in showing that it must have been darkest just before the dawn. To mitigate his gloomy account, it is well to keep in mind the advice Lady Malmesbury gave to Lady Minto when the latter's son Gilbert Elliot joined his friend 'Harry' Temple (later Lord Palmerston) at the University of Edinburgh in the spring of 1801: 'So Gilbert goes to Edinburgh. I am very glad, for Harry's sake and his, that they will be together, and as he is not a drunkard it is a very good plan for him. As to Jacobinism, it is all stuff everywhere. A boy of nineteen may be seduced by a fair face, or led into gaming or drinking, or racing, but nobody at that age cares about politics that is worth a farthing. It is, like the love of money, belonging to those who have exhausted or left behind them the light and cheerful pleasures of life. Mrs. Robinson says they learn mathematics but nothing else.' Lady Malmesbury to Lady Minto, May 19, 1801, Sir Gilbert Elliot-Murray-Kynynmound, 1st Earl of Minto, *Life and Letters, 1751–1806*, ed. Countess of Minto, III, 220.

repression which ended in the complete defeat of the reformers and the Friends of the French Revolution need not be recounted here.[1] But it is worth noting the extreme cruelty with which the Edinburgh 'Conventions' of 1792 and 1793 were put down. The name of Judge Braxfield has become as notorious as that of Judge Jeffreys of an earlier age, and the trials of Muir, Palmer, Margarot, and Gerrald are now chapters in the hagiology of British Radicalism.

The spirit of reaction ran high in Edinburgh, and the Whigs, many of them burgh reform veterans, suffered along with the Radicals. In January 1796 Henry Erskine was deposed from his office as Dean of the Faculty of Advocates by a majority of ninety-five, in spite of the fact that he had always refused to join the Friends of the People. The thirty-eight advocates who voted in favour of Erskine on that occasion came to constitute the nucleus of Scottish Whiggism at the turn of the century. 'Self-interest had converted some [to Dundas], and terror more; and the residue, which stood out, consisted only of the stronger-minded men of the party.'[2]

It was therefore a considerable triumph for the Whig members of the 'Spec'—including Jeffrey, Brougham, and Francis Horner—when a political crisis threatening the society in 1799 was resolved by the resignation of many of the Tory senior members.[3] A resolution of 1794 which had prohibited political debates was temporarily rescinded. This meant that there existed for a time a forum for the free exchange of political ideas, as well as a social situation in which the Whigs had gained the upper hand.

That kind of situation had become a rare thing, even in academic circles, after the French revolutionary terror had put a new premium on loyalty and conformity. The Edinburgh literati, with their close intellectual affinities to the French enlightenment, had initially welcomed the events of 1789. Dugald Stewart, the Professor of Moral Philosophy at the University. and Robertson, its Principal, were among the early enthusiasts.

[1] See Henry W. Meikle, *Scotland and the French Revolution* (Glasgow, 1912), for an excellent account.

[2] Cockburn, *Memorials*, 76.

[3] On this incident see *ibid.*, 68, and Dickson, *Speculative Society*, 12.

Number One

And the students did not lag behind their professors.[1] Yet in 1794 Stewart found it necessary to address an abject letter of apology to a nobleman who had attacked him for his friendly attitude towards the *philosophes*. 'I shall ever regret', he wrote, 'that I dishonoured some of my pages by mentioning with respect the name of Condorcet.'[2]

He remained a Whig nevertheless, 'too spotless and too retired to be openly renounced'.[3] It was his course in Political Economy that provided a further common intellectual experience for Jeffrey, Brougham, Horner, and the *Review*'s originator, Sydney Smith. His influence on their ideas, and thus on the *Edinburgh Review*, was considerable. And, representing a direct link with his own two intellectual mentors, Thomas Reid and Adam Smith, he constituted one more powerful mediating force between the heritage of eighteenth-century Scottish culture and the bright young men of a new generation.

To know that these bright young men lorded it over the Tories in the 'Spec', discussed science and legal reform in the Academy of Physics, and heard Dugald Stewart expound the intimate connection between the science of politics and the philosophy of the human mind is to come a little closer to the sort of environment from which the *Edinburgh Review* sprang.

The question still remains: Who founded the *Review* when? A detailed examination of this problem has been relegated to an appendix.[4] It is possible therefore to supply a succinct answer here: some time in the late winter of 1801–1802 Sydney Smith, the undisputed father of the *Review*, suggested the idea to Jeffrey and Horner, as they were discussing various possible literary projects. These three took a larger group, including Brougham, into their confidence, and the first number was planned in the spring and summer of 1802, with Smith and Jeffrey performing the bulk of the editorial chores. Brougham, though a contributor

[1] Thus see the debate in the University's Dialectic Society on December 10, 1791, when, on the question 'Will the Revolution of France be of more advantage than disadvantage to Europe?' the vote was unanimous in favour of the Revolution. *History of the Dialectic Society* (Edinburgh, 1887), 1.

[2] Dugald Stewart to Lord Craig, February 20, 1794, *Works*, X, lxxiv.

[3] Cockburn, *Memorials*, 78.

[4] See *post*, 'The Founding of the *Edinburgh Review*', pp. 186–197. What appears in this chapter is, in part, a summary of the conclusions reached in that appendix, where supporting evidence may be found.

to the first number which appeared on October 10, 1802, was not admitted into the 'inner circle' until the following year. Jeffrey became sole editor in May, 1803, but the inner circle—Smith, Horner, and Brougham—continued to be his closest and most influential editorial advisers. The motto finally adopted was *Judex damnatur cum nocens absolvitur* from Publius Syrus, which was chosen by the grave Horner after Sydney Smith's proposed *Tenui musam meditamur avena*—'We cultivate literature upon a little oatmeal'—had been found too near the truth to be admitted.

And indeed it was. For the founders of the *Edinburgh Review* were as poor as they were bright. They were young, though their respective ages—Smith thirty-one, Jeffrey twenty-nine, Brougham and Horner twenty-four—call for a fairly broad interpretation of the word 'youth'.[1] Three of them were lawyers. In embarking upon this literary project they followed that tradition of the intimate connection between literature and the law so characteristic of Scottish cultural history in the eighteenth century. Jeffrey, son of a Deputy Clerk in the Court of Session, had attended Glasgow University, then Queen's College, Oxford. He was called to the Scottish Bar in 1794, six years before Francis Horner. Horner, son of a merchant, grandson of a Writer to the Signet, had previously been a student at Edinburgh University and had succeeded in losing his Scottish accent at an English parsonage—unlike Jeffrey who never quite succeeded in doing the same. Brougham, like Horner, was called to the Bar in 1800, after study at the University of Edinburgh. He had already established a reputation for brilliance, having had two of his papers on scientific subjects read before the Royal Society and published in its *Transactions*. The Rev. Sydney Smith had come to Edinburgh as tutor to young Michael Hicks-Beach in 1797, three years after his ordination in the Church of England, which followed Winchester and New College, Oxford. His life in what he was later to call that 'energetic and unfragrant city' was taken up with his not too arduous tutorial duties and an occasional sermon.

[1] Brougham is included here not as one of the original projectors—he was not—but as the most powerful and voluminous contributor during the *Review*'s early years.

Number One

None of the four was satisfied with his lot at the time the *Review* was founded. All of them had time on their hands, and stood in need of diversion. Indeed, though the *Review* was to bring renewed cultural glory and repute to the city of its origin, it might never have been begun had its projectors not shared a feeling of discontent with their professional life in Edinburgh. In 1799 Jeffrey wrote to his brother: 'One is quite buried here, among a great crowd of men of decent ambition, and moderate expectation, and it is almost necessary that some great man, or some great accident, should pull you out of it, before you can come into any kind of desirable notice.'[1] No such man or accident seemed to appear. Little more than a year later he expressed vague thoughts of going to India in some capacity and, early in 1801, toyed with the rather odd alternative of either becoming a West Indian trader or establishing himself as an expert on Oriental literature.[2] In July of that same year Sydney Smith expressed the hope that Jeffrey might find a situation as lecturer in India.[3]

The legal profession at the turn of the century no longer constituted enough of a source of income or advancement for able and ambitious men on the wrong side of the political fence. The Edinburgh Bar as a whole was predominantly Tory.[4] And 'such was the servility of the public mind at that time that it was not considered safe to trust a Whig lawyer with the management of a case, from the supposed prejudices of the Judges against their holding those opinions'.[5] In England Fox led his unhappy few to hibernation in the comfort of their country houses. In Edinburgh the young Whig lawyers lounged year after year at a particular place at the north end of the law courts, occasionally employed, but never enough to make them feel that they were in fair professional competition.[6] Thus in March, 1802, shortly after plans for the first number of the *Edinburgh Review* had got under

[1] Francis to John Jeffrey, March 4, 1799, Cockburn, *Life of Jeffrey*, II, 37.

[2] Francis Jeffrey to Robert Morehead, July 6, 1800, *ibid.*, II, 44–45; to John Jeffrey, January 3, 1801, *ibid.*, II, 51.

[3] Sydney Smith to Francis Jeffrey, June, 1801, Nowell C. Smith, ed., *The Letters of Sydney Smith* (Oxford, 1953), I, 64.

[4] See Porritt, *Unreformed House of Commons*, II, 169, for an account of Dundas's special interest in lawyers as county electors.

[5] Lady Mary Richardson, ed., *Autobiography of Mrs. Fletcher* (Boston, 1876), 369.

[6] Cockburn, *Memorials*, 136.

way, Jeffrey wrote as follows to his friend James Grahame in Glasgow, asking for work:

'. . . Both Jardine and you are incapacitated by recent matrimony, I take it, for engaging in anything of the kind [i.e. circuit cases] and as the circuit is a good deal earlier than usual, some of the other regular attendants may perhaps be thrown out. . . . If you can get any [illegible] little case for me it will be a good work.'

The letter ends with a humble apology for having requested such a favour; which seems to indicate the necessity for the request.[1]

Brougham was no happier with his professional situation. Late in 1800 he wrote to Sir Joseph Banks that his aversion to the law as an ultimate profession had not abated, '. . . not to mention that it exposes one to the worst part of party politics, and that to succeed in it requires almost as much interest as to rise in the diplomatic line'.[2] By August, 1802, he was still so discontented with all the prospects in Edinburgh that he considered entering the army, a step he called the last resource and only for incurables.[3] Horner, too, expressed his dissatisfaction with his situation. 'Though I become daily more attached to law as a study,' he wrote in 1801, 'I become daily more averse to the practice of the Scots Court.'[4] And Sydney Smith, much as he loved Edinburgh society and scenery, had by then made up his mind that he must tear himself away—presumably because his prospects were better south of the Tweed.[5]

Thus it was partly because the professional life of its projectors neither fully occupied nor satisfied them that they were able to invest time and enthusiasm in a project which, to them, appeared to promise amusement and diversion. For if the *Edinburgh* began a revolution in periodical reviewing, then Jeffrey, Smith, and Horner were revolutionaries in spite of themselves.

---

[1] Francis Jeffrey to James Grahame, March 23, 1802, National Library of Scotland, MS. 3519, folio 11.

[2] Brougham to Bankes, December 10, 1800, *Life and Times*, I, 228.

[3] Brougham to James Loch, August 20, 1802, R. H. M. Buddle Atkinson and G. A. Jackson, *Brougham and his Early Friends* (London, 1908), I, 344.

[4] Horner's 'Journal', November 23, 1801, Leonard Horner, ed., *Memoirs and Correspondence of Francis Horner, M.P.* (London, 1843), I, 173.

[5] Sydney Smith to Francis Jeffrey, August 1, 1801, *Smith Letters*, I, 65.

Number One

To them the *Review*, while they were planning its first number was, at best, a *jeu d'esprit*. Perhaps one is not too far off the mark in comparing them to the ringleaders of some daring undergraduate prank, suddenly confronted with the experience that its execution, so blithely planned and acceded to in who knows what alcoholic or tea-sodden haze, involves hard work and difficult problems.

Jeffrey who, according to Brougham's account,[1] did not even display a great deal of initial enthusiasm, remained pessimistic all along. Thus he wrote in May of 1802:

'Our Review has been postponed till September and I am afraid will not go on with much spirit even then. Perhaps we have omitted the tide that was in our favour. We are bound for a year to the booksellers, and shall drag through that, I suppose, for our own indemnification; but I foresee the likelihood of our being all scattered before another year shall be over, and, of course, the impossibility of going on on the footing upon which we have begun.'[2]

Smith was undoubtedly the most sanguine of the original group; though, according to Jeffrey's retrospective account, he proved a most timid co-editor who demanded that editorial meetings take place secretly in a dingy room of Willison's printing-office, in Craig's Close, 'to which he insisted on our repairing singly, and by back-approaches or different lanes,'— lest the incognito of the planners be uncovered.[3] Horner regarded the *Review* as 'a matter of temporary amusement and subordinate occupation';[4] and Brougham, who for a time quit the entire project in April 1802, looked upon the articles which he finally contributed to the first number as 'little better than waste of time'.[5]

Neither he nor anyone else could have foreseen the effect created by that first number when it made its appearance, after

---

[1] *Life and Times*, I, 252.

[2] Francis Jeffrey to Robert Morehead, May 24, 1802, Cockburn, *Life of Jeffrey*, II, 63–64.

[3] Jeffrey's account as quoted in *Chambers's Cyclopedia of English Literature* (4th rev. ed., London and Edinburgh, 1893), II, 385.

[4] Horner to James Loch, December 12, 1802, *Memoirs and Correspondence*, I, 212.

[5] Brougham to James Loch, August 20, 1802, *Brougham and his Early Friends*, I, 345–346.

various postponements, on October 10, 1802, in an edition of seven hundred and fifty copies, at five shillings per copy.[1] 'The truth is,' Brougham himself was to write more than sixty years after the event, 'the most sanguine among us, even Smith himself, could not have foreseen the greatness of the first triumph, any more than we could have imagined the long and successful career the Review was afterwards to run, or the vast reforms and improvements in all our institutions, social as well as political, it was destined to effect.'[2] Mrs. Archibald Fletcher who, as hostess and confidante, played the part of a sort of 'poor man's Lady Holland' for the young Edinburgh Whigs at the start of the century,[3] speaks of the 'electrical effects' of the first *Review* on the 'public mind'.[4] And Cockburn writes that 'it is impossible for those who did not live at the time, and in the heart of the scene, to feel, or almost to understand, the impression made by the new luminary, or the anxieties with which its motions were observed'.[5]

Sales figures are perhaps more impressive than testimonials coloured by the roseate hues of nostalgic reminiscence. By November 7, 1802, a second edition of seven hundred and fifty copies was in the press;[6] and within another year 2,150 copies of the first number had been sold in Edinburgh alone.[7] The

---

[1] I am accepting the date mentioned in the *Edinburgh Review*'s centennial issue, CCCCII (October, 1902), 279. Horner actually wrote John Allen that the first number was not to appear until November 1. *Memoirs and Correspondence*, I, 201. One of the people who couldn't afford the *Review* at the price was Thomas Chalmers, later famous as preacher and theologian. See his letter to Archibald Constable, October 1, 1803, quoted in Thomas Constable, *Archibald Constable and his Literary Correspondents* (Edinburgh, 1873), I, 53.   [2] *Life and Times*, I, 253.
[3] See entry for April 27, 1838, in George Ticknor, *Life, Letters, and Journals* (Boston and New York, 1909), II, 163. He drove out to see Mrs. Fletcher, 'around whom, in the early days of the *Edinburgh Review*, Brougham, Jeffrey, and all that clique were gathered and whose talents still command their admiration and regard'.
[4] *Autobiography of Mrs. Fletcher*, 82.   [5] Cockburn, *Life of Jeffrey*, I, 131.
[6] Horner to James Loch, November 7, 1802, *Memoirs and Correspondence*, I, 204. See also Brougham to Loch on the same day, *Brougham and his Early Friends*, I, 363–364.
[7] Brougham to James Loch, December 12, 1803, *Brougham and his Early Friends*, II, 102. Brougham, citing a report made over a month previously, states that sales figures for the later numbers at that time were: No. II, 2,000; No. III, 1,900; No. IV, 1,770; No. V, 862. He points out that these figures probably underestimated total sales, since two to three hundred copies of each number were not accounted for. He adds that a new edition of the first four numbers is in the press as he is writing.

city's population then numbered around one hundred thousand. While it is hard to estimate the proportion of that number literate enough to want to read the *Review* and affluent enough to purchase it, a circulation of over two thousand certainly represented an impressive figure. One has only to keep in mind Burke's estimate, made in the 1790's, of the total English reading public as some eighty thousand, located mostly in London.[1]

What accounts for the unexpectedly striking impact of the first number? To answer this question requires a brief look backwards at the state of English periodical reviewing in the eighteenth century.[2] During this period the review had gradually assumed a position as a periodical distinct from the magazine—the latter mainly devoted to literary and antiquarian learning, miscellaneous essays, and poetry, the former to what at first amounted to mere abstracts of all the latest works on politics, literature, science, and art.[3] The emphasis on abstracts lasted, in varying degrees, throughout the century. It marked the first years of the *Monthly Review* (from 1749) which, with its principal rival, the *Critical Review* (from 1756), dominated the field. Nevertheless, the very fact that the *Critical* was established under Tory and Church patronage to combat the air of liberality displayed by the *Monthly* shows that politics and partisanship entered into book reviewing at an early date. Furthermore, the end of the century saw an increasing awareness that abstracts were not enough. In 1788 Joseph Johnson, a Radical publisher, founded the *Analytical Review* which, presumably to no one's surprise, undertook to follow an 'analytical plan' in its articles; and by the late 1790's the *Monthly*, under the influence of William Taylor of Norwich, one of its contributors, was publishing a certain amount of 'philosophical criticism' that went

[1] Quoted in Arthur S. Collins, *The Profession of Letters: A Study of the Relation of Author to Patron, Publisher, and Public* (London, 1928), 29.

[2] What follows is in the main based on the standard work dealing with this subject, Walter Graham, *English Literary Periodicals* (New York, 1930), 209–238 and *passim*.

[3] The suggestion has been made that the very earliest such series of abstracts published in Britain, entitled *Historical Account of Books and Transactions in the Learned World*, appeared in Edinburgh in 1688, some months before the first English review. *Notes and Queries*, Second Series, II (September 20, 1856), 227.

far beyond mere summary.¹ Other able men were engaged in reviewing by the turn of the century: Southey, Parr, Mackintosh. But they as well as the scores of hacks and penny-a-liners were completely dependent on the mercy of editors in their turn dependent on booksellers who financed the reviews in order to advertise the books they printed and sold. This meant that praise and blame were almost invariably bestowed on the basis of commercial rather than literary criteria. The venality that inevitably resulted put book reviewing as a profession into such bad odour that those who thought themselves gentlemen took it up only as a last resort, and then only after taking great precautions to hide their having done so.

This undoubtedly accounts for the fact that the first three numbers of the *Edinburgh Review* were 'all gentlemen, and no pay';² and that great care was taken (without total success) to preserve the anonymity of the reviewers.³ Archibald Constable, the Edinburgh publisher who had already undertaken the publication of the *Farmer's Almanac* (1800) and the *Scots Magazine* (1801), put up the money for the first three numbers.⁴ Departing

¹ Hazlitt saw the origin of the *Edinburgh Review*'s critical style in a series of articles written by Taylor in 1796 for the *Monthly Review*. See William Hazlitt, *The Spirit of the Age, or Contemporary Portraits*, ed. W. Carew Hazlitt (4th ed., London and New York, 1894), 241. Cockburn, *Life of Jeffrey*, I, 114, states that Jeffrey was an occasional contributor to the *Monthly Review*, in 1799. But the MS. notes of its editor, Griffiths, record June, 1802 as the first date of publication of an article by Jeffrey. D. Nichol Smith, ed., *Jeffrey's Literary Criticism* (London, 1910), ix. Crabb Robinson felt that Horace Walpole's *Letters* served as the stylistic model for the *Edinburgh* reviewers. Edith Morley, ed., *Henry Crabb Robinson on Books and Their Writers* (London, 1938), I, 229.

² The phrase is Cockburn's, in *Life of Jeffrey*, I, 133.

³ See letter to T. N. Longman after seeing an early copy of the first number of the *Edinburgh Review*: 'It is written (without pay) by some young men (whose names I have down, tho' they are pretended to be secret) of very great abilities.' Quoted in centenary issue of the *Review*, CCCCII (October, 1902). 279 The first London advertisement of the *Edinburgh Review* appeared in the *Monthly Magazine*, XV (April, 1803), 258. It named Smith, Brougham, Jaffray [*sic*], and Thomas Brown as 'the critics who have thus undertaken to direct the taste of their countrymen'. But the authorship of individual articles was kept a secret from the start. In a pamphlet probably written by Jeffrey in 1804 he noted 'the small number of persons who are in possession of the secret'. *Observations on Mr. Thelwall's Letter to the Editors of the Edinburgh Review* (Edinburgh, 1824), 15.

⁴ 'The projectors intrusted its [i.e. the *Edinburgh Review's*] publication to my father, as the person whom they considered most likely to promote its success. He had already become known to many of them as active, enterprising, and enlightened; his political opinions were in sympathy with their own, and he grate-

from tradition, he made it quite clear that neither he nor the booksellers would try to exert any influence over editors or contributors.[1] It was Sydney Smith who suggested to him that 'if you will give £200 p.a. to your editor and ten guineas a sheet[2] [to the contributors] you will soon have the best review in Europe'.[3] After some negotiations with Thomas Longman, a distant relative of Smith's who, after the first number, had taken over London publication rights from Joseph Mawman, a well-known bookseller, Constable accepted this advice. On May 11, 1803, Jeffrey wrote to Horner that the editor was to be given £50 a number, and the contributors paid ten guineas a sheet—terms which he rightly regarded as 'without precedent'.[4]

In the same letter Jeffrey expressed doubts as to whether he ought to accept the position of permanent editor. The job was bound to entail vexation and trouble, interference with his professional employment and character, and a risk of general degradation. But '£300 a year is a monstrous bribe to a man in my situation'.[5] And, unable to resist such a 'bribe', he accepted the post of sole editor, under conditions that did much to raise

fully accepted the commercial conduct of the work, with all its pecuniary responsibilities.' Thomas Constable, *Archibald Constable*, I, 49.

[1] Cf. Brougham's recollection that in the course of the summer of 1802 the editors received the following assurances: (1) The booksellers were to be mere instruments, entirely in subservience to the editors, and exercising not only no control but no influence of any kind. Brougham calls this 'the fundamental object of the Review'. (2) There was to be no pressure from book publishers, either to suppress or make mention of their publications, or to distribute praise or blame. (3) Jeffrey's control was not to be interfered with. *Life and Times*, I, 250.

[2] A sheet equalled sixteen printed pages.

[3] Quoted in Thomas Constable, *Archibald Constable*, I, 51. The letter is undated, but Constable's son remarks that it must have been written soon after the *Edinburgh Review* was started, and before the rate of remuneration of contributors had been settled.

[4] Jeffrey to Horner, May 11, 1803, Cockburn, *Life of Jeffrey*, II, 70–71.

[5] The discrepancy of £100 between this figure and the £200 total resulting from a computation of his salary at £50 per number may be accounted for by considering the extra money to be Jeffrey's estimate of what his own articles would bring. A note in *Notes and Queries*, Fifth Series, II (December 5, 1874), 460, states 'on authority from Edinburgh' that between 1803 and 1809 Jeffrey received a total of 200 guineas for editing each number, out of which he had to pay the contributors. For some interesting information on rates of pay later in the century, both to editor and contributors, see Cyprian Blagden, '*Edinburgh Review* Authors, 1830–1849', *The Library*, Fifth Series, VII, No. 3 (September, 1952), 212–214.

the social status of the reviewing profession as a whole. The principle that the editor and the contributors were to be paid at a high rate was linked to the principle that every contributor was bound to accept such payment.[1] Thus there was no longer any opportunity for a class division of contributors into those who disdained to write for pay on social grounds—but were willing to grind a gratuitous axe—and those who had to earn their living by reviewing. All were put on the same professional footing. The policy of anonymity, as well as lending the pronouncements of the reviewers an oracular authority derived from the appearance of an ultimate, monotheistic dispensation, also served to give some protection to those who did not want it known that they were writing for a periodical.[2]

The new status of contributors, important as it is for the later history of the *Edinburgh Review* and that of periodical literature in general, had no share in the novelty of the first number. The new plan of reviewing propounded there took as its focus the increased selectivity to be found in the new journal. The existing reviews—usually monthlies—undertook to print notices of the majority of books currently published. This meant that each number contained dozens of abstracts of patently inferior productions. Thus the October 1802 issue of the *Monthly Review* was made up of a total of forty-three reviews: sixteen fairly lengthy, taking up ninety-two pages; followed by twenty-seven short notices taking up the next nineteen pages. The corresponding number of the *Critical* contained a total of sixty reviews, sixteen major ones taking up ninety pages, forty-four minor ones taking up twenty-nine pages.[3]

[1] The minimum pay to contributors was soon raised from ten to sixteen guineas per sheet, at which it remained throughout Jeffrey's tenure as editor. He himself stated that two-thirds of the articles were bought for much more, making an average of twenty to twenty-five guineas per sheet for a whole number. *Chambers's Encyclopedia*, II, 385.

[2] As late as 1808, the Benchers of Lincoln's Inn 'made a bye-law excluding all persons who had written for the daily papers from being called to the Bar. More than twenty years afterwards a Lord Chancellor offended the propriety of his supporters, and excited their animadversions, by inviting the editor of the *Times* to dinner.' Walpole's *History of England from the Conclusion of the Great War in 1815*, quoted in Stuart J. Reid, *A Sketch of the Life and Times of the Rev. Sydney Smith* (New York, 1885), 63.

[3] *Monthly Review*, 2nd Series, XXXIX (October, 1802), 113–224; and *Critical Review*, XXXVI (October, 1802), 121–240.

It was this aspect of contemporary book reviewing that supplied the principal subject for the 'Advertisement' prefixed to the first number of the *Edinburgh Review* by its editors who wished their journal 'to be distinguished, rather for the selection, than for the number of its articles'. After admitting that most of the existing literary journals customarily rejected the very lowest order of publications the 'Conductors' announced that they proposed to carry this principle a great deal farther, by declining any attempt at exhibiting a complete view of modern literature and confining their notices mainly to works that either had attained, or deserved, a certain portion of celebrity:

'As the value of a publication, conducted upon this principle, will not depend very materially upon the earliness of its intelligence, they [the editors] have been induced to prefer a quarterly, to a monthly period of publication, that they may always have before them a greater variety for selection, and be occasionally guided in their choice by the tendencies of public opinion.'

The 'Advertisement' ended by announcing that no articles were to be continued from one number to the next, and that 'for this reason, as well as for the full discussion of important subjects, it may sometimes be found necessary to extend these articles to a greater length, than is usual in works of this nature'.[1] This was undoubtedly what one contemporary commentator had in mind when he wrote that the first two numbers of the *Edinburgh Review* were 'on an entire new plan'.[2] Yet the first number contained no fewer than twenty-nine articles. However, it ran to two hundred and fifty-two pages, more than twice the length of the corresponding numbers of the *Monthly* and the *Critical*; and five reviews exceeded fifteen pages in length, one extending to twenty-nine pages.

The impact made by the first number cannot, however, be

[1] In connection with this 'Advertisement', *Edinburgh Review*, I (October, 1802), it is interesting to note a letter of Jeffrey's to Constable, written some time before the appearance of the first number. In it he writes that he is beginning to think that there is no need for a prospectus, that a short advertisement prefixed to the first number will explain the plan of reviewing and will be safer than making promises that might not be fulfilled. He suggests an advertisement in the *Monthly Magazine*. (Jeffrey to Constable, 'Edinburgh, 1802', Constable Correspondence, National Library of Scotland, MS. 672, folio 42.) This duly appeared in April, 1803.

[2] Andrew Clephane to James Loch, February 14, 1803. *Brougham and his Early Friends*, II, 42.

explained by mere statistics such as these, important as they may be as indications of a novel approach to periodical reviewing. Nor does the fact that the more important review articles were built (in the words of the 'Advertisement') around 'the discussion of important subjects' supply this explanation. It is true that in the long run this principle opened the way to making reviews pretexts for instilling in the reader what Bagehot was to call 'suitable views for sensible persons'; and that it came to have great significance, both for the manner and extent of the *Review*'s influence. It certainly found expression in the first number which, for example, contained general discussions of the French Revolution, the Lake School of poetry, and British financial policy. But the method *per se*, not entirely original, was no insurance of quick success, of 'electrical effect'.

Nor can it be said that the first number electrified readers by the expression of startling political views. The *Review* from the very first bore the buff-and-blue colours of Fox's party, and there is no question about the generally Whiggish inclinations of its projectors. But Edinburgh Whiggism, based on opposition to the benevolently stifling despotism of Dundas, was quite different from the English parliamentary variety at the turn of the century—or what there was of it. Brougham was regarded by some as the champion of Pitt at Edinburgh University, and actually lavished high praise on Fox's rival in the first number of the *Edinburgh Review*. Horner, in December, 1802, still described himself as 'one, who cares very little about men or parties, except as connected with the fate of leading objects'[1]—a not uncommon attitude at a time when party configurations had not yet lost the legacy of amorphousness left by the previous century. Jeffrey himself, though by 1801 notorious enough as an anti-Dundas man to have failed in his attempt to obtain the office of Judicial Reporter,[2] had not been among the courageous

[1] Horner to James Loch, December 12, 1802, *Horner Memoirs*, I, 212. For Brougham see letter of Wilberforce to Lowther, May 21, 1806, *Historical Manuscripts Commission, Thirteenth Report, Appendix, Part VII: The Manuscripts of the Earl of Lonsdale* (London, 1893), 183; and *Edinburgh Review*, I (October, 1802), 237.

[2] Cf. Sydney Smith's letter to Jeffrey, August 1, 1801: '. . . I left you with a permanent and ingenuous blush for your venal city, and in a short month you deem yourself qualified in corruption to be a candidate for its honours.' *Smith Letters*, I, 65.

thirty-eight who had voted against the exclusion of Henry Erskine.[1] And Smith, while priding himself on his liberal opinions, was then as always a Whig by temperament as much as by party. So those who expected the first number to be a 'Jacobin' manifesto really had little ground for their fears.

'You will be surprised', wrote Horner to James Loch, 'that we have given a good deal of disappointment by the temperate air of our politics; nothing short of blood and atheism and democracy were predicted by some wise and fair ones, as the necessary production of our set.'[2] It is doubtless true that this moderate political tone helped the *Review* to gain a public which would have been frightened off by a violent approach. Yet at the same time it is unlikely, even in the Edinburgh of Dundas, that the mere advancement of temperate political views would have been sufficient to create a sensation akin to that created by the first number of the *Edinburgh Review*. The sensational element lay rather in a method of presentation combining cleverness, wit, and an impression of omniscience with an aptitude for literary demolition that turned no fewer than fifteen out of twenty-nine review articles in the first number into adversely critical pieces. Destructiveness in itself, again, was nothing new. The older reviews contained occasional spiteful pieces, usually directed against books published by rival booksellers or against political pamphlets of one or the other party. But the *Edinburgh* from the very first gave notice that no author, whosoever he was, could henceforth go unscathed if cant and dullness characterized his productions, and that its reviewers were willing and able to lay down the law according to their lights, with incisiveness and vigour.

A few extracts will best serve to convey an idea of this novel approach. Here is the first paragraph of Sydney Smith's review of the Rev. Dr. W. Langford's *Anniversary Sermon of the Royal Humane Society*:

[1] This was principally due to Jeffrey's filial deference to what Cockburn calls 'the gloomy intolerance of his Tory father'. Cockburn, *Life of Jeffrey*, I, 84. The influence of his father is said to have prevented him from attending Professor Millar's class at Glasgow University and Dugald Stewart's lectures on moral philosophy at Edinburgh in 1792. Cf. [Cosmo Innes], *Memoir of Thomas Thomson, Advocate* (Edinburgh, 1854), 11; and Cockburn, *Life of Jeffrey*, I, 52.

[2] Horner to James Loch, November 7, 1802, *Memoirs and Correspondence*, I, 204.

Number One

'An Accident which happened to the gentleman engaged in reviewing this Sermon, proves, in the most striking manner, the importance of this charity for restoring to life persons in whom the vital power is suspended. He was discovered, with Dr. Langford's discourse lying open before him, in a state of the most profound sleep; from which he could not, by any means, be awakened for a great length of time. By attending, however, to the rules prescribed by the Humane Society, flinging in the smoke of tobacco, applying hot flannels, and carefully removing the discourse itself to a great distance, the critic was restored to his disconsolate brothers.'[1]

Here is Jeffrey on the Lake School:

'A splenetic and idle discontent with the existing institutions of society, seems to be at the bottom of all their serious and peculiar sentiments. Instead of contemplating the wonders and the pleasures which civilization has created for mankind, they are perpetually brooding over the disorders by which its progress has been attended. They are filled with horror and compassion at the sight of poor men spending their blood in the quarrels of princes, and brutifying their sublime capabilities in the drudgery of unremitting labour. For all sorts of vice and profligacy in the lower orders of society, they have the same virtuous horror, and the same tender compassion. While the existence of these offences overpowers them with grief and confusion, they never permit themselves to feel the smallest indignation or dislike towards the offenders.'[2]

Even Horner, somewhat unjustly famous for lacking a sense of humour, managed to be amused as well as shocked:

'These eighty-six pages, of which not more than twenty are employed on the subject of Country Banks, afford an amusing specimen of plagiarism. The anonymous author appears to have met with Hume's Political Discourses, and Smith's Inquiry, a short time, probably, before the date of this pamphlet, which is made up of unacknowledged extracts from those works, mutilated both in composition and argument, and thrown together into a shapeless mass. By a diligent study of those excellent models, for a certain number of years, he may perhaps qualify

[1] Smith, *ER*, I (October, 1802), *16*, 113.
[2] Jeffrey, *ibid.*, *8*, 71.

38

himself to understand such disquisitions, and by the improvement of his taste at least, be prevented from violating, as he has done, the property of others.'[1]

And here is Brougham on the style of the author of *The Crisis of the Sugar Colonies*:

'But nothing, in these pages, is more unpleasant, than the aid which the writer constantly seeks from *marks of admiration* (!): When he wishes to eke out his phalanx of indignant or contemptuous expressions, he brings up the rear of his periods with those auxiliaries, sometimes in double rank, and sometimes three abreast, according to the strength of the position which he purposes to attack. For our part we declare ourselves impregnable to all such offensive operations. They belong not to the author, but the printer. Stratagems like these remind us of the emphatic marks, which females who are given to composition, make under every other word, or the italics that stud each page, when their works are permitted for a season to visit the world.'[2]

Compare these passages with one that may fairly serve as typical of the sort of review published in the *Monthly* and the *Critical*:

'We have thus resumed and concluded our examination of this highly and useful and interesting work, noting such passages and observations as seemed necessary to convey some suitable ideas of its extent, variety, and merits.'[3]

The *Edinburgh* blew into this rather tepid atmosphere like a gust of fresh air. This is not to suggest that all of the reviews in the first number were mainly distinguished by polemics or witticisms. Some, such as Horner's thirty-page article entitled 'Thornton on the Paper Credit of Great Britain', must have produced, first of all, an impression of competence and learning, if not of tedium. Others were still quite close to mere abstracts. But it was the daring and spirit of the first number that created the most striking impression. Mrs. Fletcher recalled that the

---

[1] Horner, *ibid.*, *14*, 106. The manuscript letters in the Horner Collection, London School of Economics, show that Horner's reputation as a humourless prig is to some extent due to a most timid editor who did a great deal of pruning before the publication of his letters.

[2] Brougham, *ibid.*, *27*, 219–220.

[3] *Monthly Review*, 2nd Series, XXXIX (October, 1802), 126.

authorship of the articles was discussed at every dinner-table.[1] The severity of some of the reviews aroused most comment, by no means all favourable.[2]

Jeffrey wanted the second number to show that the *Edinburgh* reviewers could praise, and were neither impious nor destitute of substantial science—and thus 'rather to disappoint our enemies than to delight our friends'.[3] Horner, too, duly noted the fact that the second number contained less abusive criticism and more careful disquisition than the first; but felt bound to add that it contained no articles as good as some of those in its predecessor.[4] At least one reader agreed with him, reporting that in Edinburgh the first number was still thought the better of the two.[5]

The public liked the verve and high spirits of the new review, and even those who did not approve could not fail to be impressed. There were protests, of course, mainly against the sharpness of the reviewers. In March, 1803, Jeffrey found it necessary to authorize his friend Lockhart Muirhead in Glasgow to 'deny us and our good works with a good conscience'; and, in jest, offered to prove Muirhead's innocence of connection with the *Edinburgh Review* by inserting a 'bloody review' of his book in the next number.[6] The first of many pamphlets evoked

[1] *Autobiography*, 82. Horner noted at the time that Jeffrey's articles were generally recognized. Horner's 'Journal', November 20, 1802, *Memoirs and Correspondence*, I, 205.

[2] Cf. Horner's comment in his 'Journal', November 20, 1802, to the effect that the *Review* 'is considered as respectable enough in point of talents, but the severity, in some of the papers it may be called scurrility, has given general dissatisfaction'. *Memoirs and Correspondence*, I, 205.

[3] Jeffrey to Lockhart Muirhead, February 8, 1803. Boulton and Watt Collection, Birmingham Reference Library. Quoted in Leroy H. Buckingham, 'The Authorship of the First Twenty-five Numbers of the *Edinburgh Review* (1802–1808)', Yale Doctoral Dissertation (1938), 301. Also cf. 'Note to Correspondents' at conclusion of *Edinburgh Review*, II (January, 1803), 510: 'We have to return our acknowledgements to a great number of valuable Correspondents, some of whom will perceive, from the present Number, that their hints had been anticipated.'

[4] Horner to James Loch, *Horner Memoirs*, I, 214–215.

[5] Cf. letter from Andrew Clephane to James Loch, February 14, 1803. Clephane writes that the first two numbers 'have a great character here, tho' the first one is thought, and I think justly, the best'. *Brougham and his Early Friends*, II, 42.

[6] Jeffrey to Lockhart Muirhead, Boulton and Watt Collection. Quoted by Buckingham, 'Authorship of First Twenty-five Numbers', 303.

by the reviewers warned them, in verse, not to be too severe
and to show moderation:

> *A knack of words you have, some fancy, too;*
> *But have you judgment, think you, to review?*
>
> *
>
> *Treasure this maxim in your thoughts for ever:*
> *A critic must be just as well as clever.*[1]

This admonition, repeated year after year, though usually
with much less benevolence, was to shadow the *Edinburgh
Review* throughout the early period of its career. Aggressive-
ness was as much a hallmark of the first number as its blue-and-
buff cover, and neither the one nor the other changed. In retrospect it seems hard to believe that on September 20, 1802, three
weeks before the first *Edinburgh Review* made its appearance,
Sydney Smith took as the text of his sermon at the English
Chapel in the Cowgate 'the necessity of candour and forbear-
ance towards our antagonists in opinion'.[2] Did he add the silent
qualification 'Judex damnatur cum nocens absolvitur'?

---

[1] [Sir Alexander Boswell, Bart.], *Epistle to the Edinburgh Reviewers* (Edinburgh, 1803), 4–5.

[2] Entry for Sunday, September 20, 1802, in Catherine Mackintosh's MS.
Journal of a 'Tour in Scotland by Catherine and James Mackintosh, 1802'.
Wedgwood Archives, Barlaston, No. 32631.

Francis Jeffrey:
An Editor and His Problems

In politics his views are clear,
Oppression's sway we need not fear,
For Liberty—to Scotsmen dear—
Is sacred to Frank Jeffrey.[1]

His writings long have been the dread
Of those who on the poor have fed;
Corruption ne'er dare rear her head
In presence o' Frank Jeffrey.[1]

*

Witty as Horatius Flaccus,
As great a democrat as Gracchus,
As short, but not so fat as Bacchus—
Here rides Jeffrey on his Jack-Ass.[2]

The *Edinburgh Review* was the 'jack-ass'; and Jeffrey rode it for twenty-seven years. Under his editorial guidance it became the most powerful organ of its kind, the arbiter of literary taste alike for the fashionable world and for those who aspired to that world. Napoleon, we are told, 'was not the only monarch who respected the opinions it put forth'; Stendhal's admiration knew no bounds; and Madame de Staël informed Lord Glenbervie in 1815 that 'if some being from another climate were to come to this and desire to know in what work the highest pitch of human intellect might be found, he ought to be shown

[1] Stanzas 5 and 6 of 'Hurrah! for Francis Jeffrey', *Reform Bill Handbills and Broadsides* (Edinburgh, 1832), No. 33.
[2] Ascribed to Sydney Smith in John Kay, *A Series of Original Portraits and Caricature Etchings . . . with Biographical Sketches and Illustrative Anecdotes* (Edinburgh, 1878), II, 391.

Francis Jeffrey: An Editor and His Problems

the *Edinburgh Review'*.[1] Yet it would not be altogether wrong to say that Jeffrey never considered the *Review* as anything more than a subsidiary occupation, a sort of lucrative sideline supplementing the income he derived from his legal work.

It is clear that he undertook his editorial responsibilities with some reluctance. 'I would undoubtedly prefer making the sum [£300 p.a.] by my profession,' he wrote to Horner in 1803, 'but I really want the money, and think that I may take it this way, without compromising either my honour or my future interest.'[2] Shortly afterwards he stated his feelings in no uncertain terms:

'I hope you do not imagine that I have made a *trade* of this editorship, or that I have, upon the whole, any interest in the publication that is essentially different from yours, or Smith's, or that of any of our original associates. The main object of every one of us, I understand to be, our own amusement and improvement—joined with the gratification of some personal, and some national, vanity.'[3]

As late as 1814, when the *Review* had just about reached the height of its influence and prosperity, he still considered relinquishing it in favour of exclusive concentration on what he always regarded as his real profession. Sydney Smith, commenting at that time on Jeffrey's occasional feelings of disgust with his editorial office and his 'half-formed intentions of giving it up', advised him to think twice before cutting himself off from the money he earned as editor of the *Review*. 'But', he added, 'if you can get as great an income by your profession, and the two cannot be combined, I would rather see you a great lawyer

[1] Entry for July 5, 1815, *The Diaries of Sylvester Douglas, Baron Glenbervie*, ed. Francis Bickley (London, 1928), II, 163. On Napoleon see *Selections from the Edinburgh Review*, ed. Maurice Cross (Paris, 1835), I, 28; on Stendhal, Doris Gunnell, *Stendhal et l'Angleterre* (Paris, 1909), 168.

[2] Jeffrey to Horner, May 11, 1803, Henry Thomas Cockburn, Lord Cockburn, *Life of Lord Jeffrey, with a Selection from his Correspondence* (Edinburgh, 1852), II, 72. Horner, as it happened, wrote him on the very same day, advising strongly against his assuming a permanent connection with the *Review*: 'I am sure that better and more conspicuous exertions are destined for you, if you will be true to yourself.' Horner to Jeffrey, May 11, 1803, Horner Correspondence, L.S.E., II, 8. But writing to his cousin on May 13, Jeffrey reiterated: '£300 a year is not to be lightly rejected.' *Memorials of the Life and Writings of the Rev. Robert Morehead, D.D.* (Edinburgh, 1875), 120.

[3] Jeffrey to Horner, September 8, 1803. Cockburn, *Life of Jeffrey*, II, 83.

than a witty journalist. There can be no doubt which is the most honourable and lucrative situation, and not much doubt which is the most useful.'[1] In the course of the following months Jeffrey developed 'an extraordinary fit of professional zeal', attending to little else beside the law. His efforts were of no avail. 'I cannot afford to quit yet,' he wrote to his father-in-law in America, 'but must scribble on—begging, borrowing, and coining.'[2]

Until 1829 he carried the triple burden of legal work, editing the *Review*, and writing his own critical contributions. 'Jeffrey is most entertaining', reported Lord Minto's daughter to her father during the winter of 1809–1810, 'with his miseries of writing reviews with his head full of bad law, and his law with his head full of reviews, and passing his nights scribbling and being abused for his pains.'[3] Another contemporary, writing shortly after Jeffrey's death, remarked on his extraordinary capacity for crowding into a single day law-pleadings, consultations with clients, an evening dinner party, and the composition of an article for the *Review*, 'until the morning light found him still awake and working in his study'.[4] Yet in spite of constant complaints about his busy schedule and occasional outbursts of despondency over his having to 'scribble on', Jeffrey developed and retained a strong feeling of pride in the *Review* and its superiority to the run-of-the-mill periodical literature of the day.

'The publication is in the highest degree respectable,' he wrote early in its career, 'as there are none but gentlemen connected with it. If it ever sink into the state of an ordinary bookseller's journal I have done with it.'[5] He saw to it that it never sank to such a state. On at least two occasions Constable, the Edinburgh publisher of the *Review*, complained to Longmans,

[1] Smith to Jeffrey, December 30, 1814, Nowell C. Smith, ed., *The Letters of Sydney Smith* (Oxford, 1953), I, 251.

[2] Jeffrey to Charles Wilkes, February 25, 1815, Cockburn, *Life of Jeffrey*, II, 148.

[3] Hon. A. M. Elliot to Lord Minto, winter of 1809–1810, Countess Minto, ed., *Lord Minto in India* (London, 1880), 234.

[4] David Constable in Thomas Constable, ed., *Archibald Constable and his Literary Correspondents* (Edinburgh, 1873), II, 222. Cf. also Jeffrey to Horner, May 11, 1803: 'I had reviews to write, felons to defend, visits to pay, and journeys to perform, directions to give, and quarrels to make up.' Cockburn, *Life of Jeffrey*, II, 69.

[5] Jeffrey to John Jeffrey, July 2, 1803, *ibid.*, 74. See also Jeffrey's letter to Morehead written at about the same time, complaining about the slow recruitment of reviewers: 'Our standard, to be sure, is high, as well as our bounty.' Jeffrey to Morehead, June 20, 1803, *Morehead Memorials*, 121.

then the London agent, about the inferior treatment accorded the *Review* in advertisements, warning each time of Mr. Jeffrey's particular disapproval. On the second occasion Longmans had announced the *Review* as the *Edinburgh Review and London Critical Journal*. The protest from Constable demanded how Longmans could possibly have thought of adding anything to the title of so well established a journal, and expressed the hope that Mr. Jeffrey would not see the advertisement, since he would be much displeased.[1] When a contributor complained to Constable about late payment for his contribution, Jeffrey offered ten guineas out of his own pocket, since 'it is right that the review and its management should not be liable to the imputation of shabbiness, even from the shabby'.[2] And he sounded this note of proprietary pride even more movingly in a letter to Thomas Thomson whom he left in charge of the *Review*—'that good cause for which I lived and bled with such exemplary devotion' —during his American trip of 1813–1814. 'Do not let the poor Review die till I come back, if any human exertions can keep her alive', he exhorted him from the ship.[3]

Jeffrey's proprietary tone in connection with the *Review* needs no more justification than a mere statement of the number of articles he wrote for it. To the first fifty numbers he contributed the staggering total of almost one hundred and fifty reviews. The only other contributor who even approached this total was Brougham, with less than a hundred and twenty, the great bulk of them contributions to the first twenty-five numbers.[4]

The range in subject matter of Jeffrey's contributions—those articles read and re-read by Macaulay until he knew them by

[1] Entry for January 6, 1815, Constable Letterbook, National Library of Scotland, MS. 789, folio 180. The first protest concerned listing the *Review* in an advertisement on the same page as the *Annual Register*. Constable to Longmans, December 15, 1804, National Library of Scotland, MS. 324, folio 33.

[2] Jeffrey to Archibald Constable, n.d., *Constable and his Correspondents*, II, 216.

[3] Jeffrey to Thomas Thomson, May 29, 1813 [Cosmo Innes], *Memoir of Thomas Thomson, Advocate* (Edinburgh, 1854), 139. The quotation in the previous sentence is from a letter of the same to the same, August 10, 1813, *ibid.*, 138.

[4] These statistics are based in part on Leroy H. Buckingham, 'The Authorship of the First Twenty-five Numbers of the *Edinburgh Review* (1802–1808)', Yale Doctoral Dissertation (1938), 102; in part on W. A. Copinger, *On the Authorship of the First Hundred Numbers of the Edinburgh Review* (Manchester, 1895), 16–26. Allowance must be made for disputed ascriptions and for errors in Copinger. But it may be assumed that the figures are approximately correct.

heart[1]—extended over poetry, fiction, drama, aesthetic theory, history, biography, philosophy, jurisprudence, political science, religion, geography, and current politics. He himself was to call them 'miscellaneous papers, written hastily, in the intervals of graver occupations'.[2] But to have been equally modest about his work as editor would have been more difficult. For from the very beginning of his tenure it was clear to friend and foe that, to use Brougham's words, 'if we had searched all Europe, a better man, *in every respect*, could not have been found'.[3]

The anonymous author of the first pamphlet provoked by the *Review* exclaimed:

> *To Mounier's candid critic praise is due,*
> *Make him your leader, keep him in your view.*[4]

It proved to be good advice, not least from the publisher's point of view. After reporting the satisfactory sale of the *Review* in London in 1810, Constable's partner added often-echoed words of praise for the editor: 'May the Lord long preserve Mr. Jeffrey to us and the country. He is indeed a block of pure marble, the chief pillar of the temple.'[5]

In any sense but the most abstract, 'block of pure marble' was without doubt the unaptest metaphor that could possibly have been applied to the man who reminded Hazlitt of a voltaic battery and Carlyle of an aerial little sprite.[6] George Ticknor, then a young man of twenty-three, met Jeffrey when the latter visited Boston in 1814 and, in describing him to a friend, sketched a masterly portrait:

[1] Macaulay to Macvey Napier, April 19, 1843, *Selection from the Correspondence of the Late Macvey Napier*, ed. Macvey Napier (London, 1879), 428.

[2] Francis Jeffrey, *Contributions to the Edinburgh Review* (2nd ed., London, 1846), ix.

[3] Henry Brougham, 1st Baron Brougham and Vaux, *The Life and Times of Henry Lord Brougham, Written by Himself* (2nd ed., Edinburgh and London, 1871), I, 264.

[4] [Sir Alexander Boswell], *Epistle to the Edinburgh Reviewers* (Edinburgh, 1803), 7. Jeffrey's first article (No. I, Art. 1) was a review of J. Mounier's *De L'Influence attribuée aux Philosophes, aux Francs-Maçons, et aux Illuminés, sur la Révolution de France*.

[5] Alexander Gibson Hunter to Archibald Constable, March 16, 1810, *Constable and his Correspondents*, I, 150.

[6] William Hazlitt, *The Spirit of the Age, or Contemporary Portraits* (4th ed., London and New York, 1894), 250; Thomas Carlyle, *Reminiscences*, ed. J. A. Froude (New York, 1881), 298.

Francis Jeffrey: An Editor and His Problems

'A short, stout, little gentleman, about five and a half feet high, with a very red face, black hair, and black eyes. . . . [He possesses] all the restlessness of a will-o'-wisp, and all that fitful irregularity in his movements which you have heretofore appropriated to the pasteboard Merry Andrews whose limbs are jerked about with a wire. . . . [He enters the room with] a countenance so satisfied, and a step so light and fantastic, that all your previous impressions of the dignity and severity of the *Edinburgh Review* are immediately put to flight. . . . [He] bursts upon you with a torrent of remarks.'[1]

If one adds to this Carlyle's description of Jeffrey's singular accent—'a strange, swift, sharp-sounding, fitful modulation, part of it pungent, quasi-latrant, other parts of it cooing, bantering, lovingly quizzical'—and the results of Sydney Smith's efforts to form a distinct image of the editor of the *Edinburgh Review*—'he appears to me of a stature so incredibly small, that I cannot venture to say I am awake, and my mind in a healthy and vigorous state'—one receives some impression of Jeffrey as he struck his contemporaries.[2]

Those who knew him were impressed not only by his small size, but even more by his intellectual powers. Horner could note in 1802 that 'the genius of that little man has remained almost unknown to all but his most intimate acquaintances'.[3] It was certainly known to Horner who, on leaving Edinburgh in 1803, assured Jeffrey that 'you were one of my chief masters and improvers; I shall ever consider you as such, and love you on that account over and above every other'.[4] By the time that Macaulay, more than forty years later, wrote that 'take him all in all, I think him more nearly an universal genius than any man of our time',[5] there were many who had come to share his opinion. Mackintosh probably came closer to the mark when he

[1] George Ticknor, *Life, Letters, and Journals* (Boston and New York, 1909), I, 43–44.

[2] Cf. Carlyle, *Reminiscences*, 309, and Smith to Jeffrey, April or May, 1804, *Smith Letters*, I, 95.

[3] Entry in his Journal, November 20, 1802, *Memoirs and Correspondence o Francis Horner, M.P.*, ed. Leonard Horner (London, 1843), I, 205.

[4] Horner to Jeffrey, April 19, 1803, Horner Correspondence, L.S.E., II, 7.

[5] Macaulay to Macvey Napier, December 13, 1843, *Napier Correspondence*, 453. It is worth noting that Macaulay added: 'Certainly far more nearly than Brougham, much as Brougham affects the character.'

called Jeffrey the *cleverest* person he had ever encountered;[1] though even this may seem excessive praise to those who, with Leslie Stephen, would grant him lively talent rather than original power, or, with Bagehot, invoke for him a gentle oblivion to cover his subsiding reputation.[2] There is abundant evidence that he must have possessed a rare genius for making his omniscience articulate. Sydney Smith envied Jeffrey's 'head full of arguments on all subjects',[3] while Ticknor sat entranced as he passed from subject to subject and from thought to thought with such intuitive rapidity 'that his mind [was] completely occupied and satisfied with its own knowledge and operations, and [had] . . . no attention left to bestow on the tones and manners of expression'.[4]

Glibness in conversation and cocksureness in matters intellectual were not in this instance signs of an arrogant and cold personality. To consider any critic lovable requires a certain effort of the imagination; to extend the adjective to a Whig, in this day and age, demands prodigies. Yet it must be said that all those who knew Jeffrey well seem to have agreed with Lady Holland's verdict that he was 'a very dear little man, who has the best heart and temper, although the authors of the day consider him their greatest scourge'. In spite of his fundamental, rather un-Whiggish pessimism about mankind in general and most projects, including that of the *Edinburgh Review*, in particular, his disposition was usually cheerful and even sprightly.[5] He never carried political or critical disagreements beyond the pages of the *Review*. His tragi-comic Chalk Farm duel with Thomas Moore in August of 1806 is an exception to this rule—

[1] As reported by Smith to Jeffrey, April 6, 1813, *Smith Letters*, I, 236.

[2] Leslie Stephen, *Hours in a Library* (new ed., London, 1907), III, 116; Walter Bagehot, *Literary Studies* (Everyman ed., London, 1911), I, 26.

[3] Smith to Jeffrey, July 3, 1809, *Smith Letters*, I, 163.

[4] Ticknor, *Life, Letters, and Journals*, I, 46.

[5] Lady Holland to Mrs. Creevey, September 23, 1814, *The Creevey Papers*, ed. Sir Herbert Maxwell (New York, 1904), 205. See also Mrs. Grant to Miss Fanshawe, October 6, 1810; she comments that it is almost impossible to reconcile the asperity of Jeffrey's criticism with the general kindliness of his disposition. *Memoir and Correspondence of Mrs. [Anne] Grant of Laggan*, ed. J. P. Grant (London, 1845), I, 252. See also Cockburn, *Life of Jeffrey*, I, 130, and Carlyle, *Reminiscences*, 298 and 320–321. However, in a letter to Brougham, he mentions an old nervous malady which occasionally recurred and put him in dread of apoplexy or palsy. Jeffrey to Brougham, March 19, 1810, Brougham, *Life and Times*, I, 502.

it was Moore who had issued the challenge after Jeffrey had accused him of corrupting unsuspecting readers with his poetry. But Jeffrey and Moore became fast friends shortly afterwards.[1] His affection for his large circle of friends was almost as great as that which he bore towards Scotland and Edinburgh. On one occasion he wrote from Liverpool that he would never be able to live there with any comfort. 'Indeed,' he went on to say, 'I could not live anywhere out of Scotland. All my recollections are Scottish, and consequently all my imaginations; and though I thank God that I have as few fixed opinions as any man of my standing, yet all the elements out of which they are made have a certain national cast also.'[2]

The great sorrow of his early years occurred during the year 1804–1805, when within a few months both his sister and his first wife died. Some poignant letters among the hitherto unpublished Horner correspondence reveal the extent of the personal blow he suffered at that time. No one loved and admired Jeffrey more than Horner who, from the first, was only too well aware of his own excess of high seriousness, in which he differed so much from the rest of the *Edinburgh*'s stalwarts. Thus, in 1804, he had written to Jeffrey in these pathetic terms:

'I cannot shake off this pompous tawdry sort of garb that is somehow fastened upon me, nor can I contrive to change the undertaker's funeral step I have contracted into a common walk. Do give me your secret, my dear little Jeffrey, of tripping so lightly and so nimbly; I must have been cradled, I suspect, in Warwick Lane, and articled from my birth to be "sad, slow, and profound".'[3]

Some months later he had indignantly defended himself against Jeffrey's imputations of ambition, striking a (for him) rare sarcastic note in writing that 'I have not like you mounted so high, as to despise the globe and its existing race of inhabitants, or to view this goodly frame as a sterile promontory.'[4]

---

[1] See Howard Mumford Jones, *The Harp that Once. A Chronicle of the Life of Thomas Moore* (New York, 1937), 93–99, for a detailed account of the circumstances. Byron reserved some of his most venomous shafts for his description of this duel in *English Bards and Scotch Reviewers*.

[2] Jeffrey to Lord Murray, August 20, 1813, Cockburn, *Life of Jeffrey*, II, 141.

[3] Horner to Jeffrey, October, 1804, Horner Correspondence, L.S.E., II, 74.

[4] Horner to Jeffrey, June 13, 1806, Horner Correspondence, L.S.E., III, 27.

But when he heard of his friend's depression, all other feelings gave way to one of solicitude. To their mutual friend J. A. Murray he wrote a confidential letter of inquiry:

'I would not pry into his sorrows; but yet I feel the greatest curiosity to understand what it is, that robs so much excellence of its natural reward, and leaves so unhappy the dearest man I have ever seen, yet of the most penetrating talents and the most delicate virtue.'[1]

Horner's own conjecture, as expressed in this same letter, was that while Jeffrey's wife was still alive, the 'better pleasures of domestic confidence and indolence' had filled a void created by disappointed ambition. Now this void had come to the fore again. 'He has only to give up that cursed Review, and try other things', Horner suggested. The correspondence up to this point is of interest, both in view of the light it sheds on the values of age in which two young friends, both men of outstanding probity and intelligence, 'accuse' each other of ambition; and in view of Horner's conviction that the 'cursed Review' still hindered rather than helped Jeffrey's prospects. Murray appears to have shown little discretion about the contents of Horner's letter, for in 1808 Horner may be found assuring Jeffrey that Murray should never have disclosed to him (as he evidently did) 'what fell from me upon occasion of a sort of annual heart-delivery'.[2]

The question of the relation of Jeffrey's fit or fits of melancholia to his generally pessimistic view of the world must remain matter for speculation. He did seem to find, speedily enough, certain consolations for his loss.[3] And in 1813 he crossed the

[1] Horner to Murray, November 15, 1806, Horner Correspondence, L.S.E., III, 47.

[2] Horner to Jeffrey, June 15, 1808, Horner Correspondence, L.S.E., II, 109. Omitted from published version, Leonard Horner, ed., *Memoirs and Correspondence of Francis Horner, M.P.* (London, 1843), I, 426.

[3] See Horner to Murray, Christmas, 1806, in which Horner reports a rumoured romance between Jeffrey and an Edinburgh beauty, 'large, white, with a fine neck. But her bloom must be passed now; and the six children will be more than enough even for Jeffrey's love of children.' Horner Correspondence, L.S.E., III, 53. Omitted from published version, *Horner Memoirs*, I, 386. And Sydney Smith to Lady Holland, January 10, 1809: 'Great Scandal about Jeffrey and the Dutchess [*sic*] of Gordon. He is a very amorous little gentleman, and her disposition is not I fancy wholly dissimilar; it is probable therefore they will build a nest.' *Smith Letters*, I, 152.

Atlantic in time of war to call for his second wife, a niece of John Wilkes. Cockburn calls the dangerous voyage one of love's greatest achievements and, once committed to this formulation, tactfully omits mention of Jeffrey's subsequent flirtations, 'especially with pretty young wives', as one contemporary put it.[1] Carlyle, noticing these flirtations, called them 'weakish, mostly dramatic, and wholly theoretic'.[2]

Perhaps they derived this theoretic nature from the qualities Sydney Smith found combined in Jeffrey—a violent tendency towards analysis and a consequent failure to cultivate synthetical propensities. How did these qualities affect his conception of the function of the *Edinburgh Review*? Did he see this in questioning rather than affirming hitherto accepted literary, political, and social conventions? A letter of reprimand from Smith would seem to indicate that this was so:

'What's the use of virtue? What's the use of wealth? What's the use of honour? What's a guinea but a damned yellow circle? What's a chamber-pot but an infernal hollow sphere? The whole effort of your mind is to destroy.'[3]

Horner expressed himself in similar terms. 'Do not, my dear Pyrrhonist,' he wrote Jeffrey, 'insist on disputing every position, because it is not placed in the best light, or because your prolific brain bursts with nine forms of objection.'[4]

Jeffrey had to confront this accusation of destructiveness for its own sake throughout his career as editor and reviewer. Indignant authors whose works had been adversely criticized, or

[1] J. G. Lockhart to J. W. Croker, August 27, 1840, *Notes and Queries*, CLXXXVII (Sept. 9, 1944), 114. See also Marion Lochhead, *John Gibson Lockhart* (London, 1954), 239. Lockhart seems to have made something of a hobby out of keeping Croker informed of scandal. Brougham is another reviewer who serves as a victim: 'As you like *dates*, I'll give you a couple from the parish register of the Cowgate Edinr: I take them from a copy of Chambers' *Traditions of Edinr.* annotated for me by the author. "H B's father and mother were married 25th May and himself born 19th September." . . .' Lockhart to Croker, n.d., *Notes and Queries*, CLXXXVIII (June 30, 1945), 280. For a lively account of Jeffrey's American journey, see William Charvat, 'Francis Jeffrey in America', *New England Quarterly*, XIV (1941), 309–334.

[2] Carlyle, *Reminiscences*, 287.

[3] Smith to Jeffrey, April or May, 1804, *Smith Letters*, I, 95–96. See also same to the same, February 25, 1807, in which he parodies Jeffrey with: 'Damn the solar system! bad light planets too distant—pestered with comets—feeble contrivance;—could make a better with great ease.' *Ibid.*, I, 121.

[4] Horner to Jeffrey, August 13, 1804, Horner Correspondence, L.S.E., II, 67.

whose friends had suffered the same fate, usually upbraided him
and the other *Edinburgh* reviewers for engaging in calumny and
detraction in order to increase sales of 'this journal, the genius
of which seems to consist in stroking the animal the contrary
way to which the hair lies'.[1] Thus, in 1807, a Mr. John Ring,
who demonstrated his own spirit of moderation by entitling his
pamphlet *The Beauties of the Edinburgh Review, alias the Stinkpot
of Literature*, declared that

'Our English reviewers are rather shortsighted when they
cannot discover the reason why their northern brethren make
war upon the whole tribe of authors, and mangle them for the
amusement of the public. They are not so stupid, but they know,
that authors in general have *more wit* than money; and that the
readers of *their Review* have in general *more money than wit*.'[2]

Jeffrey himself admitted the uses of asperity. 'I think we
should make one or two examples of great delinquents in every
number', he wrote to Horner in 1803.[3] The *Review* more than
lived up to this undertaking. Horner was quite capable of recommending a review for publication because it has 'the severity of
the true Edinr. tone'.[4] Yet that acidulous tone which, in the

---

[1] Smith to Lady Holland, September 9, 1809, *Smith Letters*, I, 167.

[2] John Ring, *The Beauties of the Edinburgh Review, alias the Stinkpot of Literature*
(London, 1807), 4. Perhaps the most famous pamphlet allegedly evoked by the
Edinburgh Review was Edward Copleston's *Advice to a Young Reviewer, with a
Specimen of the Art* (Oxford, 1807). But though the *DNB* and other authorities
credit the *Edinburgh Review*, in this particular instance the *casus belli* appears to
have been an article in the *British Critic*. See Richard (Archbishop) Whately, ed.
Remains of Edward Copleston (London, 1854), 6, and J. P. Owen, '*Edinburgh
Review* attack on Oxford', *Notes and Queries*, Tenth Series, VII (March, 1907),
190–191. However, it is little wonder that this pamphlet was generally thought to
have been directed against the *Edinburgh*. The 'specimen', a review of Milton's
L'Allegro, had all the hallmarks of the true *Edinburgh* arrogance and destructiveness. Thus: 'Upon the whole, Mr. Milton seems to be possessed of some fancy and
talent for rhyming; two most dangerous endowments, which often unfit men for
acting an useful part in life, without qualifying them for that which is great and
brilliant.' Copleston, *Advice*, 17.

[3] Jeffrey to Horner, October 19, 1803, Cockburn, *Life of Jeffrey*, II, 86. He had
initially tried to restrain his more bellicose colleagues. Thus Sydney Smith's reply
to Jeffrey's criticism concerning excessive levity in one of the articles for the first
number: 'As for personalities grant that the man is a proper object of punishment,
and in these literary executions I do not care for justice or injustice a fig. My
business is to make the archdeacon as ridiculous as possible.' Smith to Jeffrey,
August, 1802. *Smith Letters*, I, 73.

[4] Horner to Jeffrey, February 16, 1805, Horner Correspondence, L.S.E., II, 90.

popular estimate, became the principal hallmark of the *Edinburgh Review* in general, and its editor in particular, was in great part due as much to Jeffrey's intellectual and psychological hypersensitivity to the ludicrous as it was to the profitable connection between vituperation and good business. There are certain people for whom the very act of approbation, however well deserved, holds something intrinsically and embarrassingly comical. Jeffrey was one of these. 'I have a sort of consciousness that admirers are ridiculous,' he wrote to Horner, 'and therefore I laugh at almost everything I admire, or at least let people laugh at it without contradiction. You must be in earnest when you approve and have yet to learn that everything has a respectable and a deridable aspect.'[1] The prankish strain so apparent in the founding of the *Review* was never entirely thrown off. Thus Horner could reassure Murray about what appeared to be a grossly unjust footnote of Jeffrey's: 'I know he writes such things flippantly, and therefore did not accuse him of an intentional injury to anybody.'[2]

Jeffrey's own conception of the aim of the *Review* certainly transcended those merely destructive aspects which his personality and his response to public demand imposed upon it. It is true that there is some discrepancy between his statement in the Preface to his collected *Contributions* (1843) that the *Edinburgh Review* aimed high from the start, refusing to confine itself to the humble task of pronouncing on the mere literary merit of the work before it, and his avowal in 1804 that 'it was undertaken more for the purpose of amusement, and for collecting the scattered literature of the place, than from any other motive'.[3] For some time after the appearance of the first number Jeffrey had doubts about the advisability of using the *Review* mainly as a platform for the enunciation of sound views and first principles. A letter to a contributor shows this hesitation:

'I am sensible that you have made a peg of the Dr. and that you have hung very valuable things upon him, but we must not carry the system too far, and I confess that I have some scruples

[1] Jeffrey to Horner, September 3, 1804, Cockburn, *Life of Jeffrey*, 91.
[2] Horner to Murray, January 18, 1816, Horner Correspondence, L.S.E., VII, 4. Omitted from published version, *Horner Memoirs*, II, 286–288.
[3] [Francis Jeffrey], *Observations on Mr. Thelwall's Letter to the Editor of the Edinburgh Review* (Edinburgh, 1804), 15.

as to the legality of that very long dissertation on Indian policy which precedes your first mention of the unhappy author's name.'[1]

But shortly afterwards Horner tells Jeffrey that he hopes to shape some notes he has written on the problem of the corn bounty into a review, though he has as yet found no book to which to tack them.[2] And less than two years later Jeffrey informs a prospective writer for the *Review* that 'it is rather the object and the ambition of our review to step occasionally beyond the limits of technical details and to mingle as much general speculation with our critiques as the subject will easily admit of. To be learned and right is no doubt the first requisite —but to be ingenious and original and discursive is perhaps something more than the second in a publication which can only do good by remaining popular—and cannot be popular without other attractions than those of mere truth and correctness.'[3]

It was this function of 'doing good' by educating readers, as one of them put it, through 'explaining, in an abler way than they have been illustrated hitherto, the fundamental laws of criticism, morals, and science . . . [and] demolishing popular errors and absurdities',[4] which came to constitute Jeffrey's principal object. In trying to attain it he was well aware that he put himself in considerable danger of being attacked and ridiculed for 'our Scotch manner of running everything up to elements, and explaining all sorts of occurrences by a theoretical history of society'. But, as he wrote Horner in the same letter, 'I always profess to write for babes and sucklings, and take no merit but for making things level to the meanest capacities'.[5]

This pedagogical note is sounded again and again in Jeffrey's correspondence—whether he is defending his own inaccuracies on the grounds of popularity and comprehensibility, or asking

[1] Jeffrey to James Loch, June 21, 1804, *Brougham and his Early Friends*, ed. R. H. M. Buddle Atkinson and G. A. Jackson (London, 1908), II, 129.

[2] Horner to Jeffrey, September 12, 1804, Horner Correspondence, L.S.E., II, 69.

[3] Jeffrey to König, January 20, 1806, Add. MS. 32,439, ff. 234–235. See also Jeffrey to Morehead, May 13, 1803: 'Mere scholarship, however, we will not give a shilling for.' *Morehead Memorials*, 120. And Horner to Jeffrey, August 10, 1805: 'Ostentatious learning is a very good seasoning; but we can't dine heartily without beef and solid pudding.' Horner Correspondence, L.S.E., II, 108.

[4] Alexander Murray to Archibald Constable, January 15, 1807, *Constable and his Correspondents*, I, 258–259.

[5] Jeffrey to Horner, January 5, 1813, Cockburn, *Life of Jeffrey*, II, 139.

Horner to remember the beneficial powers of argument in a work read with some attention by fifty thousand thinking people, or telling him to make an article as full, long, 'and popular' as he can.[1]

Jeffrey's 'Greater Barons', as he called them—Brougham, Smith, and Horner—saw eye to eye with him on the educational function of the *Review*. Brougham looked back on it as having devoted itself to 'the promotion of sound and liberal opinions upon all questions in Church and State, leaving the doctrines of religion untouched, and assuming the duty of submission to the constitution as fixed and permanent, the frame of our government only being subject to decorous and temperate discussion';[2] Smith remarked on the good effects of its liberality and knowledge;[3] and Horner regarded it as 'a most useful channel for the circulation of liberal opinions very extensively among the higher and middling classes of the people of England'.[4]

But if the principal contributors were in general agreement with Jeffrey about the aim of the *Review*, they were far from sharing his sense of devotion to it. Sydney Smith had good reason for writing: 'Editoris salus, suprema lex.'[5] Smith himself informed Jeffrey that 'I have three motives for writing reviews: 1st. the love of you; 2nd the habit of reviewing; 3rd the love of money—to which I may add a fourth, the love of punishing fraud or folly.'[6] But even the combination of these motives could not prevent him from employing a tone of nonchalant condescension about his own brain-child: 'I wish it well as I do the Game of Fives or billiards if you pursue them,' he wrote to Jeffrey at the end of 1808, 'but I cannot see why I am bound in friendship to think and speak of such games with enthusiasm.'[7] On another occasion he showed little understanding for his friend's editorial troubles in chaffing him about a delay in publication. It is not hard to imagine Jeffrey's wry expression

[1] Jeffrey to Horner, February 19, 1804, December 21, 1809, July 20, 1810. The first and third in Cockburn, *Life of Jeffrey*, II, 87 and 129; the second in *Horner Memoirs*, II, 12.

[2] Brougham, *Life and Times*, I, 259.

[3] Smith to Jeffrey, January, 1808, *Smith Letters*, I, 130.

[4] Horner to Jeffrey, June 5, 1807, *Horner Memoirs*, I, 403.

[5] Smith to Jeffrey, soon after April 17, 1810, *Smith Letters*, I, 185.

[6] Smith to Jeffrey, November 18, 1807, *ibid.*, I, 126.

[7] Smith to Jeffrey, November or December, 1808, *ibid.*, I, 147.

when he read: 'Why stickest thou in the clay, Jeffrey the elastic and the gay?'[1]

It is hard to believe that the publication could have survived without the constant dunning which from the very first came to constitute one of Jeffrey's most onerous editorial duties. 'Jeffrey is inexorable to my prayers and tears, and of a truth hath no bowels of compassion within him', wrote Thomas Thomson to Horner in complaint.[2] It may be assumed that his correspondent felt more than a modicum of sympathy, for Horner proved to be 'a sort of literary tiger, whose den is strewed with ten times more victims than he can devour'.[3] Again and again, Jeffrey must plead with him for contributions, sometimes in anger, always importunately.[4] Nor were the others any more dutiful. 'My time is so much taken up by dunning my "tardy ministers",' wrote Jeffrey in 1804, 'that I can scarcely do any thing else; and begin to suspect that the office of editor should be separated from that of author, in this as in other cases.'[5] And some time afterwards, in requesting a contribution, he confessed that 'the next No. is to be published on the 18th of next month, and I have *not a single line of MS* in my possession'.[6] As more contributors were attracted by the generous payments and growing reputation of the *Review*, this sort of desperate situation tended to become less frequent. And there was always Brougham who, to use his own phrase, could and did dash off more than one article 'by an exertion about midnight'.[7]

Jeffrey's task, however, did not begin and end with soliciting contributions. The policy of anonymity meant that the editor was held responsible for the content of an entire issue. One pamphleteer, attacking what to him appeared to be the in-

---

[1] Smith to Jeffrey, November 29, 1809, *ibid.*, I, 174.

[2] Thomson to Horner, December 24, 1803, [Innes], *Memoir of Thomas Thomson*, 52.

[3] Smith to Jeffrey, November 30, 1803, *Smith Letters*, I, 91.

[4] For examples, cf. Jeffrey to Horner, April 1, 1803, May 11, 1803, September 8, 1803, September 3, 1804; Cockburn, *Life of Jeffrey*, II, 67–68, 70, 84, 93.

[5] Jeffrey to Horner, August 5, 1804, *Horner Memoirs*, I, 257.

[6] Jeffrey to William Drummond, n.d. (probably 1806), Gabrielle Festing, *John Hookham Frere and His Friends* (London, 1899), 154. Also see Horner to his mother, September 10, 1806: 'Jeffrey left us on Monday [i.e. September 8]; he has a review to produce on the 25th of next month, and not a word is written yet.' Horner Correspondence, L.S.E., III, 35.

[7] Brougham to Rev. Dr. Shepherd, September 19, 1814, *Life and Times*, II, 108.

creasingly objectionable political tone of the *Review* in 1811, admitted that some of the articles to which he was taking exception might not have been written by Jeffrey; '. . . but they have been published with your sanction, and I am entitled to consider them as your own'.[1] This was one important part of his responsibility. Another was his decision as to what each number was to contain, his quest for the right reviews at the right time, and the exercise of his power of rejection. 'You must have a delicate as well as laborious task', Horner wrote to him on this subject, 'in pacifying the mortified pride of these well meaning volunteers.'[2] And there was the even more delicate matter of revising contributions once received. In advising the prospective editor of the *Quarterly Review* concerning his duties, Walter Scott cited Jeffrey's work in this regard as an example worthy of emulation:

'One very successful expedient of the Editor and on which his popularity has in some measure risen is the art of giving life and interest even to the dullest articles of the Review. He receives for example a criticism upon a work of deep research from a person who has studied the book and understands the subject and, if it happens to be written, which may often be the case, in a tone of stupefying mediocrity he renders it palatable by a few lively paragraphs or entertaining illustrations of his own or perhaps by generalising and systematising the knowledge which it contains. By this sort of *finessing* he converts without loss of time or hindrance of business an unmarketable commodity into one which from its general effect and spirit, is not likely to disgrace those among which it is placed.'[3]

As an instance of the care Jeffrey took in making editorial changes Brougham recalled that James Mill's article on the *Memoirs* of Prince Eugene was first sent to Dr. Ferrier, of Manchester, for revisions; 'and when he [Jeffrey] got it back from Dr. Ferrier, he himself corrected it, and added the moral reflections and the concluding observations on the new Paris edition of the work'.[4]

[1] *A Letter to Francis Jeffrey, Esq., Editor of the Edinburgh Review by an Anti-Reformist* (Edinburgh, 1811), 1.
[2] Horner to Jeffrey, July 12, 1804, Horner Correspondence, L.S.E., II, 64.
[3] Scott to Gifford, October 25, 1808, *The Letters of Sir Walter Scott*, ed. Herbert J. C. Grierson (London, 1932–1937), II, 104.
[4] Brougham, *Life and Times*, I, 264–265.

Francis Jeffrey: An Editor and His Problems

As long as editorial changes were mainly stylistic and enlivening there was little ground for dispute by contributors. Jeffrey's right to make changes was, after all, part of his editorial function. In asking him to look out especially for certain possibly imprudent passages in one of his review articles and to remove these if he felt it necessary, Horner remarked: '. . . not as if you had not full powers to change every thing that offends you'.[1] Even so privileged a person as Sydney Smith bowed to recognized superior authority: 'I think you have spoilt many of my jokes,' he wrote to Jeffrey in 1807, 'but this, I suppose, every writer thinks, whose works you alter; and I am unfortunately, as you know, the vainest and most irritable of human beings.'[2]

The situation became more delicate when editing an article entailed changing its political purport. Rather early in the history of the *Review*, Jeffrey made it clear that some tenets were sacred and inviolable. Thus, in 1806, he issued a friendly warning to Macvey Napier who was to review a book on Ireland:

'You are aware, I believe, that we are all decided in favour of Catholic Emancipation, and impressed with a strong conviction of the lamentable misgovernment of Ireland through the whole reign. Perhaps the book may not require you to express any opinion of these subjects, but if it should, I am afraid I cannot agree to print anything very hostile to the tenets we have hitherto maintained. *I give full licence of speculation to all my contributors, provided they are tolerably ingenious; but I never will publish anything which I believe to be pernicious as well as unsound.*'[3] [Italics mine.]

---

[1] Horner to Jeffrey, September 28, 1805, Horner Correspondence, L.S.E., II, 114.

[2] Smith to Jeffrey, November, 1807, *Smith Letters*, I, 128. Smith's attitude was not always so accommodating. In sending Jeffrey an article two years later, he wrote rather testily: 'I shall be obliged to you to alter this review as little as is consistent with Safety, and Grammar. I forget whether I have told you the Scrape you have got me into by the alterations in Perceval's curate Bill [*ER*, XXV, October, 1808]; you have put into my mouth the most extraordinary assertions respecting English benefices which ever were heard. . . .' Smith to Jeffrey (November or December, 1808), *Smith Letters*, I, 148. In the *Quarterly*'s review of Cockburn's *Life of Jeffrey*, Smith is quoted as saying to the author of the review: 'The first, the most imperative, and the most offensive duty of an editor is to strike his pen through the Preface and the eloquence.' *Quarterly Review*, XCI (June, 1852), 124.

[3] Jeffrey to Napier, '1806', *Napier Correspondence*, 2.

Francis Jeffrey: An Editor and His Problems

What this meant in practice was that when Jeffrey felt that any contribution had 'pernicious' tendencies, he gave its author a choice between allowing changes to be made or not having his article published. A letter to a contributor who had just submitted a review of an American pamphlet illustrates this procedure: Jeffrey here requests permission to add with his own hand a few cautious illustrations or additional remarks which appear to him to be important and to fall in with the general tenor of the author's doctrine. If permission be granted, the article is to appear in the next number. If not, 'I must beg leave to consider further about inserting it at all—you know how very severely we are watched and scrutinized as to our political opinions—and I do perceive some few things in your paper which I think might embarrass us hereafter or give the enemy a present advantage. You will excuse me also for adding that it is unusual to make extraordinary concessions to an *unknown* correspondent and that the powers I ask from you are only those which I exercise over the oldest and most respectable of our contributors.'[1]

Did Jeffrey really exercise these powers over *all* his contributors? If so, it would follow that in so far as its articles were concerned with controversial questions of politics, the *Edinburgh Review* reflected the opinions of its editor alone. However, it is clear that this was not invariably the case. Jeffrey himself repeatedly emphasized the fact that his authority was limited. Subjects of delicacy and importance such as 'Peace' or 'Parliamentary Privilege', he wrote Twiss in 1810, 'are usually regarded as the exclusive province of the *original* and leading authors in the Review by whose suggestion and advice I am in a great degree governed in the management and among whom I do not by any means lay claim to the first place'.[2] The implication here seems to be that Smith, Horner, and Brougham acted as a sort of inner cabinet in which Jeffrey was no more than *primus inter pares*. Yet only ten days later, in a letter to one of these very same 'original and leading authors', he reiterated his

[1] Jeffrey to Horace Twiss, March 30, 1810, National Library of Scotland, MS. 2257, folios 63–64.
[2] Jeffrey to Twiss, July 10, 1810, National Library of Scotland, MS. 2257, folios 65–66. Cf. similar sentiments in the same to the same, October 25, 1810, MS. 2257, folios 67–68.

complaint. 'You judge rightly of my limited power, and of the overgrown privileges of some of my subjects', he wrote to Horner. 'I am but a feudal monarch at best, and my throne is overshadowed by the presumptuous crests of my nobles.'[1]

It is most unlikely that Jeffrey here meant to imply that one of those presumptuous crests belonged to the ancient and honourable house of Smith.[2] The Reverend Sydney did occasionally give free rein to his critical sentiments, as when he wrote to Jeffrey that one of Brougham's reviews was 'long yet vigorous, like the penis of a jackass'.[3] But he never took it upon himself to dictate policies—in fact, he once confessed to Jeffrey that he did not even read the *Edinburgh Review* as diligently as he should.[4]

Horner kept up a constant stream of letters of suggestion, caution, and cajolery on various matters connected with the *Review*. 'I have always made a duty of saying what I thought of your articles as well as of telling you what I found to be the general opinion of others', he tells Jeffrey.[5] But he is very much aware of Jeffrey's superior powers. Of his own editorial suggestions he writes: 'I tell you these little things, not to guide you, but that you may not overlook wholly what has most struck others.'[6] After recruiting two new reviewers he asks Jeffrey to tell him what he thinks of this assumption of his prerogatives.[7] On the question of preventing the appearance of a certain politically weighted article in the *Review*, he confesses to Murray that he is reluctant to use his influence, since 'I think Jeffrey dislikes an interference of this sort from me'.[8]

Jeffrey's real mayor of the palace—the *Sieur* Brougham, as Smith once referred to him—had no such scruples. Brougham's

[1] Jeffrey to Horner, July 20, 1810, Cockburn, *Life of Jeffrey*, II, 129.
[2] Cf. Brougham's reminiscence of Smith's jokingly saying: 'The Smiths have no right to crests or coat-armour, for they always sealed their letters with their thumbs.' Brougham, *Life and Times*, I, 247.
[3] Smith to Jeffrey, December 26, 1809, *Smith Letters*, I, 178.
[4] Same to the same, July 4, 1805, *ibid.*, I, 106.
[5] Horner to Jeffrey, September 30, 1807, Horner Correspondence, L.S.E., III, 84.
[6] Same to the same, May 3, 1805, Horner Correspondence, L.S.E., II, 98.
[7] Same to the same, May 16, 1804, Horner Correspondence, L.S.E., II, 54.
[8] Horner to Murray, December 23, 1809, Horner Correspondence, L.S.E., IV, 80. Omitted from published version, *Horner Memoirs*, II, 14–15.

brilliance did not always make up for his contentious personality. Some hitherto unpublished letters make it clear that from the very first his association with the *Edinburgh Review* spelled trouble. His own published *Life and Times* had already shown that in 1802 he had temporarily withdrawn his co-operation, because he had not received adequate assurances about the subservience of the booksellers to the editors and about Jeffrey's control which, he was afraid, might have been interfered with 'by certain of our body, in whom the same confidence could not be reposed, either as regarded their opinions or their discretion'.[1] By September of 1802 he was again, according to Horner's testimony, 'an efficient and zealous member of the party'.[2] Yet by the end of May, 1803, Horner, writing from London, tells of hearing rumours of Brougham's intrigues for a rival review and assures Jeffrey that as far as he is concerned, he will never have anything to do with any other than the *Edinburgh*.[3]

In a letter dated June 27, 1803, which Brougham himself calls 'infernally long', he gives Horner a full account of his grievances.[4] It appears, according to this letter, that ever since Brougham had had anything to do with the *Review* he had noticed the existence of certain prejudices against himself '. . . and had also discovered very plainly the revd. quarter whence these came'. In other words, Sydney Smith was the villain who had caused all the trouble. Brougham assures Horner that no question of pride of authorship is involved. As far as his [Brougham's] reviews are concerned, 'I write them easily and care not a d—n about them'. But he considers it singular that someone 'to whom the review was indebted for nothing but its worst parts' should have so much weight, and that 'cyphers' like Thomas Thomson should count more than 'those who have provided the sums'. In short, 'my ideas of the infinite unimportance of the concern

---

[1] Brougham, *Life and Times*, I, 250. Also see Appendix.

[2] Horner to Allen, September 1, 1802, *Horner Memoirs*, I, 201. Significantly enough, in view of the incident that was to follow, the published version omits the words 'in consequence of Smith's residence in the country' which in the original precede 'Brougham'. Horner to Allen, September 1, 1802, Horner Correspondence, L.S.E., I, 79.

[3] Horner to Jeffrey, May 30, 1803, Horner Correspondence, L.S.E., II, 11.

[4] Brougham to Horner, June 27, 1803, Horner Correspondence, L.S.E., II, 14.

being equally like your own', Brougham had offered his resignation. For he will not think of continuing in an unacknowledged
capacity, 'only consulted when so many pp. were required within a certain No. of hours and then *worked out* with very little
ceremony'.

Jeffrey, according to Brougham, had countered that if the
latter resigned, he, too, would have nothing more to do with the
Review. In fact, Brougham boasts that he had won a complete
victory over 'the parson'. For John Allen, later to achieve fame
as a Holland House factotum, had been put in charge of the
scientific department—apparently, Brougham did not think that
science should be any of Smith's concern[1]—and Smith told 'in
plain terms that from the beginning to the end I had as much
the management as if I had been formally considered one of the
set'.[2] Apparently, Horner, in his conciliatory way, had advised
Brougham not to expend energy on becoming 'headman of a
village'. 'You are wrong', Brougham replies; 'always be headman of your own village—unless you are thereby prevented
from getting to the head of a larger town or city.' Both advice
and letter are typical of the man.

Brougham was a person of boundless ambition—brilliant, un-
predictable, incredibly energetic—who regarded the *Edinburgh
Review* from the very start as an instrument for his personal
political advancement and the dissemination of whatever political views he happened currently to espouse. Up to 1806 these
views did not by any means fit a single party label. Horner felt
that Brougham would always be inclined towards the party
really in power, or strong enough to seem at the point of getting
it. 'I cannot much respect the man', he wrote to Murray, 'who
could write both the review of Lord Chatham's letters, and the
late State of the Nation, who reviewed Lord Lauderdale [most
unfavourably] and gives that author an opportunity of expressing his surprise at the familiarity of old acquaintance with which

---

[1] This is borne out in Brougham's *Life and Times*, where, in denying that Smith
was ever appointed editor of the *Review*, even for a short period, Brougham recalls
that 'with all his other rare and remarkable qualities, there was not a man among
us less fitted for such a position. He was a very moderate classic; he had not the
smallest knowledge of mathematics or of any science.' Brougham, *Life and Times*,
I, 246–247.

[2] See Appendix, pp. 186–197, for a discussion of 'the set'.

his critic now accosts him.'[1] After 1806 Brougham threw in his lot with the Whigs; but his involvement in the day-to-day business of London politics and in the continual manœuvrings of Whig splinter groups which marked the lean years of the party meant that both temperamentally and in practice he departed farther and farther from Jeffrey's beloved first principles and general maxims. Why, then, did Jeffrey tolerate his interference?

One answer is obvious, but none the less important. While Horner and Smith had to be dunned for each one of their not very numerous contributions, Brougham, at extremely short notice, could always be counted on to supply any number of articles on almost any subject under the sun. There is no doubt that, like the sorcerer's apprentice, he eventually came to be more of a nuisance than help to Jeffrey who could call himself master only in spite of him. But it is equally certain that, had it not been for Brougham, the *Review* might well have died in infancy. 'I am in the greatest distress for MSS, and if it were not for my reliance on Brougham, I should have no hope of salvation.'[2] Thus Jeffrey in June, 1804. Shortly afterwards, as Brougham was on the point of leaving for Holland and Italy, Jeffrey thanked him for the six sheets [ninety-six printed pages] he had contributed to Number VIII of the *Review*, apologized profusely for the liberty he had taken in making certain minor editorial changes, and assured him that 'you see of what importance you are to me by the number of questions I am obliged to ask when you are going away'.[3] Six years later it is still the same story. 'What I am most anxious about', Jeffrey tells Brougham, 'is your own contribution on which I depend more completely, perhaps, than at any former period.'[4] Figures speak

[1] Horner to Murray, May 26, 1806, Horner Correspondence, L.S.E., III, 25. This was putting things a little more kindly than one of Creevey's correspondents who, some months before, had called Brougham 'a notorious prostitute—setting himself up to sale'. Dr. Currie to Creevey, October 2, 1804, *Creevey Papers*, 30. Earlier that year Horner had expressed his resentment at Brougham's intimacy with the Saints. He wrote Jeffrey that Brougham had spent a night at James Stephen's house, where he had had to join family worship morning and evening. 'Would not you have given all your hopes of heaven, (not a great price on your part) for a sight of Brougham upon his knees?' Horner to Jeffrey, March 29, 1804, Horner Correspondence, L.S.E., II, 47.

[2] Jeffrey to Loch, June 21, 1804, *Brougham and his Early Friends*, II, 130.

[3] Jeffrey to Brougham, August 5, 1804, Brougham, *Life and Times*, I, 269.

[4] Jeffrey to Brougham, March 19, 1810, *ibid.*, I, 503.

even more eloquently than words: to the first twenty-five numbers of the *Review* Brougham contributed a maximum of ninety-eight articles, Jeffrey a maximum of ninety-one. No other contributor can be credited with half so many.[1] It is no wonder that Brougham felt more than a little proprietary interest in a publication which was so largely dependent upon him. By 1807 Jeffrey was forced to resort to subterfuge. He asked a new contributor not to mention his connection with the *Review* to Brougham, since 'he has all along had a strange jealousy of our admitting any new associates, and the experience I have had has satisfied me of the prudence of not making him acquainted with the names of any such contributors'.[2]

Jeffrey had good reason to be cautious, since Brougham, from some notion of his own, had not so long before circulated rumours in London to the effect that Jeffrey was definitely about to give up the *Review*'s management.[3] Nevertheless, as Horner pointed out to Jeffrey some years later, 'Brougham has been too useful and powerful an ally, to make it easy for you to point out any change you might wish for'.[4] Jeffrey, unable as well as unwilling to precipitate a break, had to resign himself to Brougham's indiscretions and to what Sydney Smith called his 'bolting out of the course'.[5] Brougham, for his part, felt so sure of his power over Jeffrey that he was able to write Lord Grey concerning a certain book to be reviewed: 'It is too delicate to trust Jeffrey with, so I intend to give him general reasons for begging he will leave it wholly in my hands. And I know he will, as a matter of course.'[6]

[1] Some of these ascriptions are in dispute, others apply to collaborative efforts. The figures are taken from Leroy Buckingham, 'The Authorship of the First Twenty-five Numbers of the *Edinburgh Review*', 102.

[2] Jeffrey to Napier, '1807', *Napier Correspondence*, 3.

[3] Murray to Constable, August 22, 1806, and November 28, 1806, *Constable and his Correspondents*, I, 249 and 250–251. Also see Horner to Jeffrey, November 2, 1806: 'I hope you will not come to any sudden resolution of giving up the Review, without letting me know in time.' Horner Correspondence, L.S.E., III, 44.

[4] Horner to Jeffrey, July 16, 1810, *Horner Memoirs*, II, 53.

[5] Smith to Lady Holland, after Christmas, 1808, *Smith Letters*, I, 151. Smith here proposes that Brougham should always have two tame elephants, Abercrombie and Whishaw, by his side, 'who might beat him with their tusks when he behaved in an unwhiglike manner'.

[6] Brougham to Grey, October 13, 1811, *Life and Times*, I, 530. See also Brougham's letter to Shepherd, September 19, 1814: he had at first meant to send

Francis Jeffrey: An Editor and His Problems

Jeffrey could not afford to precipitate a break with Brougham. If his hands had not been tied, would he have done so? Their difference over the function of the *Edinburgh Review* as a political journal was not so fundamental as one might be led to expect, or as has sometimes been assumed. Both regarded the *Review* as an engine for the dissemination of learning and liberal opinions. It was to take all knowledge for its province and to attempt to educate as large a group of readers as it was possible to reach. Needless to say, where politics was concerned, sound views and first principles generally matched the blue-and-buff colours which enclosed them. This held for Brougham even more than for Jeffrey, once the former had terminated his flirtation with the Tories. Any difference between the two concerned the degree rather than the fact of the *Review*'s political character. That Jeffrey was not 'unpolitical', and that he knew what he wanted, is shown by the manner in which he requested an article from a prospective reviewer. 'Dear Reddie,' he wrote, 'could you undertake a review of Stevens Frauds of the Neutrals [*sic*] for us? The subject is much in your way and of great interest and importance besides. I think the author wrong—or at least I suspect him—and I think it would illustrate our journal if we were learnedly and convincingly to disavow national usurpations and candidly espouse a cause which must be sooner or later successful.'[1]

What principle governed the acceptance or rejection of any particular political line? Some years after he gave up the management of the *Review*, Jeffrey wrote an extremely revealing letter to his successor, Macvey Napier, in which he laid down three considerations by which an editor must be guided in the admission or refusal of important articles of a political sort. The first was the effect of the editor's decision on the principal

Shepherd's book to Jeffrey, with instructions and hints. 'But I changed my plan, and was unwilling to run any risks, so, deviating from my rule of only handling general subjects, and those but few, I have done the deed myself.' *Ibid.*, II, 108.

[1] Jeffrey to James Reddie, February 28, 1806, National Library of Scotland, MS. 3704. Horner had written Jeffrey a few weeks earlier, asking him to review this pamphlet—James Stephen's *War in Disguise or the Frauds of the Neutral Flags*—himself, since 'I trust you are now too well aware of the influence your Review possesses to leave an opportunity like this in unworthy hands.' Horner to Jeffrey, December 6, 1805, Horner Correspondence, L.S.E., II, 118. As it turned out, Jeffrey *did* write the review. Jeffrey, *ER*, XV (April, 1806), *1*, 1–35.

contributors; the second, its effect on the sale, circulation, and just authority of the work with the great body of its readers; the third, the editor's own deliberate opinion as to the safety or danger of the doctrines maintained in the article under consideration, 'and its tendency either to promote or retard the practical adoption of those liberal principles to which, *and their practical advancement*, you must always consider the journal as devoted'.[1] Throughout his tenure as editor Jeffrey attempted to maintain a delicate equipoise between these three considerations, but there is no doubt that Brougham often forced him to pay more attention to the first than he would have wished.

In 1810 Horner, complaining to Jeffrey about the increasing intrusion of party politics into the *Review*, distinguished between 'that general tone of politics, which, when it was the transcript of your sentiments, it almost uniformly preserved', and 'the turn it has taken of late, by descending to questions between ministry and opposition'.[2] The early years of the *Review* were marked, with some exceptions arising from Brougham's Pittite phase, by the 'general tone of politics' so nostalgically evoked by Horner.[3] Wilberforce, Scott, and other Tories contributed; discussion of current party questions and personalities was kept down to a minimum; and Jeffrey was able to confine his function to keeping out what he considered to be pernicious sentiments, such as attacks on Catholic Emancipation or on the Abolitionists. Brougham had not yet found his *métier* as Whig publicist and self-appointed troubleshooter.

Lord Holland recalled that it was Jeffrey's article on Cobbett's

[1] Jeffrey to Napier, December 27, 1837, *Napier Correspondence*, 219.

[2] Horner to Jeffrey, July 16, 1810, *Horner Memoirs*, II, 52.

[3] Even then, Horner's gentlemanly caution had on occasion been severely tried. As an instance, see his letter to Jeffrey, October 15, 1803, in which he expressed a suspicion (based on something Sydney Smith had told him) that Smith had given a Treasury pamphlet unmerited praise: 'I sicken at the idea of our contaminating ourselves with politics; still more, of showing mercy to such a stupid, blackguard production as that. But Sidney [*sic*] would make up his mind upon it, between his second and third cups of tea.' Horner Correspondence, L.S.E., II, 23. A statistical examination of some sample issues during the early years of the *Review* shows the following percentage of pages devoted to politics: October, 1802: 10 per cent; January, 1803: 5 per cent; October, 1808: 30 per cent; January, 1809: 44 per cent; November, 1814: 27 per cent; February, 1815: 13 per cent. The curve certainly coincides admirably with the intensity of Whig crises and manœuvres in this period. Literature, travel, and science follow and at times top politics as principal subjects treated.

Political Register (July, 1807), written at the instigation of Brougham—who managed the Whig press campaign during the General Election of that year—which irrevocably stamped the *Review*'s character as a political publication.[1] Brougham maintained later that 'in 1808, Cevallos on Spain and the war generally first made us conspicuous as Liberals'.[2] He himself, however, had noted some weeks before the article on Cevallos appeared that:

'The last *Edinburgh Review* and some former ones have put the ministerial folks here [Edinburgh] out of all patience. They storm beyond bounds and as I am accused of it, Jeffrey being no partizan, I have the whole brunt of it to bear now. . . . I maintain, however, that it is in the main quite impartial, and tho' most frequently hostile to Govt., because Govt. is generally worse than opposition, yet I contend that it is above both sides and acts justly by each.'[3]

The letter is interesting, not only because of its characterization of Jeffrey as 'no partizan', but also because it is a contemporary version of a view Brougham was to reiterate many times in retrospect, to the effect that during its early years the *Review* had at no time been a Whig party tool.[4] In one sense this statement is certainly correct: the Whigs, in or out of office, were never completely immune from critical comment in the *Review*; and Brougham's ideas of what Whig party politics ought to be did not always coincide with those of Lords Holland and Grey. In another sense, the statement is quite misleading: for from 1807 on, the *Review* took considerable interest in concrete and short-term political issues and concerned itself increasingly, to use Jeffrey's words, 'with questions which might be considered as of a narrower and more factious description'.[5]

What was Jeffrey's attitude towards this trend? There is no

[1] Henry Richard Vassall Fox, third Baron Holland, *Further Memoirs of the Whig Party, 1807–1821*, ed. Lord Stavordale (New York, 1905), 387.

[2] Brougham to Napier, October 27, 1839, *Napier Correspondence*, 308. The article on 'Don Pedro Cevallos' appeared in October, 1808.

[3] Brougham to Loch, August 19, 1808, *Brougham and his Early Friends*, II, 319–320.

[4] Cf. Brougham to Napier, September 26, 1835, October 19, 1837, October 29, 1837, January 1, 1838, and October 27, 1839; Napier Correspondence, 168, 202, 210, 228, and 308–309. Also Brougham, *Life and Times*, I, 263.

[5] Jeffrey to Horner, March 12, 1815, Cockburn, *Life of Jeffrey*, II, 151.

doubt that he did not like his enforced dependence on Brougham, who must have been deceiving himself if he really believed what he wrote in self-defence to Napier in 1837:

'I only wish Lord Jeffrey would show you one per cent of the letters he used to get once a month all the time he held the office, and from, I believe, *all* the original founders of the work, and I will venture to say that he never once, during that quarter of a century, expressed the least impatience of advice, and of the strongest and often angriest remonstrance.'[1]

Jeffrey's continually repeated references to himself as a limited monarch, unable to do what he wanted, and his admission that 'the youthful ardour of some of our associates . . . carried them farther than I could approve of'[2] indicate that he was not always altogether happy about the advice he received from Brougham. On one occasion, at least, he came close to pathos: 'When I have more power', he wrote to a prospective contributor, 'I shall consider it as a piece of great good fortune if I have the same good opportunities for exerting it as seem now to present themselves.'[3]

Yet, granted that Jeffrey without Brougham would probably have followed more cautious policies, it must be said that he himself gradually became less reluctant to engage in political infighting than he had been during the early years of the *Review*, far less so than Horner, who sent repeated warnings to desist.[4] In defending himself against Horner's charges Jeffrey admitted that he had allowed too much mischief from mere indifference and love of sport.[5] Is this the whole explanation?

[1] Brougham to Napier, October 29, 1837, *Napier Correspondence*, 209.

[2] Jeffrey, *Contributions*, I, xvii.

[3] Jeffrey to Twiss, October 25, 1810, National Library of Scotland, MS. 2257, folios 67–68.

[4] See Horner to Jeffrey, December 29, 1804, Horner Correspondence, L.S.E., II, 84; same to same, January 14, 1807, June 12, 1809, *Horner Memoirs*, I, 391 and 464; Horner to Murray, October 21, 1812, Horner Correspondence, L.S.E., V, 105, omitted from published version in *Horner Memoirs*, II, 132–135; Horner to Murray, December 16, 1812, *Horner Memoirs*, II, 139; same to same, January 19, 1815, Horner Correspondence, L.S.E., VI, 65; Horner to Jeffrey, April 19, 1815, *Horner Memoirs*, II, 250.

[5] Jeffrey to Horner, December 6, 1808, *Horner Memoirs*, I, 439. It appears that the original letter contained Brougham's name in this passage. Elisabeth Schneider, Irwin Griggs, and John D. Kern, 'Brougham's Early Contributions to the *Edinburgh Review*: A New List', *Modern Philology*, XLII, No. 3 (February, 1945), 170.

Francis Jeffrey: An Editor and His Problems

As Brougham pointed out, Jeffrey, unlike himself, was not a 'partizan'. Yet it is not without significance that Sydney Smith could write to him in 1807: 'You take politics to heart more than any man I know; I do not mean questions of party, but questions of national existence.'[1]

Rightly or wrongly, 'questions of national existence' came to be identified by Jeffrey more and more with questions of party, partly because the years from 1802 to 1815 witnessed an increasing polarization of 'Government' and 'Opposition'. By 1808 the Whigs had tasted office and were eager for another taste. Meanwhile, military strategy had become a major party issue, and one which held a special appeal for the peace-loving editor of the *Edinburgh Review*. It is not surprising that Jeffrey should have extended his definition of 'national existence' to include questions hitherto considered 'partizan'. Writing to Horner in 1815, he admitted that the *Review* might have been more firmly conducted, and greater circumspection used to avoid excesses of all sorts. 'Perhaps', he continued, 'it would have been better to have kept more to general views. But in such times as we have lived in, it was impossible not to mix them, as in fact they mix themselves, with questions which might be considered as of a narrower and more factious description. In substance it appeared to me that my only absolute duty as to political discussion was, to forward the great ends of liberty, and to exclude nothing but what had a tendency to promote servile, sordid, and corrupt principles.'[2]

In denying that in 1808 he had promised Scott that the *Review* would henceforth relinquish party politics, Jeffrey recalled that while he might have joined Scott in regretting the amount of violence and personality in the *Review*, and might even have promised to do all in his power to reduce it, the notion that he should have offered to renounce politics altogether at that time was 'palpably ridiculous'.[3] He remembered telling Scott on one occasion that 'the *Review*, in short, has but two legs to

[1] Smith to Jeffrey, November, 1807, *Smith Letters*, I, 127.
[2] Jeffrey to Horner, Cockburn, *Life of Jeffrey*, II, 151.
[3] Cf. Scott to Ellis, December 15, 1808: 'Jeffrey has offered terms of pacification, engaging that no party politics should again appear in his Review.' *Letters of Walter Scott*, II, 138. Also see Jeffrey to Napier, October 4, 1843, *Napier Correspondence*, 434–435.

stand on. Literature no doubt is one of them. But its *Right leg* is Politics.'[1] Undoubtedly Jeffrey often wished for a steadier leg than Brougham's—but had he found one among the Whigs of those years, it might well have turned out to be wooden. Sydney Smith, a master at having the last word, shall have it here. In 1812 he wrote to Jeffrey: 'If I reconcile the interests of *truth* with the feelings of party, so much the better.'[2] For the sorely tried rider of his Jack-Ass, this was ever a reconciliation devoutly to be wished.

[1] Jeffrey, *Contributions*, I, xix.
[2] Smith to Jeffrey, September, 1812, *Smith Letters*, I, 226.

[3]

The Whig Party and the
Edinburgh Reviewers[1]

In his essay on Chatham, Macaulay uses Dante's account of a strange battle that took place in Malebolge between a human form and a serpent to illustrate the transformation undergone by the two English parties in the course of the reign of George I. Each gradually took the shape and colour of his foe, 'till at length the Tory rose up erect the zealot of freedom, and the Whig crawled and licked the dust at the feet of power'. In some ways it would not be inappropriate to say that by the beginning of the following century the wheel had again come full circle: the very mention of the names of Pitt, of Eldon, of Sidmouth, brings to mind reaction, persecution, and intolerance; while those of Fox and Grey conjure up visions of wickedness denounced, slave trade abolished, and that grand though gradual crescendo which was to end in the C-major chord of 1832.

Yet we are told that in 1815, 'the political passions exploited by the Tory leaders, the catchwords so frequently on their lips, differed in no essential point from the mass of sentiments and commonplaces which had composed the Whiggery of sixty years

---

[1] The first section of this chapter is, for the most part, based on the following authorities: Lewis B. Namier, *England in the Age of the American Revolution* (London, 1930); George M. Guttridge, *English Whiggism and the American Revolution* (Berkeley and Los Angeles, 1942); Michael Roberts, *The Whig Party 1807–1812* (London, 1939); Keith Feiling, *The Second Tory Party, 1714–1832* (London, 1938) and *A History of England* (London, 1950); Henry W. C. Davis, *The Age of Grey and Peel* (Oxford, 1929); George M. Trevelyan, *Lord Grey and the Reform Bill* (New York and London, 1920); Arthur Aspinall, *Lord Brougham and the Whig Party, 1807–1812* (Manchester, 1927); Elie Halévy, *England in 1815* (second revised ed., London, 1949). In this and the next chapter I am particularly indebted to Professor Roberts's authoritative monograph, a brilliant study of a most difficult subject.

71

earlier. In 1815, as in 1760, the party in office—though Whig then and Tory now—was the party of war, and moreover of war with France, and a Protestant party resolved to maintain the penal laws enacted against the Catholics. The Tories of 1815, in their struggle against the Jacobin Revolution and the Empire, posed, as the Whigs had done formerly in their struggle against the Bourbons, as the defenders of the freedom of Europe, threatened with French domination.'[1] Furthermore, as Halévy points out, the Tories had been supported through the greater part of the Napoleonic wars by those progressive elements in the country—finance, commerce, and industry—which had formerly supported the Whigs. In short, the 'Tory reaction' did not amount to very much. What, then, had happened to the Whig party? One thing is certain: if, between 1802 and 1815, it still deserved to be called a serpent, it was one whose fangs had been removed.

The story of the Whigs during those years is one of confusion, frustration, and ineffectuality. It was a period, not yet, in the mid-nineteenth-century sense of the word, of parties, but of groups and connections vying for the favour of the monarch and supported, when in power, not only by their own parliamentary followers, but by the all-important 'floating strength' of the House of Commons as well. 'Ins' and 'outs' were terms more commonly used than party labels by political observers, though 'Pittites' and Foxites' survived the death of the leaders who had inspired the names. While those leaders were still alive, there had occurred what has been called a false dawn of two-party government, in which the powerful personalities of the two men supplied a kind of polarization. But Pitt's party had already begun to disintegrate at the turn of the century, and the years that followed were marked by efforts to bring about its reintegration. Some of its crumbling components performed for the Foxites the rather dubious service of (on the one hand) holding out constant hopes of accretion and (on the other) threatening their Ark of the Covenant which sheltered that peculiarly Whiggish preserve of high principle so frequently put to the test by betrayal and concession.

The most memorable betrayal of this sort had, of course, been

[1] Halévy, *England in 1815*, 199.

Fox's coalition with North in 1783. It was only Fox's radiant personality, investing with a 'golden haze' the noble illusions and aspirations of his century,[1] that could—in part—overcome such a flagrant breach of principle. And it was this same powerful personality—dare one call it charismatic?—which remained the essence of the Whigs' 'middle section' even after his death. The origin of this section may be traced back to the year 1780, when the Rockinghams adopted economic reform as an important plank in their platform and, in the words of Sir Lewis Namier, set out to destroy the edifice which the Pelhams had built for their party and which George III had taken over with most of its residents.[2] But its real test came with the French Revolution whose effects produced not only the dramatic parting of the ways of Fox and Burke, but also the split resulting in 1792 from Grey's founding of the reformist Friends of the People, with Fox's silent acquiescence. The Portland Whigs went over to Pitt, while Shelburne and the Duke of Bedford stayed with Grey, who brought in his second motion for parliamentary reform five years later. Its failure was followed by the retreat of the Whigs to their country houses, from which they were just beginning to drift back at the time of the founding of the *Edinburgh Review*.

What bound the Foxites together in the years that followed was above all the memory of their having jointly defended a difficult cause, while everyone else (who mattered) had deserted that cause to fight the Revolution at home and abroad. It goes without saying that Fox himself, Lansdowne (formerly Shelburne), Grey, and Fox's nephew Holland—the most prominent names among them—remained aristocratic to the core. They saw themselves not as innovators and certainly not as Painites, but as guardians of the sacred Whig heritage of toleration, liberties and rights, and opposition to the encroachments of the Crown, a heritage which still survived, though it had suffered not a little during the long Whig tenure of power in the first half of the eighteenth century.

The real heirs of these pre-Rockinghamite Whigs in the early years of the nineteenth century were the Grenvillites, most

---

[1] Davis, *Age of Grey and Peel*, 43.
[2] Namier, *England in the Age of the American Revolution*, 219.

oligarchical of oligarchs. Their leader, Lord William Grenville, who had moved the first reading of the Bill to suspend Habeas Corpus, had refused to join Pitt's ministry of 1804 out of loyalty to Fox with whom he and his small but territorially immensely powerful group had been in alliance against Addington. Grenville's band, known paradoxically enough as the 'new opposition', was tied to the Foxites (or 'old opposition') by its support of Catholic Emancipation and by little else. Grenville's fond memories of the fight he had waged at the side of his cousin Pitt against the French Revolution did not help to endear him to men like Grey or Fox's nephew, Lord Holland. And if relations were strained between Foxites and Grenvillites, they hardly existed at all between Grenville's group and the third section of the Whigs, their left wing or 'Mountain'. This section, which included men like Creevey, Romilly, and (eventually) Brougham, was led by Grey's brother-in-law, the brewer Samuel Whitbread who, in spite of his aristocratic connections, never ceased to take 'a bourgeois delight in uncovering the scandals of High Life'.[1]

It could hardly be expected that these three groups, uncomfortably allied, would be able to reach any great degree of homogeneity. Their problems, however, by no means ended with this difficulty. After Fox's death, the Whigs could find no outstanding figure to lead them in the House of Commons; for Lord Howick went to the Lords as Lord Grey in 1807, and Ponsonby who was given the job was qualified for it only by negative capability—he offended nobody. He could well serve, as Mr. Roberts justly points out, as the symbol of Whig sterility during these years.[2] Whitbread, a far abler man, was not only completely unacceptable to the Grenvillites, but had been mortally offended when his brother-in-law did not include him in the Ministry of All the Talents (1806–1807), the only tenure of power by the Whigs in this period and (except for the abolition of the slave trade) a complete failure.

The failure of this Ministry—'there had rarely been, in the history of English ministries, so glaring a contrast between promise and fulfilment'[3]—brings into focus the three principal

---

[1] Roberts, *Whig Party*, 206.
[2] *Ibid.*, 328.
[3] Aspinall, *Lord Brougham and the Whig Party*, 38.

issues confronting the Whigs during this period. For while in office, they failed to make peace, and failed to take up the question of parliamentary reform; and they fell over Catholic Emancipation. The last may be taken up first, since it was the issue which at one and the same time cemented the various Whig groups and helped keep them out of office on all the occasions when they had a chance for it.

Emancipation of the Irish Catholics was by no means a naturally clear-cut party issue. After all, Pitt had resigned over his inability to proceed with it in 1801, and there was no more warm-hearted supporter of the Catholics than 'despotic Dundas'. But it was the only major point on which all Whigs could agree —Holland House and the Mountain felt more strongly about it than Grenville, Grey, Lansdowne and Tierney—and thus it became a sort of self-imposed albatross round their necks.

Grey wanted to solve the problem in conjunction with the particular exigencies of day-to-day Whig politics. Thus he was quite annoyed over Irish Catholic objections to the King's retention of veto power against episcopal candidates, feeling all the time that the Irish ought to be grateful for what they were about to receive. And when the Whigs fell in 1807, they had already consented to abandon the Emancipation Bill, and were only saved from complete ignominy over this desertion when George III, indignant at their sharp practice in their dealings with him, drove them from office; thus giving their fall 'an air of nobility wholy fictitious'.[1] They continued to press the question, but were hampered by the fact that emancipation was simply not a popular issue. The election of 1807 gave convincing evidence of the strong 'No-Popery' sentiment which continued to exist, more or less violently, among all classes. The truth was that the country was not behind the Whigs on this question, and that they made things worse by compromising on it when it suited their political convenience.

Even more unpopular was the Whig stand on the war. Grenville, who had vigorously attacked the Peace of Amiens, continued to press for vigorous action. The other Whigs, in varying degrees, followed Fox's pacific line—though their inability to reach any satisfactory settlement while in office disillusioned

[1] Roberts, *Whig Party*, 32; see also 64–65.

them somewhat. It was to take them until 1812 to grasp the fact
that England was engaged in a fight to the finish. Before that
they outdid each other in dire prophecies about the fate of under-
takings like the Peninsular War, and retained—many of them—
an indestructible faith in the possibility of accommodation with
Napoleon. Thus here again they were swimming steadily against
the currents of public opinion which increasingly came to regard
the war as a patriotic struggle for the very existence of the
country.[1]

It might be assumed that in parliamentary reform the Whigs
had a more popular issue than Catholic Emancipation or Peace
—for while it is true that the turbulent 'nineties were followed
by a few years of general apathy on this question, the period
from 1807 was marked by Cobbett's popularity as a reformer,
the Radical Burdett's election for Westminster, and great public
indignation at scandals like that of the sale of army commissions
by the Duke of York's mistress. But it was on this question that
the three principal groups which constituted the party were
fundamentally and hopelessly split. The Grenvillites, who
gloried in the unreconstructed Whiggism of the age of Walpole,
would not hear of reform, economical or otherwise. Grey and
the bulk of the Foxites were at this point themselves not especially anxious to recall the dim, distant days of the Friends of
the People. Only the 'Mountain' brought any enthusiasm to
reform, and its efforts were hampered by the hostility and indifference of the other groups. Whitbread was perfectly willing to
exploit popular sentiment against the Duke of York and to
cultivate relations with the Burdettites and with the extra-
parliamentary, non-aristocratic elements agitating for reform.
And the founding of the Hampden Club in 1812 presaged the
future in its mingling of the right wing of the Radicals with the
adjacent left wing of the Whigs. But even Whitbread was
frightened by prospects of riots and cautioned by prospects of
office. And between 1812 and 1817 the subject of reform was not
raised among the parliamentary Whigs.

Bentham, who joined the Burdettites in 1809, had no difficulty

[1] A rather extreme but not altogether unjust view of the Whigs as bumbling
appeasers may be found in Arthur Bryant, *Years of Victory, 1802–1812* (New York
and London, 1945).

in pointing out what he considered to be the real reason for Whig reluctance in this matter: Whigs and Tories alike were out to preserve the predominance of landed property; and however much the Whigs, being 'out', might raise the cry of 'reform' in order to get 'in', they had no intention of cutting their own throats by abolishing abuses which seemed to be the essential prerequisite for such predominance. As for their claim that the introduction into the House of Commons of the joint influence of Crown and peers had saved the hallowed balance of the Constitution, 'leave that to Mother Goose and Mother Blackstone!'[1]

There was certainly a great deal of difference between Burdett, with his genuinely democratic ideas, and Lord Holland, less concerned with increasing the power of the people than with restoring the influence of the House of Commons. This process of restoration the Foxites felt to be necessary because the Crown, by means of corruption and influence, seemed to be threatening once again the sacred equipoise of the balanced constitution. The adverse popular reaction to the Duke of York's scandal of 1809 showed that this issue of corruption could obtain for the Whigs the extra-parliamentary support they lacked on most other issues. But while the 'Mountain' was all for taking advantage of such situations, even if this involved co-operation with the Radicals, Grey and Grenville held disdainfully aloof. Most Whigs, in fact, had no intention of fundamentally undermining a system from which—if only they were 'in'—they still expected to derive considerable benefit. There was more than a little sour grapes involved in those measures of 'economical reform' which they continued to advocate during this period. But to blame the Whigs too severely for timidity and self-interest is, as Halévy justly remarks, to confuse 1809 with 1832.

Before any sweeping reform of the representation could be taken up by the Whigs, they would have to be frightened into it by the realization that a powerful Radical agitation arising from economic distress as well as from intellectually convinced democrats might pose a bigger threat to both the principles and the society established by 1688 than the allegedly increasing

[1] Jeremy Bentham, *Works*, III, 450; quoted in Roberts, *Whig Party*, 263.

influence of the Crown. For the latter was really a myth, a battle cry from the previous century which had lost all meaning. The Tories remained in office during this period because the country and the 'floating strength' of the House of Commons were behind them, not because of bribery or corruption, either on their part or on the part of the Crown. When George III finally went completely mad, the Prince Regent—from whom the Whigs had expected so much—concluded quite correctly that a vigorous war and 'No Popery' were more likely to find widespread support than the high-principled hesitations of a party divided against itself. So the Whigs were left to protest their virtue. They had remained demi-virginal, with all the handicaps and advantages of that position.

What of the Tories in this period? They, too, had their share of warring factions and intrigues—but their constituent elements, unlike those of the Whigs, agreed on fundamentals, and their generally successful prosecution of the war gave them a sort of national standing. Furthermore, thanks to the heritage of Pitt's advanced economic policies, they had the moneyed and commercial interests behind them, much to the alarm of the Whigs for whom 'even the Treasury and the Crown—seemed preferable to the City man and the East India magnate'.[1] It is true that by the time of Waterloo, this state of things had already begun to change. 'They [the Tories] were on the way to becoming once more a party narrowly conservative, rural, out of touch with the progressive forces of the nation.'[2] But the Whigs, for the most part, had not yet allied themselves with these progressive forces, and could do no better than to oppose a force that existed largely in their imaginations—the influence of the Crown—with one that had already begun to become anachronistic—the influence of landed property. The age of oligarchy and faction was dead. The future of the Whig party lay not with the Grenvillites, who were soon to break away, but with that very Radicalism which Grey and most of his friends held for so long in contempt, and which was one day to help them to their greatest triumph.

. . .

[1] Roberts, *Whig Party*, 236.
[2] Halévy, *England in 1815*, 193.

The Whig Party and the 'Edinburgh' Reviewers

Within a few months after the establishment of the *Review*, Brougham, Horner, and Smith had left for London and all of them were soon involved in the politics of the capital. Brougham immediately became active in the abolitionist movement under the aegis of Wilberforce, and in June, 1804, Pitt delivered one of his speeches on the subject holding in his hand Brougham's pamphlet entitled *A Concise Statement of the Question regarding the Abolition of the Slave Trade.*[1] Until 1806 Wilberforce was convinced that Brougham was a loyal supporter of the Tory cause, and, as Mr. Aspinall writes, 'had the Government had the discernment to put him into harness, he might have become permanently associated with the Tory party, and within a few years he might possibly have come to dispute with Canning for the leadership of the rising school of new Tories'.[2]

The Tories, however, missed their great opportunity. In July, 1805, Brougham's name first appeared on the dinner books of Holland House, where he owed his introduction to Dr. John Allen, the physician and scholar who had become a permanent resident there in 1802, and to Francis Horner, a constant visitor since his arrival in London in April of 1803.[3] Thenceforth he cultivated friendships with Holland, Grey, and other prominent Whigs, though for another year he kept one foot in the Tory camp. The Whigs were in no hurry to bring him into Parliament, but put him in charge of their press campaign of 1807, waged in connection with the General Election which followed the formation of the Duke of Portland's cabinet. Lord Holland

---

[1] Aspinall, *Lord Brougham and the Whig Party*, 11. Brougham must have swallowed the words he wrote to Horner in 1803, about his having sent Pitt a copy of his *Inquiry into the Colonial Policy of the European Powers*: 'Billy Pitt (whom I conscientiously think the ablest of them all) has also got a copy—but I fancy he forgot to keep up his reading when in place and is too old to learn again. . . .' Brougham to Horner, June 27, 1803, Horner Correspondence, L.S.E., II, 14.

[2] Aspinall, *Lord Brougham and the Whig Party*, 13.

[3] Giles Stephen Fox-Strangways, 6th Earl of Ilchester, *The Home of the Hollands, 1605–1820* (London, 1937), 309, 318. See also Lord Minto to Lady Minto, August 22, 1805: 'I have seen most of the Edinburgh Reviewers there [i.e. at Holland House] and amongst the rest is Mr. Horner.' Sir Gilbert Elliot-Murray-Kynynmound, 1st Earl of Minto, *Life and Letters, 1751–1806*, ed. Countess of Minto (London, 1874), III, 361. And see Sydney Smith to Sir James Mackintosh, October 1, 1805: 'She [Lady Holland] has taken hugely to the Edinburgh Reviewers, particularly little John Horner—whose reputation as well as Brougham's are so high for political oeconomy that they are fêted everywhere.' *The Letters of Sydney Smith*, ed. Nowell C. Smith (Oxford, 1953), I, 107.

later recalled the energy and ingenuity with which Brougham threw himself into this campaign.[1] By this time he had become a well-known figure in Lady Holland's salon, but that he failed to mingle devotion with discretion is shown by the following extract from a letter of Lady Bessborough's:

'Think of Mr. Brougham, the protégé of Lord Holland, and apparent toad-eater and adorer of Lady Holland, abusing her violently to Corisande and saying he *detested* her.'[2]

The letter is revealing not only in that it supplies proof (hardly needed) of Brougham's indiscretion, but in that it shows the position that a young man without wealth or family was expected to fill. One of Brougham's biographers has used the terms 'Amateur' and 'Professional' to distinguish between those 'who entered on public life as their birthright' and those who 'had to fight their way into politics by their ability and their cunning, or sometimes by their wealth'.[3] Brougham, like Burke and Sheridan before him, was one of the 'Professionals', and, like them, had to pay the price of his origin. Grey (by 1809) was calling Brougham 'the first man this country has seen since Burke's time'.[4] Yet it was only in 1810, when the Whigs began to fear that he might leave them if they neglected him much longer, that they finally brought him into Parliament for the Duke of Bedford's close borough of Camelford. It is true that his opportunism, his egocentricity, and his sharp tongue had a great deal to do with his difficulties. Horner was quite right when he wrote to Murray that Brougham tended to ignore the 'staid and reserved correctness, the systematic principles, the slow approach to honours, which, in this lazy order of things, are required of every political man who has not a hereditary name and fortune to give in earnest of all those requisites'.[5] He was too proud and independent to suit the Whig magnates, a heritage he may have owed to his mother, whose refusal to

[1] Henry Richard Vassall Fox, 3rd Baron Holland, *Memoirs of the Whig Party during my Time*, ed. Henry Edward Lord Holland (London, 1852–1854), II, 228.

[2] Lady Bessborough to Leveson-Gower, October 28, 1807, Granville Leveson-Gower, 1st Earl Granville, *Private Correspondence, 1781–1821*, ed. Countess Granville (London, 1916), II, 300.

[3] Geoffrey T. Garratt, *Lord Brougham* (London, 1935), 17–18.

[4] *The Creevey Papers*, ed. Sir Herbert Maxwell (New York, 1904), 108.

[5] Francis Horner to John Archibald Murray, October 25, 1804, Horner Correspondence, L.S.E., II, 76.

receive the scandalously divorced Lady Holland led to her son's virtual estrangement from Holland House for a period of over six years (1809–1815).[1]

In Parliament he soon distinguished himself as a forceful and intelligent speaker, but was not permitted by the Opposition leaders to act in any but a back-bench capacity. Even so, he was able, in 1811, to bring in and have successfully passed a Bill strengthening the existing legislation against the slave trade and, in the course of the following year, attacked the Orders in Council with such brilliance, energy, and effectiveness that the Tories under Liverpool were forced to repeal them. His triumph in this cause, which was the cause of the new industrial interests, shows that his path had led him far away from the basically agricultural economic interests of the Foxites to a now unaccustomed alliance of Whiggism and trade, which was to be prophetic of the future. It is no wonder that when the Duke of Bedford, perhaps the greatest of the Whig landowners, suddenly sold the borough for which Brougham sat, there was some speculation that the Duke's motive was to get rid of its representative. Actually, this was not the case.[2] But in any event, Brougham found himself without a seat, was defeated at the General Election of October, 1812, was not given another close borough by the Whigs, and remained out of Parliament for four years.

He had been moving ever closer to the Burdettite Radicals, and now that he had been—so to speak—given his walking papers by the regular Opposition, he definitely aligned himself with them. In 1814 Francis Place and the Benthamites supported his unsuccessful attempt to obtain nomination as a parliamentary candidate for the famous Radical constituency of Westminster. By that time Brougham had built up a considerable popular reputation through his activities as a lawyer. He twice (1811 and

---

[1] Henry Brougham, 1st Baron Brougham and Vaux, *The Life and Times of Henry Lord Brougham, Written by Himself* (Edinburgh and London, 1871), II, 100–101. Lord Holland himself later called the estrangement 'unaccountable', and claimed it was political as well as personal (Henry Richard Vassall Fox, 3rd Baron Holland, *Further Memoirs of the Whig Party, 1807–1821*, ed. Lord Stavordale [New York, 1905], 45.) But the Holland House MSS. quoted by Aspinall, *Lord Brougham and the Whig Party*, 25–27, show that the two men continued to correspond, at least until 1811.

[2] Aspinall, *Lord Brougham and the Whig Party*, 26.

1812) defended John and Leigh Hunt who were being prosecuted by the Government for libel, and in 1812 managed to obtain the acquittal of thirty-eight working-class Manchester Radicals who had been brought to trial in connection with the Luddite riots. It speaks for Lord Grey's sagacity that in spite of Brougham's activities in this period—and they were certainly left of the 'Mountain'—he still maintained cordial relations with him and, in 1816, helped him to obtain another seat in Parliament. Whatever Grey's own shortcomings in matters that required boldness and imagination, he may well have seen the importance of Brougham as an electric spark binding together, however intermittently, popular Radicalism and the Whig party.

Brougham's relation to the Whigs of 1815 has been aptly compared to that of Joseph Chamberlain to the Liberals sixty-five years later.[1] Both men wanted to take politics out of the control of the country houses, and both saw correctly which way the political winds were blowing and to what extent they owed their strength to economic forces. The fact that Brougham could remain within the Whig party shows that the efforts of Whitbread and the 'Mountain' had not been entirely in vain.

If Brougham was the bad boy of the Whigs, Horner was certainly their good boy. Unlike his voracious namesake in the nursery rhyme, he did not exclaim over this fact in public—and, in any event, would never have permitted himself to pull out even the tiniest plum. He was brought into Parliament by the Grenvillites, with whom he shared views favourable to Catholic Emancipation and to free trade, and throughout his parliamentary career (terminated by his premature death in 1817) he managed to advocate these and other principles in which he believed without stepping on anyone's toes. He owed this accomplishment partly to his monumental honesty, partly to a sense of caution worthy of Fabius himself. Unlike the latter, however, he did not have it in him to strike hard at any time, and one must grant some justice to Scott's comparison of him with Obadiah's bull 'who, though he certainly never did produce a calf, nevertheless went about his business with so much gravity, that he commanded the respect of the whole parish'.

[1] 'The Rise and Fall of Brougham', *The Times Literary Supplement*, No. 1737, (May 16, 1935), 305–306.

His two outstanding parliamentary activities involved his chairmanship of the great Bullion Committee of 1810 which recommended (for the time in vain) the resumption of cash payments, and his opposition to the Corn Law proposals of 1815, which earned him a vote of thanks from the City of London. He was an indefatigable exponent of Adam Smith's economics and has been called the first man to make the doctrines of political economy intelligible to the House of Commons whose members 'suspended for him their habitual dislike of lawyers, of political adventurers, and of young men of *conseederable taalents* from the North'.[1] Horner, too, though less flamboyantly than Brougham, epitomized a new kind of Whig—one who preferred financial and commercial statistics to the social whirl of the great country houses, and whose hagiology was headed not by Algernon Sidney but by Adam Smith.

Which brings us, in a manner that he might not have found entirely without merit, to 'the Sid'.[2] His name appeared on the dinner books of Holland House as early as 1799;[3] and when he settled in London four years later he became a regular and welcome guest there. In politics his principal contribution to the Whig cause—a cause in support of which 'I find as I see more of the World all the truly honest and able men (who are of any party at all) ranging themselves'[4]—was undoubtedly his publication of the *Letters of Peter Plymley* (1807–1808), a devastating indictment of Protestant intolerance regarding the emancipation of the Catholics. On other political questions he kept well to the right of the 'Mountain' and well to the left of Lord Grenville, of whose candidature under the Whig auspices for the Chancellorship of Oxford University he remarked to a large gathering at Holland House:

'The Whig canvass for Lord Grenville at Oxford is like the trustees of the Madgdalen applying to place a reclaimed prostitute at a bawdy house.'[5]

[1] Sydney Smith to Leonard Horner, August 26, 1842, *Memoirs and Correspondence of Francis Horner, M.P.*, ed. Leonard Horner (London, 1843), II, 436. See also Sydney Smith to Lady Holland, July 31, 1817, *Smith Letters*, I, 278–279.

[2] As Horner called him in a letter to Jeffrey, January 26, 1804, Horner Correspondence, L.S.E., II, 42.

[3] Ilchester, *Home of the Hollands*, 177. Lord Holland's aunt was Sydney Smith's sister.   [4] Smith to Jeffrey, January 30, 1806, *Smith Letters*, I, 111.

[5] Quoted in Hesketh Pearson, *The Smith of Smiths* (London, 1934), 141.

In 1809 when residence of clergy was enforced, Smith left London for his living in Yorkshire; and from then on, though he struck up a close friendship with Lord Grey and continued occasionally to visit London and Holland House, he was pretty much out of the main stream of Whig party politics.

The same held true, in a different sense, for Jeffrey. Between 1802 and 1815 he visited London a few times and took his American trip in order to call for his new wife—but apart from these journeyings he stuck to the Law Courts of Edinburgh. Scottish politics in this period bore little relation to the shifting tides and eddies that marked the last age of faction at Westminster. The power of Dundas (now Melville) was reinforced by patriotic fervour, and while it is true that his impeachment shattered the myth of his inviolability, his acquittal in 1806 produced widespread rejoicing, illuminations, and festive dinners in Edinburgh. Lady Minto, a resident there at the time, reported that the whole country considered Melville as its chief, that even while out of power he had never lost control of patronage, and that there was no such thing as an opinion between one political party and another: 'There are merely *Melvilleites*, without an idea that any other man can *serve Scotland*, as they call it.'[1]

The official leaders of what Scottish Whigs there were—the 'Seniors', as Cockburn calls them—were Lauderdale, Erskine, and Clerk. They had little use for Jeffrey and the young Whig lawyers in his circle; during the administration of All the Talents, none of the latter was even considered for office. And never were Jeffrey, Horner, or Brougham consulted on the affairs of the Scottish party by its older, far more conservative leaders.[2] During the brief Whig tenure of power, this split was dramatically illustrated, when Jeffrey and all the 'Juniors' opposed the reform of the Court of Session projected by Grenville and supported by the 'Seniors'. Partly through the growing reputation of the *Review*, the younger Edinburgh Whigs came to surpass their elders in social and literary influence, though they were unable to accomplish much in the realm of Scottish

[1] Lady Minto to Lord Minto, May 30, 1806, *Minto Letters*, III, 383–384.

[2] Henry Thomas Cockburn, Lord Cockburn, *Memorials of his Time* (Edinburgh and London, 1910), 200. Lord Lauderdale never forgave the *Review* for its unkind treatment of his book on the origin of public wealth. (Brougham, *ER*, VIII [July, 1804], 8.)

politics. Neither burgh nor parliamentary reform found much support during the war years and, as in England, the Whigs made themselves unpopular by their lack of consistent patriotic ardour for the war.[1]

It is worth noting that an Edinburgh meeting held in protest against West Indian slavery in July, 1814 was 'the first assembling of the people for a public object that had occurred here for about twenty years'.[2] A visitor observed in 1810 that the only political party in Edinburgh was one of obedience and loyalty; that there were few downright reformers among the better people; and none among the lower classes, for whom Whiggism was said to constitute rank democracy.[3]

Thus the situation was not at all comparable to that in London, where popular opinion could always make itself felt, and where, except for a very few years, Radicalism found active support from among the left wing of the parliamentary Whigs. The first respectable meeting held in Edinburgh, 'within the memory of man', for the avowed purpose of controlling Government on a political matter did not take place until after the war, when, in February, 1816, a public gathering protested against the income tax. Appropriately enough, the principal speaker was Francis Jeffrey.[4] For by that time he and the younger Whigs, bound together by the *Edinburgh Review*, had pretty well supplanted the 'Seniors' and had become the only political group which could, with any degree of effectiveness, put itself in opposition to that all-pervasive Scottish Toryism only then beginning to suffer its first inroads.[5]

[1] For an unsympathetic view of the Scottish Whigs, in sharp contrast to Cockburn's, see Sir Henry Craik, *A Century of Scottish History* (Edinburgh and London, 1901), II, 230–270. There is at present no satisfactory work on the history of Scotland between 1795 and 1815.

[2] Cockburn, *Memorials*, 271.

[3] [Louis Simond], *Journal of a Tour and Residence in Great Britain during the Years 1810 and 1811* (New York, 1815), I, 363–364.

[4] Henry Thomas Cockburn, Lord Cockburn, *Life of Lord Jeffrey, with a Selection from his Correspondence* (Edinburgh, 1852), I, 252.

[5] See Walter Scott's letter to Sir William Knighton, September 12, 1822, *The Letters of George IV*, ed. Arthur Aspinall (Cambridge, 1930), II, 539–543, for a succinct and valuable account of Scottish Whiggism in the early nineteenth century.

[4]

The Politics of the *Edinburgh Review*

I cannot say but I have a sneaking kindness for them. They have
done a great deal of good in lashing the boobies and bastards that are
fastened upon the public; but, what has long appeared to me evident,
is, that they want to supplant them, and to fasten *themselves* upon us;
rather than which I, for my Part, would have to maintain the boobies
and bastards, who, being somewhat gorged already, are likely to suck
our blood less unmercifully than those northern leeches would.

COBBETT on the *Edinburgh* reviewers[1]

Both Brougham and Smith, as they looked back on the
achievements of the *Edinburgh Review*, pointed out that
its importance could not really be understood without remembering the state of things at the time the *Review* was started.
'Protection reigned triumphant,' Brougham recalled, 'parliamentary representation in Scotland had scarcely an existence—
the Catholics were unemancipated—the test acts unrepealed—
men were hung for stealing a few shillings in a dwelling-
house, no counsel allowed to a prisoner accused of a capital
offence—the horrors of the slave-trade tolerated, the prevailing
tendencies of the age, jobbery and corruption.'[2] In this
remembrance of things past he may have had in mind Smith's
very similar statement which had appeared nearly thirty years
before:

'To appreciate the value of the Edinburgh Review, the state
of England at the period when that journal began should be had
in remembrance. The Catholics were not emancipated, the Corporation and Test Acts unrepealed, the Game Laws were hor-
ribly oppressive, Steel Traps and Spring Guns were set all over

[1] *Political Register*, XII, No. 15 (October 10, 1807), 556.
[2] Henry Brougham, 1st Baron Brougham and Vaux, *The Life and Times of Henry
Lord Brougham, Written by Himself* (Edinburgh and London, 1871), I, 253.

the country, Prisoners tried for their Lives could have no Counsel, Lord Eldon and the Court of Chancery pressed heavily upon mankind, Libel was punished by the most cruel and vindictive imprisonments, the principles of Political Economy were little understood, the Law of Debt and of Conspiracy were upon the worst possible footing, the enormous wickedness of the Slave Trade was tolerated, a thousand evils were in existence, which the talents of good and able men have since lessened or removed; and these effects have been not a little assisted by the honest boldness of the Edinburgh Review.'[1]

Both Brougham and Smith may doubtless be criticized for arrogating unto the *Review*—and thus themselves—too much of the credit for the removal of abuses whose effects were perhaps never quite as dire as they later pictured them. But if one attempts to arrive at a definition of those 'sounder and larger views of the great objects of human pursuit' whose dissemination Jeffrey considered to have been the most successful part of the *Review*'s function,[2] one finds that the reform of existing evils was from the very beginning a part of the reviewers' canon. And, in their eyes, the greatest of those evils lay in two unpalatable facts: the slave trade was still legally sanctioned, and the Irish Catholics were as yet unemancipated.

Paradoxically enough, the first call for the abolition of the slave trade—in the first number of the *Edinburgh Review*—came in conjunction with an article by Brougham which looked forward to the success of a French military expedition sent out to put down the independent negro republic of Santo Domingo, whose continued existence would, he thought, put in jeopardy the European balance of power. Brougham, who took the same line in his *Inquiry Into the Colonial Policy of the European Powers* (1803), here expressed the hope that England, Holland, and Spain would join the French in their struggle against 'the Jacobins of the West India Islands'.[3] After this, his demand for the total abolition of the slave trade, 'the root of all the evils',

[1] *The Works of Sydney Smith* (Boston, 1854), 3–4.
[2] Francis Jeffrey, *Contributions to the Edinburgh Review* (2nd ed., London, 1846), I, xi.
[3] Brougham, *ER*, I (October, 1802), 27, 226–227.

comes almost as an anticlimax.[1] Similar strictures on the attempts of the West Indian negroes to gain their freedom were expressed by the reviewers twice again in the course of the next four years.[2]

Dr. Aspinall regards the *Review*'s attitude on this question as proof that its influence was not invariably exerted on the side of progress and enlightenment.[3] One must certainly not approach it with this expectation. In this as well as many other instances the *Edinburgh* followed prevailing winds of doctrine. After the Peace of Amiens British opinion was largely in favour of Bonaparte's attempt to reconquer Santo Domingo, and Brougham shared the general fear of a threat to white hegemony in the West Indies.[4] As late as November, 1814, when the Congress of Vienna had already begun to settle the fate of the defeated enemy, the *Review* recalled that twelve years earlier the interests of France and England had required the reduction of the West Indian negroes, though it was now inclined to doubt the advisability of this line of action.[5]

By this time, however, the *Review* had come to oppose slavery as well as the slave trade[6] and was certainly justified in priding itself on twelve years of unremitting opposition to the latter.[7] Jeffrey quite correctly called the slave-trade question unpolitical;[8] but it is a measure of the *Review*'s change of line towards Pitt that in 1802 it praised him for his devotion to the cause, while eight years later it attacked him for having done nothing

[1] *Ibid.*, 233.

[2] Jeffrey, *ER*, VIII (July, 1804), *17*, 477; and *ER*, XV (April, 1806), *3*, 52. (Note: Identifications, when given, only apply to the individual citation and are not carried over. Thus the second article cited in this note is *not* by Jeffrey.)

[3] Arthur Aspinall, *Lord Brougham and the Whig Party* (Manchester, 1927), 47.

[4] Cf. Frank J. Klingberg, *The Anti-Slavery Movement in England* (New Haven, 1926), 120–121; and cf. Lord Holland's statement after the passing of the abolition measure that 'whilst, on the one hand, it was essentially just that the trade should be abolished, it would on the other hand, be injustice to the slaves in the islands to give them emancipation, because it could only tend to their own injury'. And even Wilberforce on this occasion declared himself against immediate emancipation. William Smart, *Economic Annals of the Nineteenth Century, 1801–1820* (London, 1910), 132.

[5] *ER*, XLVII (November, 1814), *6*, 127.

[6] *ER*, XLII (July, 1813), *11*, 474.

[7] *ER*, XLVII (November, 1814), *6*, 132.

[8] Jeffrey, *ER*, VIII (July, 1804), *17*, 476.

about it beyond making speeches.[1] However, shortly afterwards, Canning and Perceval received praise for their steady abolitionism.[2] Credit for passing the great measure itself could, of course, be given to the Ministry of All the Talents: Brougham had properly hailed the event, adding that this was one of those public questions on which men had only differed because they had not fully discussed them.[3] Brougham's formulation here is significant. For it would not be wrong to say that the *Edinburgh* reviewers, enviably convinced of their ultimate verities and of the power of reason to arrive at them, saw their periodical as a forum for discussion from which truth universally acknowledged must inevitably result.

In 1810 the *Review* announced its patronage of the African Institution—whose leading members included Brougham as well as all the prominent 'Saints'—and asked readers to send information about infractions of the abolition law to the *Edinburgh* publishers or to Zachary Macaulay, the secretary of the Institution.[4] It steadily continued to support the Institution, to review its publications, and to deplore the fact that the Spaniards and the Portuguese were carrying on the trade.[5] Its special interest in this question was no doubt largely due to Brougham whose connection with Wilberforce dated from 1803 and whose enthusiasm in the abolitionist cause never flagged. But, more important, the reviewers found that the slave trade was that issue which 'alone, perhaps, of all political topics, has afforded a point of union for the wise and good of every class,—alone, in the mighty fluctuation of human affairs, has displayed a ground where men might conscientiously hold the same straightforward course, without being inconsistent'.[6]

.   .   .

[1] Brougham, *ER*, I (October, 1802), *27*, 237; Brougham, *ER*, XXX (January, 1810), *14*, 486.
[2] Brougham, *ER*, XXXII (August, 1810), *9*, 441.
[3] Brougham, *ER*, XIX (April, 1807), *13*, 206. For an interesting comment on Sydney Smith and the liberal logic of assuming basic concepts of truth and justice, with a concomitant belief in the efficacy of discussion, see W. H. Auden, 'Portrait of a Whig', Mario Praz, ed., *English Miscellany*, III (Rome, 1952), 141–158.
[4] Brougham, *ER*, XXX (January, 1810), *14*, 498–501.
[5] Cf. Brougham, *ER*, XXVIII (July, 1809), *2*, 322; Brougham, *ER*, XXXII (August, 1810), *9*, 430 and 443; and *ER*, XXXIX (July, 1812), *5*, 61.
[6] *ER*, L (October, 1815), *2*, 345.

Could not the same be said of Catholic Emancipation? After all, this was the question on which Burke, Fox, and Pitt agreed —and the *Review*, noting this agreement, promised solemnly that no considerations of party would ever enter into its views in discussing the Catholic question.[1] Shortly afterwards, Jeffrey expressed the hope that the 'liberal part of the community' would be able to distinguish the advocates of the Catholic cause from the zealots of a party.[2] But since this very non-partisan cause constituted, as has been noted, the only major policy on which all sections of the Whigs were in agreement during this period, it is not surprising that on occasion the Tories aided and abetted by the Methodists were given a major share of the blame for the unfortunate state of the Irish Catholics.[3]

Nevertheless, it is certainly true that the pros and cons of the question were generally argued on a far higher level than that of party. Typical of the many articles published on this subject is one that bears brief analysis in illustration of a frequent method of argument employed by the reviewers.[4] At the start comes the statement of a general principle ('We may venture to lay it down as a general proposition, that all restrictive laws, which exclude certain classes of men from political stations, are, in their immediate operation, oppressive and impolitic'); there follows an appeal to the pride presumably felt by the readers in their contemporary civilization ('Do we laugh at the hereditary casts of the old Egyptians, which kept the son of a cobler [sic] to his father's awl, and checked a passion for laying bricks in the young basketmaker, like felony or sacrilege?'); this in turn is followed by the utilitarian argument ('. . . such restrictions must be defended, not as beneficial in themselves, but as means of purchasing some essential good, or warding off some evil, more important than those which they bring with them'); which puts the burden of proof wholly on those who want to retain the restrictions. This and a great many of the other reviews concerned with the Catholics point out the absurdity of fearing that they constituted, actually or potentially, a dangerous force. 'We

[1] *ER*, XIX (April, 1807), *9*, 136.
[2] Jeffrey, *ER*, XXI (October, 1807), *8*, 117.
[3] For example, cf. *ER*, XXXVIII (February, 1812), *9*, 465.
[4] *ER*, XVI (July, 1806), *6*, 311–313.

should as soon dream', wrote Sydney Smith in the first number, 'that the wars of York and Lancaster would break out afresh, as that the Protestant religion in England has any thing to apprehend from the machinations of Catholics.'[1]

And on this question the *Review* never wavered—though in 1807, after the fall of the Talents, it was forced to concede that opponents of the Catholic claims unfortunately comprehended too large a portion of the public to be reviled or turned into ridicule—a wonderfully revealing comment on the self-imposed limits of the *Review*'s function and method.[2] For its implication appears to be an admission that those weapons were to be employed only when minority views were clearly involved, with reader opinion automatically assumed to be in harmony with editorial views; and that sweet reasonableness must be resorted to when this was not the case. When the absurdity he ridicules is taken seriously by the majority, it is only too easy for the critic himself to appear absurd—and to lose his readers. The favourite *Edinburgh* device of setting timeless common sense against temporary absurdity had its limitations.

Unlike Lord Grey and many of the Foxites, the reviewers did not feel that the condition for meeting the Irish Catholic claims was to be their recognition of royal veto power in the appointment of Bishops.[3] It was their opinion that complete emancipation should precede discussion of special provisions and expedients.[4] The Whig leaders, however, never adopted the *Edinburgh*'s advice on this point and stuck to their attitude of compromise. Professor Roberts rightly feels that they would have done more justice to their good intentions by adopting more extreme views from the start.[5] The *Review*, at any rate, deserves credit for its consistent defence of an unpopular cause, on which it conceded very little to party politics.

Brougham and Smith were fully justified in praising the exertions of the *Edinburgh Review* on behalf of slave-trade abolition

[1] Smith, *ER*, I (October, 1802), *9*, 90.
[2] *ER*, XIX (April, 1807), *9*, 124–125.
[3] Smith, *ER*, XXVII (April, 1809), *5*, 63–64; also *ER*, XXVII (April, 1809), *12*, 169, and Jeffrey, *ER*, XXXIII (November, 1810), *1*, 30.
[4] *ER*, XL (November, 1812), *5*, 368–369.
[5] Michael Roberts, *The Whig Party, 1807–1812* (London, 1939), 101.

and Catholic Emancipation. Did it equally merit their praise as
an organ that opposed all the abuses associated with the age of
Eldon? And to what extent did it disseminate the ideas of the
most prominent fighter against those abuses, Jeremy Bentham?
It is easy to list instances of the reforming spirit: opposition to
the sale of army commissions;[1] to flogging in the British army
and navy;[2] to the enforcement of the Test and Corporation Acts
—partly for the very good reason that all Scotsmen holding
offices in England, 'a pretty numerous band', would be affected;[3]
and enthusiastic support for Romilly's proposed legal reforms[4]
and for Howard's plans for reforming the prisons.[5]

More interesting as a subject for analysis is the *Review's*
general attitude in this period towards utilitarian—and, specifically, Benthamite Utilitarian—ideas. In the very first number
Sydney Smith praised Dr. Parr for maintaining (against Godwin) that our actions cannot be justified by being 'natural', but
that a principle of general utility must be sought to regulate
them.[6] Jeffrey, reviewing Bentham's *Principles of Legislation*
some months later, accepts as a truism the doctrine that laws
are made to promote the general welfare of society, and that
nothing should be enacted which has a different tendency.[7] He
had previously declared himself in agreement with Millar's
maxim that the principle of authority was everywhere giving
way to the principle of utility, so that even the Tories were
arguing for an enlargement of royal power on the basis of its
tendency to promote good order and the ultimate happiness of
the community.[8] But in commenting on the obvious nature of
Bentham's doctrine, Jeffrey feels bound to add that 'we can
scarcely remember any one of his [Bentham's] practical maxims

[1] *ER*, XVI (July, 1806), *5*, 311.
[2] Brougham, *ER*, XXXVI (August, 1811), *2*, 324–325.
[3] *ER*, XXXVII (November, 1811), *6*, 162.
[4] Brougham, *ER*, XXXVIII (February, 1812), *7*, 389–415. Cf. especially page
403, where the repeal of capital punishment for felonies is approved, and page 409
where bankruptcy and debt law reforms are welcomed.
[5] *ER*, XLIV (January, 1814), *7*, 385–400. With this article the reviewers atoned
for the rosy view of prison life which they had presented eleven years earlier. Cf.
Aspinall's criticism, *Brougham and the Whig Party*, 48.
[6] Smith, *ER*, I (October, 1802), *2*, 19–20.
[7] Jeffrey, *ER*, VII (April, 1804), *1*, 10.
[8] Jeffrey, *ER*, V (October, 1803), *13*, 177.

that can possibly be conceived to be overlooked for a moment by the legislature for whose illumination this work is intended'.[1] He accuses Bentham of forgetting that there is such a thing as common sense in the world and of exaggerating the frequency and extent of abuses.[2] In a similar vein Horner had paid homage to the 'resolute unclouded calmness of English justice which . . . is the last [in Europe] to retain a sense of ancient rights, a veneration and observance of ancient maxims'.[3]

This Burkean strain of awe before established institutions is, on the whole, confined to the *Review*'s early years. A definite tendency towards Benthamite ideas begins to manifest itself in the course of the year 1806, when the trial of Melville and the proposed reform of the Scottish Court of Session brought the issues of corruption, abuses, and their amendment squarely into the foreground.[4] In his article on Scottish legal reform Jeffrey asks whether it is better to bear with habitual inconvenience out of respect for what is established than to purchase respite by a series of great and periodical disorders. His answer is that the hazards of reformation are to be preferred to the accumulation of established evils. He comments on the characteristic English faculty for praising everything peculiarly their own, and quotes Bentham at length to show how mistaken this attitude becomes when applied to existing legal institutions.[5] Dumont reported to Bentham about this article that 'after some praises (you may see his part in this) he [Jeffrey] desires you should be engaged on this subject'.[6] And a few weeks later, Horner expressed his satisfaction with Jeffrey's conversion to his own favourable view of Bentham's book on French judicature.[7]

[1] Jeffrey, *ER*, VII (April, 1804), *1*, 17. Dumont was shocked by the 'scandalous irreverence of the article'. Elie Halévy, *The Growth of Philosophic Radicalism*, trans. Mary Morris (new ed., London, 1934), 298.

[2] Jeffrey, *ER*, VII (April, 1804), *1*, 19.

[3] Horner, *ER*, IV (July, 1803), *18*, 477.

[4] Also cf. the revealing correspondence between Jeffrey and Horner after the death of Fox: Horner to Jeffrey, September 15, 1805, *Memoirs and Correspondence of Francis Horner, M.P.*, ed. Leonard Horner (London, 1843), I, 373–377; Jeffrey to Horner, September 18, 1806, Henry Thomas Cockburn, Lord Cockburn, *Life of Lord Jeffrey, with a Selection from his Correspondence* (Edinburgh, 1852), II, 110–113.

[5] Jeffrey, *ER*, XVIII (January, 1807), *14*, 464–465, 481.

[6] Dumont to Bentham, February 10, 1807, Jeremy Bentham, *Works*, ed. Bowring (Edinburgh, 1843), X, 422.

[7] Horner to John Archibald Murray, April 7, 1807, *Horner Memoirs*, I, 400.

James Mill, at this time an advanced Whig, who may have known Jeffrey in his student days, began to contribute to the *Edinburgh Review* in 1808. After his fateful meeting with Bentham, he used the *Review* as a means for the propagation of the latter's ideas. 'Jeffrey', Halévy writes, 'considered that James Mill was abusing his rights as a writer, and he suppressed Bentham's name in some article or other while retaining his ideas—this resulted in Mill's being treated at Holland House as an "impudent plagiarist".'[1] The important thing was, of course, the fact of Jeffrey's retention of Benthamite ideas. Thus the Spanish colonies in South America were warned not to be duped by the 'vague and inaccurate' division of the powers of government into legislative, executive and judicial;[2] only those actions of mankind from which good or evil might arise were recognized as the proper objects of legislators who were told to look to Bentham as the only source for the calculation of goods and evils;[3] and Bentham himself was lauded as one 'who, with all his dogmatism and irreverence for existing institutions, has treated the whole subject of legislation with a spirit, a precision, and a profundity which entitle all his suggestions to the most deliberate and respectful consideration'.[4]

By the time these articles appeared, Bentham himself, disgusted by the failure of his schemes for legal reform, had already joined the Radical Burdettites. Needless to say, the *Edinburgh Review* did not follow him in thus accepting the full consequences of his doctrines. But it was surely in consonance with his spirit when it condemned the common (and Whiggish) mode of arguing *à Gulielmo*, i.e. by referring every problem to the hypothetical actions of those involved in the Glorious Revolution

---

[1] Halévy, *Growth of Philosophic Radicalism*, 301. The article must have been *ER*, XXIX (October, 1809), *6*, 88–109, a review of Scipion Bexon, *Application de la Théorie de la Legislation pénale etc.* Horner wrote to Jeffrey about this article that the true Benthamites 'consider you as having committed plagiarism in taking the doctrines and even the very language of their master, without acknowledgement'. Horner to Jeffrey, December 7, 1809, Horner Correspondence, L.S.E., IV, 78. See also Michael St. John Packe, *The Life of John Stuart Mill* (London, 1954), 12.

[2] *ER*, XXVI (January, 1809), *2*, 308. This article was, in part, the work of James Mill.

[3] *ER*, XXIX (October, 1809), *6*, 98, 101–102.

[4] *ER*, XXXIII (November, 1810), *4*, 114.

of 1688.[1] And less than ten years after Jeffrey had accused Bentham of being a manufacturer of truisms, the *Edinburgh Review* made handsome amends by reprimanding its 'cursory' readers for wrongly making the very same accusation.[2]

Burke's veneration for established institutions found occasional echoes in the early years of the *Edinburgh Review*; and it is possible to cite instances which seem to point to a negatively Burkean attitude towards the French Revolution. Thus Sydney Smith, in the first number, berates a traveller in France reporting Robespierre's tenure of power for perpetually bursting into tears at the thought of the iniquities of the feudal system, when the scenes passing before his eyes exceeded in horror all that had gone before;[3] another writer in the same issue assures the readers of the new periodical that 'nobody can more thoroughly detest and despise that restless spirit of political innovation, which we suppose is meant by Jacobinism, than we ourselves do'.[4] A little later Horner blames the French revolutionaries for 'forgetting that the arrangements of nature are developed and perfected imperceptibly with the lapse of ages';[5] while Jeffrey remarks about them that 'in legislating for their country, they seem to have forgotten that they were operating on a living and sentient substance, and not on an inert and passive mass, which they might model and compound according to their pleasure or their fancy'.[6]

But instances of this kind are few and far between. On the whole, the reviewers consistently devoted their efforts to a reasoned defence of what they considered to be the positive aspects of the French Revolution, a defence whose corollary was vigorous condemnation of anti-Jacobinism as a rationale for opposition to liberal views and moderate reforms.

One important reason for the frequency and vehemence with which these sentiments occur lies in the particularly unhappy

[1] Smith, *ER*, XLI (February, 1813), *4*, 99–100. See also Brougham, *ER*, XXXVIII (February, 1812), *7*, 389–390.

[2] Brougham, *ER*, XLIII (October, 1813), *1*, 30. The Panopticon finds approbation in this same article.

[3] Smith, *ER*, I (October, 1802), *10*, 92.   [4] *ER*, I (October, 1802), *12*, 97.

[5] Horner, *ER*, V (October, 1803), *17*, 225.

[6] Jeffrey, *ER*, XI (April, 1805), *12*, 142.

The Politics of the 'Edinburgh Review'

experiences of the Scottish reformers in the 1790's under Pitt's
repressive policies, and in the traumatic jolt which the small
band of Edinburgh Whigs had sustained in consequence. Perhaps the most personal note struck in thirteen years of reviewing may be found in an article which recalls the Government
persecutions of those years:

'We speak not from hearsay—or from fancy [Brougham
writes]—but from distinct and personal recollection. . . . We
speak from a feeling recollection;—for, where did this unutter-
able baseness—this infinite misery—this most humiliating curse,
fall so heavily as in the city where we now write?—and for no
other reason, but because Scotland has no popular spirit, from
having no popular elections—and because her courts of justice
were, at that time, considerably behind the courts of Westminster.'[1]

Cockburn, reminiscing about Edinburgh in the late eighteenth
and early nineteenth centuries, writes that 'everything rung, and
was connected with the Revolution in France; which, for above
twenty years, was, or was made, the all in all. Everything, not
this or that thing, but literally everything, was soaked in this
event. . . . Jacobinism was a term denoting everything alarming
and hateful, and every political objector was a Jacobin.'[2] All
this must be kept in mind in considering the preoccupation of the
reviewers with the French Revolution, and their disagreement
with Burke's view of it.

Possibly the most effective feature of the Edinburgh's campaign against hysterical anti-Jacobins was its deliberate cultivation of a tone of bored exasperation on the subject of 'the horrors
of the French Revolution'. Sydney Smith first strikes this note in
considering himself 'long since wearied with this kind of discourses, bespattered with blood and brains, and ringing eternal
changes upon atheism, cannibalism, and apostasy'.[3] And it is
struck many times more—whether a philosopher is reprimanded
for the irrelevant introduction of 'crimes of mobs, and encyclopedists, and guillotines',[4] one traveller accused of enlivening his

[1] Brougham, ER, XXXI (April, 1810), 5, 120.
[2] Henry Thomas Cockburn, Lord Cockburn, Memorials of His Time (Edinburgh, 1910), 73 and 75.
[3] Smith, ER, I (October, 1802), 9, 87.
[4] (Jeffrey possibly co-author), ER, II (January, 1803), 1, 257.

estimate of the Chinese character with 'puerile and misplaced invectives on the atheism and wickedness of revolutionary France',[1] or another attacked for the bad taste of the 'silly rancour' with which he is pleased, in 1806, to attack the levelling doctrines of the French republicans.[2] Nor is Gentz permitted to escape without stricture for calling the enormities of the French Revolution 'unparalleled'.[3] In the very first article of the *Edinburgh Review* Jeffrey had looked forward to a time when men would recover from the apprehensions and contests engendered by the Revolution and would begin to study its moral tragedy.[4] And throughout its early career the *Review* valiantly attempted to put the discussion of the Revolution on a higher and non-polemical level.

An important part of this attempt was the defence of the great figures of the French Enlightenment against the obscurantist attacks of the anti-Jacobins. Turgot, Mirabeau, and Quesnay, 'friends of mankind', are not to be included in 'that undistinguished reprobation of the past, which in the feelings of the populace has very naturally succeeded to fanaticism and terror'.[5] Nor is any single volume of Arthur Young's to be exalted, as one author suggests, over cartloads of Voltaire, D'Alembert, Diderot, and Rousseau.[6] In 1802 even Jeffrey had commented on the harmful tendency of the 'presumptuous theories and audacious maxims' of Rousseau, Mably, and Condorcet.[7] But seven years later the *Review* praised Condorcet as one of the most original writers of his age, surpassed by none of his contemporaries in brilliancy of genius and variety of his acquirements.[8] Similar praise was accorded Voltaire who was defended against ignorance and prejudice, and called unrivalled for the extent and variety of his genius.[9]

---

[1] Jeffrey, *ER*, X (January, 1805), *1*, 288.
[2] Jeffrey, *ER*, XVII (October, 1806), *1*, 2.
[3] Brougham, *ER*, XVIII (January, 1807), *1*, 264.
[4] Jeffrey, *ER*, I (October, 1802), *1*, 17; also cf. Jeffrey (and Brougham), *ER*, III (April, 1803), *1*, 1; and Jeffrey, *ER*, XXIV (July, 1808), *1*, 278.
[5] Horner, *ER*, II (January, 1803), *16*, 431–432.
[6] Brougham, *ER*, IX (October, 1804), *1*, 4.
[7] Jeffrey, *ER*, I (October, 1802), *1*, 11.   [8] *ER*, XXVII (April, 1809), *15*, 240.
[9] Jeffrey, *ER*, XXXIV (February, 1811), *2*, 300–301. Cf. also the comment on the impetus given to scholarship in the mathematical sciences by the Revolution, *ER*, XXX (January, 1810), *9*, 396.

This defence of the *philosophes* by the *Edinburgh Review* is all the more significant, since Jeffrey insisted from the start that they had indeed a great deal to do with the causes of the French Revolution.[1] The question of causation was important, not only because it supplied an example of the influence of ideas on political events, thus enhancing the significance of the *Review's* own function, but also because it opened the way for a comparative analysis of social and political conditions in France and England. Where is the man, asks a reviewer in 1805, who will not confess the difficulty of clearly delineating the line of public duty which a French patriot should have followed at the start of the Revolution?[2] A question which, for the readers of the *Review*, must have taken on special import when they considered it in conjunction with Jeffrey's repeated assertions that the true cause of the French Revolution was the exclusion of the main body of the French people from places of distinction and authority.[3] For it was, of course, quite true that the Revolution 'has tended more to fix the attention of mankind upon the political circumstances of society, than all the facts which occupy the pages of antecedent history'.[4] And in the case of England the peculiar vigour of a society in which the privileged orders did not arrogate too much power and influence to themselves might perhaps be infused by 'an enlightened administration of her existing government'.[5]

The French Revolution had had the effect of creating an unreasonable and undiscriminating dread of all alteration and reform.[6] But the very strength of France lay in the singular display of talents in every department of human affairs which the Revolution had occasioned.[7] In England, meanwhile, all the great offices in the state were virtually monopolized by a few great families and much talent was suppressed, merely because everyone knew that it was impossible to get anywhere without making

[1] Jeffrey, *ER*, I (October, 1802), *1*, 6–11.
[2] *ER*, X (January, 1805), *13*, 422.
[3] Jeffrey, *ER*, XIX (April, 1807), *1*, 12; and Jeffrey, *ER*, XXI (October, 1807), *8*, 125.
[4] *ER*, XLIII (October, 1813), 7, 109.
[5] Jeffrey, *ER*, XIX (April, 1807), *1*, 13.
[6] Jeffrey, *ER*, XI (April, 1805), *12*, 138.
[7] Brougham, *ER*, XVIII (January, 1807), *1*, 275.

use of 'influence'.[1] It was in this way that the French Revolution was used by the reviewers as a spur to reform. 'Even those among us', wrote one of them in 1808 after deploring the illiberal and partial views which the Revolution had produced in England, 'who would prize the Epicurean delights of property under a certain gentle servitude which they picture in their imaginations, and are afraid even to breathe a sentiment in favour of liberty, lest it should shake the security of their darling possessions, would do well to consider what has become of the property of those degenerate nobles, who, in the various countries which the French have overcome, had made themselves the agents of corruption and despotism.'[2]

Here the armies of Napoleon are seen as a reforming force, fighters against the degenerate remnants of European feudalism. This view shows more than a certain amount of historical insight on the part of the reviewer. It reveals a rare degree of objectivity towards an enemy who was at that moment still threatening to make himself master of the world. It also implies a respect for the power of Napoleon characteristic of the strong strain of appeasement which runs through the *Review* until the Napoleonic wars entered their final stage. Brougham was to write many years later:

'I believe in my conscience that it [the *Edinburgh Review*] has, since 1802, done more for peace and against war, than all other engines of public good, the pulpit certainly included. It is our most glorious title to general esteem. It is one of our corner-stones, and the "head corner-stone".'[3]

This was certainly not the view taken by the general public at the time. At the end of 1807 a pamphleteer asked what motives had induced the reviewers to introduce into their work so many elaborate and anxious essays on the subject of peace, and accused them of being 'apologists for the excesses and crimes of the greatest miscreant and tyrant that ever scourged Europe'.[4] And

[1] Jeffrey, *ER*, XIX (April, 1807), *1*, 14–16.
[2] *ER*, XXV (October, 1808), *12*, 188–189.
[3] Brougham to Macvey Napier, December 23, 1837, *Selection from the Correspondence of the Late Macvey Napier, Esq.*, ed. M. Napier (London, 1879), 217.
[4] 'Cornelius Scipio', *A Sketch of the Politics of the Edinburgh Reviewers as Exhibited in their First Three Numbers for the Year 1807* (London, 1807), 69.

it is true that the *Edinburgh's* campaign for a negotiated peace
had been pressed with special vigour ever since early in 1806,
when All the Talents—from whom the reviewers expected
much in this direction—had come into power after Pitt's last
war ministry.[1]

The Whigs, while in office, were forced to change their mind
about the chances of peace. Even Fox commented on the French
negotiators that 'the shuffling, insincere ways in which they act
show me they are playing a false game'.[2] But the *Review* continued to advocate the necessity for attempts at accommodation
with Napoleon, and lived up to its self-appointed role as the
Cassandra of the Whig party by issuing an unending series of
gloomy predictions about the outcome of the Spanish Revolt
and the Peninsular War, and dwelling on the ever-increasing
invincibility of the French.[3] Lord Grey, himself a reluctant
warrior at best, was far from enthusiastic about the despondent
line of the *Edinburgh Review*. Lady Bessborough reported in the
late summer of 1808 that he was 'quite right about, and quite as
much out of patience as I was at the Ed. review of Whitbread's
letter [XXIV, *11*]—he has none of the cold despondency of
Castle Howard, and said today quite as heartily as you could:
"Now for some good news from Wellesley, and we will fire a
feu de joie and drink bumpers."'[4]

Jeffrey who in private company seems to have had the capacity for setting off a continual series of *feux de joie* as well as for
drinking bumpers never carried his cheerfulness into his prog-
nostications on matters military and political. It might almost

[1] Cf. Brougham, *ER*, XV (April, 1806), *15*, 198–206; Brougham, *ER*, XVIII
(January, 1807), *1*, 278; *ER*, XVIII (January, 1807), *11*, 427–432; Jeffrey, *ER*,
XIX (April, 1807), *1*, 1–27; Brougham, *ER*, XX (July, 1807), *1*, 271; and
Brougham, *ER*, XX (July, 1807), *8*, 368–385.

[2] Quoted in Smart, *Economic Annals*, 111.

[3] On Spain, cf. especially Brougham, *ER*, XXIV (July, 1808), *11*, 434–445; *ER*,
XXVI (January, 1809), *9*, 459–460; Brougham, *ER*, XXVII (April, 1809), *16*,
254–264. The famous 'Don Cevallos' review, Jeffrey and Brougham, *ER*, XXV
(October, 1808), *14*, 215–234, is more enthusiastic about the chances of the
Spanish patriots, but also concludes with a call for negotiations.

[4] Lady Bessborough to Granville Leveson-Gower, August 22, 1808, Granville
Leveson-Gower, 1st Earl Granville, *Private Correspondence (1781–1821)*, ed.
Castalia Countess Granville (London, 1916), II, 320–321. On Grey's optimism on
Spain, cf. also Brougham to James Loch, July 30, 1808, R. H. M. Buddle Atkinson
and G. A. Jackson, *Brougham and his Early Friends* (London, 1908), II, 315.

seem as if these affairs served to bring out his melancholy strain. In 1810 he wrote that as long as the Napoleonic system retained its energy it was bound to continue its triumphs over 'diseased and decrepit masses of corpulent impotence'[1]—a nicely turned compliment to His Royal Highness the Prince Regent. At that time he offered the interesting suggestion that if resistance to the French would only cease on the Continent—Britain, meanwhile, was to keep up her naval supremacy but engage in no military operations—then France, like Rome after her era of conquest, would go into a decline.[2] Here was historical theory applied to present practice—with a vengeance!

It was no wonder that the *Review* soon saw a need for defending itself against charges of sympathy with France and Napoleon.[3] It would be hard to substantiate either charge. The reviewers never lost their positive view of the achievements of the French Revolution—but neither did they indulge in Lord Holland's hero-worship of Napoleon. In the early days of the *Review* Sydney Smith defended him against lightly brought charges of poisoning sick French soldiers at Jaffa;[4] and that was just about the extent of the favourable notice he personally received in the periodical. Jeffrey had a healthy respect for the power of France whose institutions, he thought, owed their resilience in great part to the Revolution. But even though Napoleon 'must be acknowledged to have entwined himself with the existing institutions', his individual genius could not explain their strength, just as his death would not restore the independence of Europe.[5] The *Review* continued to predict doom and to advocate pacific policies at every critical juncture;[6] but after Waterloo it had some justification for criticizing the 'sort of hankering' after Napoleon 'which we can trace among some of our good

---

[1] Jeffrey, *ER*, XXXI (April, 1810), *1*, 19. [2] *Ibid.*, 25–29.

[3] Cf. Brougham, *ER*, XXXII (August, 1810), *4*, 354; *ER*, XXXV (May, 1811), *9*, 235–236. For an attack on the *Review* for placing Napoleon not far from the level of Frederick the Great and Catherine the Great see *A Letter to Francis Jeffrey, Esq., Editor of the Edinburgh Review by an Anti-Reformist* (Edinburgh, 1811), 68 and 71.

[4] Smith, *ER*, III (April, 1803), *4*, 62–63; and Smith, *ER*, IV (July, 1803), *4*, 331–333.

[5] Jeffrey, *ER*, XXXI (April, 1810), *1*, 20–24.

[6] Cf. Brougham, *ER*, XXXIX (July, 1812), *12*, 214–234; and after Napoleon's return from Elba, *ER*, XLVIII (February, 1815), *7*, 394–396.

Whigs', and in maintaining that 'to us, he has always appeared a most pernicious and detestable tyrant, without feeling, principle, or concern for human sufferings or honour—and such he appears to us still.'[1]

At the same time it was thus summing up its judgment of the defeated enemy the *Review* objected to the restoration of so many of the old sovereigns (without safeguards for their peoples) in countries where abuses had been most manifest, and expressed fears that their resumption of indefeasible and hereditary rights was being given precedence over the re-establishment of the balance and tranquillity of Europe.[2] The *Edinburgh*, from its very beginning, had steadfastly upheld the importance and desirability of the European balance of power. Brougham in 1803 looked back with ill-concealed nostalgia to the eighteenth century when, in areas especially set aside for this purpose, a few useless lives and some superfluous millions in money were all that was to be lost in war. Britain, he wrote, must participate in any balancing system in order to protect her international commerce.[3] But what of the argument that the balance of Europe had now been entirely overthrown by the enormous power of France, and that Europe's future was to be entirely dependent on French caprice? In reviewing Friedrich Gentz's *Etat de l'Europe*, in which this pessimistic view was advanced, Jeffrey disagreed with it, calling the principle of the balance of power something immortal that would apply itself in any combination of circumstances.

At this point (1803) he was still optimistic enough to believe in the probable effectiveness of an Austro-Prussian coalition against France.[4] But Napoleon's victories soon destroyed the hopes of an automatic adjustment in the style of the previous century. It could still be maintained that the recent subversion of the European balance simply proved that the influence of

[1] Brougham, *ER*, L (October, 1815), *11*, 511. In 1814, Jeffrey had called Napoleon a creature to be abhorred, but not to be despised: 'History, we think, will not class him quite so low as the English newspapers of the present day.' Jeffrey, *ER*, XLV (April, 1814), *1*, 4.

[2] *ER*, L (October, 1815), *9*, 477.

[3] Brougham, *ER*, II (January, 1803), *9*, 345–381; especially pp. 348 and 355.

[4] Jeffrey, *ER*, III (April, 1803), *1*, 22–23.

The Politics of the 'Edinburgh Review'

unforeseen accidents could not be wholly excluded from the direction of human affairs.[1] It was possible to express the wish that new principles might be found to create a barrier against French usurpation and preserve what was left of the old system.[2] But the unfavourable events taking place on the Continent left the reviewers to look back 'with regret' to the imperfect arrangements of the last century, when the two extremes of Europe were connected not only by ties of general humanity, but also by those of domestic feeling.[3] In this as in other articles the First Partition of Poland was held responsible for the real beginning of the end of 'that glorious system of equipoise by which the nations of Europe had . . . been so long protected and distinguished'.[4]

By 1809 it has become clear that 'we must lay our account with finding the rest of Europe no longer free, and accommodate our conduct to the novelty of our circumstances. . . . France has conquered Europe. This is the melancholy truth.'[5] And the best safeguard against the complete subjugation of the Old World is now the neutrality of the New World: 'While America covers the ocean with her ships, England may defy the conqueror of Europe. England must remain at peace with America, and America at peace with the rest of the world.'[6] This policy of friendship with the United States was one the *Edinburgh Review* had strongly urged in favouring the abandonment of the British claim to search ships of war, as well as in its attack on the Orders in Council;[7] and it was one that it continued to expound in its opposition to the American war.[8] But when Jeffrey discussed the political consequences of the liberation of Europe, he saw no need for mentioning the place of the New World in the new international order. For once he permitted himself to be

[1] *ER*, XVI (July, 1806), *5*, 298.
[2] Brougham, *ER*, XVIII (January, 1807), *1*, 255.
[3] *ER*, XXVI (January, 1809), *9*, 457.
[4] The quotation from (Brougham), *ER*, XXVIII (July, 1809), *8*, 404. On the Partition of Poland, cf. also Brougham, *ER*, XIII (October, 1805), *15*, 243.
[5] Brougham, *ER*, XXVIII (July, 1809), *11*, 470–471.
[6] *Ibid.*, 475.
[7] Brougham, *ER*, XXI (October, 1807), *1*, 30; Brougham, *ER*, XXIII (April, 1808), *13*, 245–246.
[8] Cf. (Brougham), *ER*, XXXVIII (February, 1812), *2*, 291–317; and *ER*, XLVII (November, 1814), *12*, 243–265.

optimistic, concluding that recent events had proved the utter impracticability of any future scheme of universal dominion, that Louis XVIII and the other sovereigns who were to be restored had learned their lesson, and that a new European order based on the necessity for the recognition of public opinion—that 'grand moral' of the French Revolution—was about to be established.[1]

It was in this way that the *Review* tried to combine the teachings of the French Revolution with the new principle on which another European balance of power could be built. But the refusal of the Allied Governments to take a strong line on the restoration of an independent Poland and their similarly ill-advised intentions with regard to Norway and Greece did not augur too well for the brave new Europe which Jeffrey, for once so confident, foresaw.[2] A few months after he had expressed his high hopes, the *Review* admitted that it had been deluding itself with the notion that disinterestedness sometimes appeared among absolute sovereigns.[3] The new and better balance of Europe did not, after all, seem to be rising phoenix-like from the ashes of war and destruction.

The European balance of power was not the only political balance the *Edinburgh* reviewers wished to uphold. In July of 1807 the *Review* published Jeffrey's famous review of Cobbett which enunciated the classic Whig doctrine of the balance of the Constitution. It was this article which Lord Holland recalls as having first irrevocably stamped the *Edinburgh Review*'s character as a political publication.[4] Jeffrey (who, according to Lord Holland, had undertaken to review the first eleven volumes of Cobbett's *Political Register* at the suggestion of Brougham and against the better judgement of Horner) here concluded that all of Cobbett's arguments could be reduced to a single proposition: all evils in the state are produced by an improper composition

---

[1] Jeffrey, *ER*, XLV (April, 1814), *1*, 4–5, 14–17, 25.
[2] On Poland, cf. Brougham, *ER*, XLIV (January, 1814), *3*, 294–331; Jeffrey, *ER*, XLV (April, 1814), *1*, 38–39; *ER*, XLVI (September, 1814), *13*, 493–499;on Norway, Jeffrey, *ER*, XLV (April, 1814), *1*, 38; on Greece, *ER*, L (October, 1815), *9*, 477.
[3] *ER*, XLVII (November, 1814), *6*, 124.
[4] Henry Richard Vassall Fox, 3rd Baron Holland, *Further Memoirs of the Whig Party, 1807–1821*, ed. Lord Stavordale (New York, 1905), 387.

of the legislative bodies, especially the House of Commons, where members are not chosen by the people, but nominated by the influence of the great families or allowed to purchase seats from a junto of venal electors, and where placemen and pensioners are allowed to hold seats.[1] Jeffrey admits that there is too much scrambling for place and emolument, too much buying and selling of votes. But this, he says, has nothing to do with the existence of placemen and pensioners, with venality in certain boroughs, or with the interference of peers in elections. Alteration of these parts of the system would not cure these evils; indeed, it would have a contrary effect.[2]

In a previous article he had laid it down that 'no representative legislature . . . can ever be respectable or secure, unless it contains within itself a great proportion of those who form the natural aristocracy of the country, and are able, as individuals, to influence the conduct and opinions of the greater part of its inhabitants'.[3] Now he reiterates this view, adding that in England rank, wealth, and office constitute the chief sources of influence over individuals. It follows that any parliament, however chosen and however constituted, which contains a proper representation of these three elements, which has freedom of speech, and which can meet frequently, efficiently protects the freedom of the people. There is no question but that the House of Commons contains a sufficient number and variety of persons to represent all the different opinions and maintain all the different views of policy existing in the country at large—and this is not due to the form of the election. There are, no doubt, some 'subordinate advantages' to be gained from making the people electors of their lawgivers. But the franchise has so little to do with the essence of constitutional freedom that Parliament would not be less useful or valuable were it composed of persons chosen mostly by lot or by rotation from among individuals of a certain fortune and education in each of the counties.[4]

[1] Jeffrey, *ER*, XX (July, 1807), *9*, 405–406. [2] *Ibid.*, 406–407.
[3] Jeffrey, *ER*, XI (April, 1805), *12*, 143.
[4] Jeffrey, *ER*, XX (July, 1807), *9*, 408–410. It is interesting to note that recent revisionist scholarship is not so far from upholding Jeffrey's contentions. Thus L. B. Namier: 'Were it decided that the 615 heaviest men in the country should constitute the House of Commons, the various interests and parties could be trusted to obtain their proportionate weight in it.' (*England in the Age of the American*

The Politics of the 'Edinburgh Review'

Because the great increase of power of the House of Commons endangered the checks supplied by King and Lords, these checks had to be transferred into the Commons itself—so that a certain infusion into it of placemen and of royal and aristocratic influence had become essential to the existence of mixed government. The balance of the constitution now resided within the House of Commons.[1] There was no need to fear the undue influence of the aristocracy; the landed interest, either in Parliament or in society, was scarcely a match for the moneyed interests, and, 'as it is the basis of a more steady and permanent, as well as a more liberal and exalted dependency, we wish rather to see peers concerned in elections, than stockjobbers or nabobs'.[2] Cobbett's schemes of reform were thus both unnecessary and deplorable.

Why did the *Review* choose to advance what Professor Roberts calls 'that beautiful Whig fiction' of the balance of the constitution at this time, when, as he points out, even in the eyes of the Whigs it had become the shadow of a shade? His own explanation is that the Whigs were at the moment the party of agriculture, defending the sacred influence of landed property against Pitt's *nouveaux riches*. 'Even the Treasury and the Crown, which they were soon to attack so bitterly, seemed preferable to the City man and the East India magnate.'[3] There is no doubt a great deal of truth in this. But the Tories by no means disliked Jeffrey's doctrine. 'Have this evening read Edinburgh review of Cobbett,' Leveson-Gower, then a Pittite, writes to Lady Bessborough: 'it is ably done, and though there is nothing new in his notion of the practice of the Constitution, he has stated it in a more forcible and intelligible *manner* than I have before seen.'[4] And Sydney Smith reports to Jeffrey from

---

Revolution [London, 1930], 3.) And thus Halévy: 'The unreformed House of Commons already represented to a large extent the opinion of the country.' (*England in 1815* [2nd rev. ed., London, 1949], 147.) Which leads to the curious reflection that a contemporary Whig interpretation of institutions may find confirmation, over a hundred years later, by what Mr. A. J. P. Taylor has called the Tory interpretation of history. (Cf. his review of Feiling's *History of England*, *New Statesman and Nation*, XLIX, No. 1,000, May 6, 1950.)

[1] Jeffrey, *ER*, XX (July, 1807), *9*, 414–416.   [2] *Ibid.*, 417.
[3] Roberts, *Whig Party*, 236.
[4] Granville Leveson-Gower to Lady Bessborough, September 25, 1807, *Granville Correspondence*, II, 299.

London that 'Your notions of the English Constitution delight the Tories beyond all belief. . . . The Whigs like that part of your review which attacks, or rather destroys, Cobbett; but shake their heads at your general political doctrine.'[1]

It is easy to see why the Whigs were delighted with the attack on Cobbett's democratic sentiments. For, as Sir Samuel Romilly noted in his diary during the same month in which Jeffrey's article appeared, it was Cobbett who had been mainly responsible for the propagation of the opinion, 'spreading very fast through the country', that 'all public men are corrupt, and that the true interests of the country are disregarded in an unceasing struggle between contending factions for power and emolument'.[2] The Whigs, who had only recently been turned out of office and some of whose leading members, ejected from popular constituencies at the April elections, had been forced to resort to close boroughs,[3] were in no mood for any talk of reform. They themselves, in fact, were on the defensive in regard to this question; for they had not introduced any proposals for parliamentary reform during their tenure of power. A correspondent in the *Political Register* acutely pointed out that the object of the publication of the Cobbett article in the *Review* was to support the credit of the late ministry, in order to turn out the present. 'For if they can demonstrate, that what we call abuses, are real improvements, reform is out of the question, Mr. Fox was no apostate, and the Whig ministry was justified in respect of everything but its *former professions*.'[4]

But there may be a special reason for Jeffrey's particularly rigid formulation of anachronistic political theory over which, according to Sydney Smith, some of the Whigs were shaking

---

[1] Sydney Smith to Francis Jeffrey, November 18, 1807, Nowell C. Smith, ed., *The Letters of Sydney Smith* (Oxford, 1953), I, 126–127. Little more than a year before, Horner had professed himself shocked by the 'revolutionary doctrine' of one of Jeffrey's letters to him. (Presumably Jeffrey to Horner, September 18, 1806, Cockburn, *Life of Jeffrey*, II, 110–113.) 'You and Cobbett are turned true Jacobins!' he had written him. Horner to Jeffrey, September 26, 1806, Horner Correspondence, L.S.E., III, 39.

[2] Entry for July 17, 1807, *The Life of Sir Samuel Romilly, Written by Himself* (3rd ed., London, 1842), II, 63.

[3] Aspinall, *Lord Brougham and the Whig Party*, 16. In painful contrast, Burdett and Cochrane had triumphed at Westminster.

[4] John Cotton Worthington, 'Three Letters to the Edinburgh Reviewers', *Political Register*, XII, No. 25 (December 19, 1807), 982.

their heads. At the start of his article Jeffrey stated that the last number of the *Political Register* which had reached him for review purposes was that of July 18, 1807.[1] Now it is this number which contains the report of a debate in the House of Commons in the course of which Perceval, the Chancellor of the Exchequer, attacked the patronage of the last Whig administration, mentioning specifically the office of Gazette Writer for Scotland, especially created by the Whigs as a sinecure paying three hundred pounds a year. The person for whom this office was created was none other than Professor Dugald Stewart, principal preceptor of the young Scottish Whigs. Canning, replying to Lord Henry Petty who defended the sinecure, acknowledged the high literary merit of Dugald Stewart who, he added in characteristic fashion, 'had besides the merit, and he thought it no light one, of having educated the noble lord'.[2] But Cobbett comments without much sympathy that 'his former income could have kept body and soul together; and, if not, would it not have been better to have let them separate a few years sooner, than become, at last, the subject of a wrangle in the honourable House?'[3]

What is more natural than that Jeffrey, student and admirer of Dugald Stewart, should take special offence at this gibe, and come to the aid of his teacher and fellow charter member of the Edinburgh Friday Club? And that he should do so by quoting from the master himself? For in his Lectures on Political Economy (which Jeffrey attended during the session of 1801–1802),[4] Stewart outlined the very same theory of the constitution which appears in Jeffrey's article. The House of Commons, he said, had become supreme, but the Constitution was still perfectly sound since the three powers of Crown, Lords, and Commons were now blended in the Lower

[1] Jeffrey, *ER*, XX (July, 1807), 9, 404.

[2] *Political Register*, XII, No. 3 (July 18, 1807), 76. The complete report of the debate begins on p. 65.

[3] For other comments on this sinecure, cf. Scott's letter to Lady Abercorn, July 20, 1807, *The Letters of Sir Walter Scott*, ed. Herbert J. C. Grierson (London, 1932–1937), I, 369; *Morning Chronicle*, July 4, 1807; and John Veitch, 'Memoir of Dugald Stewart', *The Collected Works of Dugald Stewart*, ed. Sir William Hamilton (Edinburgh, 1854–1860), X, lxxix.

[4] Cf. Dugald Stewart, *Works*, VIII, xxii, where the editor thanks a Mr. J. G. Craig for supplying him with Jeffrey's notes of these lectures.

Chamber.[1] Furthermore, he continued, as long as the influence of King and Peers was not carried further than necessary to preserve a due balance among the three powers—then, so far from being an abuse, this influence was absolutely requisite for preserving the ancient spirit of the British government.[2] It is not possible to offer conclusive proof for the hypothesis that the controversy over Stewart's sinecure had some influence on Jeffrey's exposition of constitutional theory, but, if true, it helps to explain its rather academic character. None of the previous articles on representative theory and practice had been so flagrantly conservative in tone—though all of them had contained solemn warnings against the dangers of democratic tendencies.[3] And from the time of the publication of the Cobbett article, the political line of the *Review* moves increasingly to the left.

It is possible that this shift was due to Brougham's influence, as Dr. Aspinall surmises.[4] For Brougham, in spite of his energetic management of the Whig press campaign in the General Election of June, 1807, had not been rewarded by a seat and was taking an increasingly less respectful view of the Whig aristocracy. But Jeffrey, too, never added a second quite so ferivd verse to his hymn in praise of the balanced Constitution. Just a year after his attack on Cobbett, he attacks 'our indolent reliance upon the imperishable virtue of our constitution' and objects to the 'monstrous patronage' of the government;[5] and Brougham, in the same number, condemns an author's excessive sympathy for a Venetian Countess who must support herself by giving music lessons as coming from the kind of persons who 'must really be as blind as a mole, or as aristocratic as a city peer or a Whig patriot'.[6] 'The last E. Review and some former ones have put the ministerial folks here out of all patience', Brougham writes to Loch shortly after the appearance of the July number. 'They storm beyond bounds, and as I am accused of it, Jeffrey being no partizan, I have the whole brunt of it to bear

[1] Dugald Stewart, 'Lectures on Political Economy', *Works*, IX, 445.
[2] *Ibid.*, 450–451.
[3] Cf. Smith, *ER*, II (January, 1803), *10*, 382–395; Jeffrey, *ER*, XI (April, 1805), *12*, 143–148; and *ER*, XVIII (January, 1807), *7*, 360–369.
[4] Aspinall, *Brougham and the Whig Party*, 19.
[5] Jeffrey, *ER*, XXIV (July, 1808), *1*, 273–275.
[6] Brougham, *ER*, XXIV (July, 1808), *3*, 321.

now.'[1] But the real shock to the ministerial as well as a great many of the Opposition 'folks' was yet to come.

In the issue of October, 1808, appeared the review entitled 'Don Pedro Cevallos on the French Usurpation of Spain' which mingled praise of the Spanish patriots who had risen against Napoleon with bitter criticism of the upper classes, English as well as Spanish, and a demand for reform of the British Constitution. The article appears to have been a collaborative effort by Jeffrey and Brougham, though the latter was universally (dis)credited with it at the time.[2] The Spanish revolt had broken out in May of 1808 and had made its first impact on British opinion in the course of the following month. From Jeffrey's point of view—and this may help to account for his change of line on constitutional issues—this revolt, directed against the common enemy, and thus, unlike the French Revolution, posing no potential threat to the safety of Britain, represented a cure for those pathological fears of Jacobinism against which the *Review* had warned from the start. This is the keynote of the article: 'We can once more utter the words *liberty* and *people*, without starting at the echo of our own voices, or looking round the chamber for some spy or officer of the government.'[3]

But it went much further than that, probably due to the part Brougham took in writing it. Not only was it suggested that if the Spaniards wanted a new monarch, 'a new stock' could be 'brought from Germany for a breed'[4]; but praise was bestowed upon the lower orders in this fashion:

'The bulk, the mass of the people,—nay the very odious, many-headed beast, the multitude—the mob itself—alone, uncalled, or unaided by the higher classes, and in direct opposition to them, as well as to the enemy whom they so vilely joined,—

[1] Brougham to James Loch, August 19, 1808, *Brougham and his Early Friends*, II, 319–320.

[2] For a summary of the latest evidence on the authorship of this article, cf. Elisabeth Schneider, Irwin Griggs, and John D. Kern, 'Brougham's Early Contributions to the *Edinburgh Review*: A New List', *Modern Philology*, XLII (1945), 170–171.

[3] Jeffrey and Brougham, *ER*, XXV (October, 1808), *14*, 222. Cf. Horner to Murray, October 27, 1808, *Horner Memoirs*, I, 435, and *Morning Chronicle*, September 1, 1808, for similar statements.

[4] Brougham and Jeffrey, *ER*, XXV (October, 1808), *14*, 221.

raised up the standard of insurrection,—bore it through massacre and through victory, until it chased the usurper away, and waved over his deserted courts.'[1]

And for the first time the *Review* clearly states that 'reforms in the administration of our affairs must be adopted, to prevent more violent changes', and anticipates a recurrence of wholesome popular feelings and a state of public opinion which will view 'radical improvements in our constitution' without horror.[2]

It is not surprising that these sentiments shocked the Tories. Walter Scott immediately cancelled his subscription (as did about twenty-five other persons of consideration in Edinburgh)[3] and began to hurry his plans for the *Quarterly*;[4] a correspondent in the Tory *Courier* assailed the *Review* as 'a quarterly Cobbett', conducted by 'a club of hungry Scotsmen, with each a mouthful of learning, [who] have established at the Edinburgh Review office, a house of call for day-labouring statesmen, a colony of whom have settled in London';[5] and a Tory Member of Parliament was moved to indite a pamphlet which he entitled *Remarks on the Jacobinical Tendency of the Edinburgh Review*.[6] One pamphleteer declared that public resentment was so strong and loud that all he could say was to express the hope that the reviewers were ashamed of what they had done.[7] 'Now did ever Thomas Paine preach or wrote doctrines more revolutionary?' asked another.[8] A third demanded the retraction of the insult to

[1] *Ibid.*, 220.

[2] *Ibid.*, 222.

[3] Jeffrey to Horner, December 6, 1808, *Horner Memoirs*, I, 438. Earl Gower writes to Charles Kirkpatrick Sharpe that he has heard of two hundred copies of the *Review* countermanded 'in consequence of the democratical principles of Mr. Brougham in the last number. He was certainly rather indiscreet in throwing off the mask so suddenly, and 'tis just as well that he has let people see what sort of a fellow he is.' Earl Gower to Charles Kirkpatrick Sharpe, January 28, 1809, Alexander Allardyce, ed., *Letters From and To Charles Kirkpatrick Sharpe* (Edinburgh and London, 1888), I, 359. Scott writes hopefully that 'subscribers are falling off like withered leaves'. Walter Scott to John Murray, November 15, 1808, *Scott Letters*, II, 75.

[4] Scott to Gifford, October 25, 1808, *Scott Letters*, II, 102–108.

[5] *Courier*, December 1, 1808.

[6] By Richard Wharton (2nd ed., London, 1809).

[7] [Anon.], *Expostulatory Letter to the Editor of the Edinburgh Review* (London, 1809), 61.

[8] 'Mentor', *The Dangers of the Edinburgh Review; or a Brief Exposure of its Principles in Religion, Morals, and Politics* (London, 1808), 37.

George III [i.e. the reviewers' reference to a 'royal stock'] and significantly added: 'If you suppose that the Whig party, the present Parliamentary Opposition of this country, go along with you in this extreme violence, you are greatly mistaken. It is generally understood, that they have expressed a very strong disapprobation of some of your late disquisitions.'[1] 'Senex' had hit the nail exactly on the head; the Whigs were shocked. Indeed, the eccentric Earl of Buchan, a veteran of the radicalism of the 1790's, kicked himself into at least that version of immortality represented by the *Cambridge History of English Literature* in booting the twenty-fifth number of the *Edinburgh Review* into the street, to be trodden under foot by man and beast.[2] Brougham later recalled that:

'In 1808, Cevallos on Spain and the war generally first made us conspicuous as Liberals, and called the *Quarterly* into existence in three months, an event sure to happen as soon as we took a bold line. But that very article, I can assure you, offended Lord Grey and Holland House as much as it did the Tories.'[3]

And at the time, he reported to Grey that 'in Edinburgh I learn both friends and foes are offended'.[4] It was no wonder that this was so. The Whigs, with the exception of the 'Mountain', were in no mood for talk of 'radical improvements in our constitution'. Grey and the Foxites were at this point completely apathetic about the subject of parliamentary reform, and the attitude of the Grenvillites was typified by Windham who wrote to Mrs. Crewe in January, 1809:

'You may be assured that there is no more pestilent doctrine than that which would reproach the Spaniards for not having corrected what are called abuses.'[5]

Horner who, like everyone else, assumed that the review was entirely the work of Brougham, called it 'most reprehensible in its tone and spirit' and asked his friend Murray: 'Are all the

[1] 'Senex', *A Letter to the Young Gentlemen who Write in the Edinburgh Review* (London, 1809), 22.

[2] On this incident and the Whig reaction in general, see John Clive, 'The Earl of Buchan's Kick: A Footnote to the History of the *Edinburgh Review*', *Harvard Library Bulletin*, V, No. 3 (Autumn, 1951), 362–370.

[3] Brougham to Napier, October 27, 1829, *Napier Correspondence*, 308–309.

[4] Brougham to Grey, December 2, 1808, Brougham, *Life and Times*, I, 420.

[5] William Windham to Mrs. Crewe, January 21, 1809, *Life and Correspondence of William Windham, 1750–1810* (Boston, 1913), II, 343.

fruits of a long continued study of politics, great opportunities of seeing both affairs and men very near at hand, and the best talents nature had to give, to be thrown away upon slashing declamations to suit a temporary purpose or give vent to the humour and fit of the day?'[1]

Jeffrey was frightened by the violent reaction to the 'Cevallos' article. Scott reported to George Ellis on November 18, 1808, that 'Jeffery [sic] is I think not unlikely to resign the management of the Review here. He told me he did not feel himself at liberty to alter Brougham's articles although he thought those on Spain greatly too strong and that he cared very little about the publication.'[2] What Jeffrey did not tell Scott was that he himself had had a considerable share in the authorship of the offending piece. Writing to Horner he showed more frankness, admitting his 'love of sport' as part of the cause for the 'mischief' done, but asking him to use nothing but exemplary moderation and impartiality on all politics in his next article.[3] But what was done could not be undone. For the first time the *Review* had put itself squarely into the progressive wing of the Whig party; for the first time it had begun to fulfil the function of acting, to use Professor Roberts's term, as its 'radicalizer'. The *Courier* recalled the 'courtly and measured' language of the Cobbett review and compared it with the inflammatory tone of 'Cevallos', remarking that 'Thomas Paine never published any thing more seditious than the last No. of the Edinburgh Review'.[4]

'Cobbett' and 'Cevallos' constitute the two poles between which the political line of the *Review* was to oscillate in the course of the following years. Never again would the theory of the balanced constitution be presented to the readers of the

[1] Horner to Murray, December 9, 1808, Horner Correspondence, L.S.E., III, 131.

[2] Scott to George Ellis, November 18, 1808, *Scott Letters*, XII, 307.

[3] Jeffrey to Horner, December 6, 1808, *Horner Memoirs*, I, 438–439. Sydney Smith had actually received the impression, both from Jeffrey and other quarters, that there were to be no more politics of any kind in the *Review*. In a subsequent letter Jeffrey explained that what he had meant was no more *party* politics. All this emerges in a letter from Smith to Jeffrey, November or December, 1808, *Smith Letters*, I, 147–148.

[4] *Courier*, December 2, 1808.

Review in a tone quite so complacent as that of the first. Never again would the many-headed beast, the mob, be exalted as it was in the second. Instead, one tends to find an amalgam whose ingredients vary according to the general political situation at the time of writing. It is clear that the reaction to 'Cevallos' convinced Jeffrey that the bulk of the *Review*'s readers was willing to swallow any sort of 'mountainous' sentiments or proposals only if properly sugar-coated with anti-democratic sentiments. Jeffrey himself was far from being a democrat; but he became convinced, in the course of 1809, that the Whigs would have to pluck their flower safety out of the democratic nettle itself—by means of a strategic popular alliance.

In July of that year he reiterated his ideas concerning the importance of the balance of the Constitution within the House of Commons, adding that if that House were to represent only yeomanry in the counties and tradesmen in the boroughs (Jeffrey wrote 'burghs'), 'it would infallibly convert the government into a mere democracy'.[1] At the same time he declared that if the people were generally desirous of a reform of parliament, 'we think the time is come when it ought to be no longer withheld'. He felt that no harm could be done by increasing the number of Members from populous boroughs—at the same time raising the pecuniary qualification for the borough and county franchise, with the proviso that in the counties property other than land be taken into account for its calculation. It would still be possible to pay 'a due tribute to the superior weight and respectability of the landed interest by making the qualification lower for them than for other proprietors'.[2] All this, Jeffrey reassured anxious readers, would not materially touch the state of taxation or influence. Indeed, if it served to exclude from the House of Commons all who were sent there through the interest of the Ministry and the noble families, 'we should think it our duty to strive against it; as against a measure which would deprive us of all the practical blessings of our constitution'.[3] As for Burdett and Cobbett, Jeffrey pointed out quite astutely that their intent was to strengthen the royal prerogative, to unite

---

[1] Jeffrey, *ER*, XXVIII (July, 1809), *1*, 300.
[2] *Ibid.*, 299.
[3] *Ibid.*, 300.

King and people against the aristocracy. However, by following the course of raising the qualifications of electors in counties and boroughs, aristocratic influence would actually be increased.[1]

It was in this guise that the *Edinburgh Review* first presented a specific plan of parliamentary reform. A few months later it came back to the subject in an article criticizing the management of the Peninsular War by the Ministry. If, wrote the reviewer, the House of Commons were (as he assumed) pure and in no need of reform, then it would undoubtedly censure the Ministry. If not, then 'we will venture to predict, not that the government is acquitted, but that the Parliament stands condemned; and we shall *most unwillingly* [italics mine] be compelled to appear in the foremost rank of those who must acknowledge that they are convinced and converted'.[2] It must be remembered that 1809 was the year of Corunna, Walcheren, and the scandals over the sale of army commissions by the Duke of York's mistress. The *Review* was in the vanguard of those who wanted to take advantage of the government's embarrassment and unpopularity.

It must also be remembered that 1809 was the year of an extremely poor harvest, high wheat prices, and a great deal of popular suffering and discontent. In a particularly outspoken letter, Jeffrey wrote to Horner in October of 1809 that as long as the people were suffering and angry, they would have no indulgence for 'the ornaments and weaknesses of refined life'. And every attempt to uphold them would be felt by the people as an insult. Grey and Grenville were 'too aristocratical, and, consequently, likely to be inefficient'. The only course for the Whigs to follow was to coalesce with the people, to assist them to ask with dignity and with order all that ought to be granted, and to try to persuade them not to ask more. In any event, it was up to the aristocracy to give way.[3]

Jeffrey feared that unless 'something be done upon a great generous system', Cobbett and Burdett would take the field against the 'base Court party'. The Whigs were standing between 'the timid, sordid, selfish worshippers of power and adherents of the Court, and the dangerous, discontented, half noble,

---

[1] *Ibid.*, 303–304.   [2] Brougham, *ER*, XXIX (October, 1809), *14*, 234–235.
[3] Jeffrey to Horner, October 26, 1809, Cockburn, *Life of Jeffrey*, I, 195–197.

half mischievous advocates for reform and innovation'.[1] If they
did not make some sort of coalition with the democrats, 'they
are nobody, and the nation is ruined, internally as well as from
without'.[2] Jeffrey was probably especially concerned over the
isolation of the Whigs, since Grey and Grenville had just
(September, 1809) refused Perceval's approach to join his
cabinet, after the Canning-Castlereagh conflict had led to the
possibility of a coalition. 'Cry aloud, and spare not, against
Walcheren', he exhorted Horner; 'push Ireland down the
throats of the Court and the country; and do not let us be lost
without something like a generous effort, in council as well as in
the field.'[3]

His own contribution to the 'generous effort' was an article
in the *Review* entitled 'State of Parties', in which he urged the
old constitutional Whigs of England to join forces with the more
respectable members of the popular side, in order to save the
constitution, the monarchy, and the Whig aristocracy itself 'by
which that Monarchy is controlled and confirmed, and exalted
above all other forms of polity' from democratic excesses.[4]
Since the people seemed to want parliamentary reform, let
them have a modicum of it, though 'we can neither approve of
such a reform as some very popular persons have suggested, nor
bring ourselves to believe that any reform would accomplish the
objects that seem to be in the view of its most zealous advocates'.[5] The article called forth from Leigh Hunt a *Reformist's
Answer to the Article Entitled 'State of Parties' in the last Edinburgh Review*, in which he expressed his amusement at the Holland House party in the character of the Sabine women parting
the combatants;[6] and it shocked 'the Sid' who accused Jeffrey
of taking his notions of the state of British opinion from the
state of opinion among the commercial and manufacturing population of Scotland, and of ignoring the great mass of English

[1] Jeffrey to Horner, December 21, 1809, *Horner Memoirs*, II, 12–13.
[2] Jeffrey to John Allen, December 22, 1809, Cockburn, *Life of Jeffrey*, II, 127.
[3] Jeffrey to Horner, December 21, 1809, *Horner Memoirs*, II, 12.
[4] Jeffrey, *ER*, XXX (January, 1810), *15*, 505.
[5] *Ibid.*, 520.
[6] Quoted in Roberts, *Whig Party*, 282. Hunt recalls that he wrote the pamphlet
in defence of the *Edinburgh*'s own reforming principles, 'which it had lately taken
it into its head to renounce as impracticable'. J. E. Morpurgo, ed , *The Autobiography of Leigh Hunt* (London, 1949), 227.

landed proprietors who would always rally around the Constitution and moderate principles in any state of emergency. 'Why do you not scout more that pernicious cant that all men are equal?' he asked Jeffrey.[1] He need not have worried. As Professor Roberts points out, there was certainly no democratic conviction in Jeffrey's views which essentially reflected the desire for a *mariage de convenance*—and nothing more—with the Reformers.[2]

But is it fair to expect democratic sentiments from Jeffrey? He at least saw which way the wind was blowing and advised the party accordingly. And the *Edinburgh Review* may perhaps claim some credit for the fact that in May, 1810, 115 Members of Parliament voted for Brand's plan of electoral reform. Shortly before this vote, Brougham, now in Parliament, had solemnly pledged the *Review* to the constant support of parliamentary reform. He promised that it would never lose sight of the subject 'until our feeble efforts, in conjunction with those of abler men, shall have awakened the country and its government to a sense of its situation, and a desire to attempt its improvement in good earnest'.[3]

By the summer of 1810 the *Review* had again managed to alienate friend and foe. A pamphleteer defending Pitt's memory against some derogatory remarks of the reviewers, accused the periodical of attempting to effect a junction with the demagogues and to propagate the doctrine that place-men could not be patriots.[4] Scott wrote to a correspondent that in Edinburgh 'folks on both sides are quarrelling with the Edinburgh for being neither democratical nor (what shall I call them) Whiggish'.[5] And Horner informed Jeffrey that Holland, Allen, and Tierney agreed with him that the *Review* should never have engaged in the discussion of questions being debated between Ministry and

---

[1] Smith to Jeffrey, soon after April 17, 1810, *Smith Letters*, I, 186.

[2] Roberts, *Whig Party*, 276.

[3] Brougham, *ER*, XXXI (April, 1810), 8, 212.

[4] [Anon.], *A Vindication of the Character of the late Rt. Hon. William Pitt, from the Calumnies against him, Contained in the Fifth Article of the Edinburgh Review for April, 1810* (Edinburgh, 1810), 27. Cf. also 'An Englishman', *Advice to the Whigs: with Hints to the Democrats and Cautions to the Edinburgh Reviewers* (London, 1810), 30, where the reviewers are warned not to emulate the French Encyclopedists who ended up by being hated by their country.

[5] Scott to George Ellis, June 16, 1810, *Scott Letters*, XII, 321.

Opposition, and that it should reassume a 'general tone' of politics.[1] Jeffrey had admitted to John Allen that in his State of Parties article he had knowingly 'stated the dangers of the thing coming to a crisis too strongly', but asked whether all that was doing in London, Westminster, and Middlesex [i.e. the Burdett Riots] did not prove him right. 'My own opinion certainly is', he wrote, 'that nothing can save them [the Whigs] or the country, but their becoming very popular in their principles to the full extent of Whitbread's speeches in Parliament.'[2]

Did this mean that the *Edinburgh Review* was becoming an appanage of the 'Mountain'? Hardly. Jeffrey, always very sensitive to adverse reaction, assured Horner in July that the 'overgrown privileges of some of my subjects' [obviously Brougham] had been responsible for the increasing factiousness of the *Review*, and that he was issuing 'laudable edicts, inculcating moderation and candour'.[3] Actually, Whitbread himself had shrunk from the alliance between 'Mountain' and Radicals recommended by Leigh Hunt—and by the end of the year, the King's madness and the Regency Bill had replaced reform as the major subject of public interest. The *Review* continued to advocate its old proposals—increase of both the number and the qualification of voters—but in a more respectably Whiggish manner, emphasizing the overgrown influence of the Crown as the chief impetus to reform.[4]

In August, 1811, Jeffrey had the satisfaction of quoting two lines from Scott's *Don Roderick*, upbraiding the Spanish nobles for their lack of spirit in the Spanish revolt. Recalling 'Cevallos', its co-author commented: 'It is amusing to see how things come round.'[5] But on the whole, the *Review* followed the official Whigs in their regression, due to prospects of office, 'from a position to which in 1809 popular excitement and political disappointment had driven them'.[6] The reviewers shared the general

[1] Horner to Jeffrey, July 16, 1810, *Horner Memoirs*, II, 52.

[2] Jeffrey to Allen, May 4, 1810, Cockburn, *Life of Jeffrey*, II, 127–128.

[3] Jeffrey to Horner, July 30, 1810, Cockburn, *Life of Jeffrey*, II, 129.

[4] Jeffrey, *ER*, XXXIV (February, 1811), *1*, 256–290, especially page 258. This was in line with Brougham's article in *ER*, XXXI (April, 1810), *8*, 187–213, which traced all calamities, foreign and domestic, to the enormous influence of the Crown.

[5] Jeffrey, *ER*, XXXVI (August, 1811), *6*, 384.

[6] Roberts, *Whig Party*, 291.

Whig indignation over the Prince Regent's 'betrayal' in retaining the Tories. Brougham, upbraiding Grey and Grenville for refusing the Wellesley-Moira coalition offers of May and June, 1812, commented lugubriously and with self-righteous pathos that 'the lot of the Whigs is merely to modify and palliate the mischievous proceedings of the Tories, by their opposition, and to come in, for a few months or weeks, once or twice in a reign, to carry through some great and salutary measure, which it goes against the consciences of the said Tories to adopt—and then to go back again to the unpopularity and conscious virtue, which are so obviously their portion in this world'.[1]

Brougham himself, on a platform of moderate reform proposals, was defeated at Liverpool at the General Election of October, 1812, an election which the Tories had called, as he commented sarcastically in the *Review*, to give the people an opportunity 'of pronouncing that mature and flattering judgment respecting the Prince Regent's demeanour in public and private (if indeed Princes have any privacy) which it is quite well known every man in the Kingdom *must* have formed'.[2] In the same number Jeffrey reiterated the advantages of a balance of the constitution in the House of Commons.[3] It was almost the last mention the *Review* made of parliamentary theory or practice in this period. The Hampden Club (founded in 1812), which actually witnessed that union between Whig and popular reform which Jeffrey had desired in 1810, found only one reference in the *Review*—and that sarcastic.[4]

For the bulk of the Whig party at Westminster the subject was dead for fully five years. Brougham, out of Parliament, veered sharply to the left, but wrote very little indeed for the

[1] Brougham, *ER*, XXXIX (July, 1812), 2, 35.

[2] Brougham, ER, XL (November, 1812), 8, 408. For other disrespectful comments on the Royal Family (which become increasingly frequent) cf. *ER*, XLIV (January, 1814), 5, 370–371; Brougham, *ER*, XLVI (September, 1814), 10, 460–467; and *ER*, XLVII (November, 1814), 6, 113, where the Prince Regent is described as 'the great potentate who fills so large a space in the eye of the country; whose weight in the State is undoubted; and to whom, it is supposed, we are indebted, under Providence, for all the blessings and victories we enjoy'.

[3] Jeffrey, *ER*, XL (November, 1812), 4, 335–336. Cf. Horner's comment: 'Allen is delighted with the orthodoxy of the review of Leckie's pamphlet, and says it is the best constitutional article Jeffrey has ever written.' Horner to Murray, December 16, 1812, *Horner Memoirs*, II, 139–140.

[4] *ER*, XLVI (September, 1814), 5, 372.

The Politics of the 'Edinburgh Review'

Edinburgh between November, 1812, and December, 1818; Jeffrey was away in America for almost a year and when he returned, early in 1814, victory and peace were his main concerns. In March, 1815, summing up the political role of the *Review*, he admitted that it might have been better if it had been less factious and had put more emphasis on general views, but added that 'in such times as we have lived in', it was impossible to keep these two approaches apart.[1] His tone is that of a man satisfied with what he has done.

To what extent was this satisfaction justified? In the first number of the *Westminster Review* (January, 1824) James Mill described the *Edinburgh* and the *Quarterly* as organs, respectively, of the Opposition and Ministerial sections of the aristocracy, and accused the *Edinburgh* of writing alternately on both sides of every question which touched the power or interest of the governing classes. Perhaps Mill might have made some allowance for the bare possibility that contradiction could on occasion mirror the search for truth as faithfully as the unchanging verities of the gospel according to St. Jeremy. But the article, on which his son collaborated, certainly struck a telling blow. 'So formidable an attack on the Whig party and policy', recalls John Stuart Mill in his autobiography, 'had never before been made.'[2] One who seeks to find in the *Edinburgh Review* between 1802 and 1815 an advanced liberal organ, commending to a reluctant aristocracy the democratic wave of the future, will certainly be disappointed. The balanced Constitution smacks of the eighteenth rather than the nineteenth century; and there is something very prim and old-maidish about Jeffrey's politics, even when he is most aware of the need for co-operation with 'the people'. By to analyse the political views disseminated by the *Edinburgh* in its early years from the vantage point of 1824 is perhaps not altogether fair.

[1] Jeffrey to Horner, March 12, 1815, Cockburn, *Life of Jeffrey*, II, 151.
[2] *The Autobiography of John Stuart Mill* (first complete ed., New York, 1924), 66. Mill was by no means the first to accuse the *Edinburgh* of tergiversation. This was a favourite weapon of assault during the early years. See the epigraph of this chapter; also Southey to Taylor, January 15, 1809, J. W. Robberds, ed., *A Memoir of the Life and Writings of the late William Taylor of Norwich* (London, 1843), II, 264, and *A Letter to Francis Jeffrey*, especially 3–12.

The Politics of the 'Edinburgh Review'

In advising his successor on the considerations by which he should be guided in his policy of admitting or rejecting important political articles Jeffrey listed three which he considered legitimate: the effect of the editor's decision on the other contributors upon whom he was mainly relying; its effect on the sale and circulation of the *Review*, and on the just authority of the work with the great body of its readers; and the editor's own deliberate opinion as to the safety or danger of the doctrines maintained in the article under consideration, 'and its tendency either to promote or retard the practical adoption of those liberal principles to which, and *their practical advancement*, [the editor] must always consider the journal as devoted'.[1] Judged on the basis of these criteria, the *Edinburgh Review* does not come off so badly. A previous chapter has shown the extent of Jeffrey's dependence on Brougham whose political career followed a zigzag pattern which, in some measure, the *Review* was bound to reflect. For Jeffrey could not afford to lose him as a contributor. Neither could he afford to alienate those he wanted to convert. The word is used advisedly. The reviewers—and Jeffrey in particular—were very much aware of the proselytizing function of their periodical: they wanted to inculcate liberal opinions.

This was simple enough when it was a matter of condemning the slave trade, or of advocating the emancipation of the Catholics, or even of adopting certain parts of the Utilitarian creed. These were questions which, to some extent, transcended party and class, and which could be argued on general humanitarian grounds. But for Jeffrey the cornerstone of liberalism was an understanding of the real meaning of the French Revolution. In reprinting an article on this subject (originally written in 1805) in his *Collected Contributions* nearly forty years later, he added this footnote:

'I have been tempted to let this be reprinted . . . to show at how early a period those views of the character of the French Revolution, and its first effects on other countries, were adopted—which have not since received much modification.'[2]

---

[1] Jeffrey to Napier, December 27, 1837, *Napier Correspondence*, 219.
[2] Jeffrey, *Contributions*, I, 548.

121

What were those views? In brief, that the Revolution, in spite of the excesses in which it eventuated, was the result of certain legitimate grievances and the cause of certain salutary changes. To regard sympathy with these grievances and changes as 'Jacobinical' was both unenlightened—a capital crime for the reviewers—and dangerous. It was unenlightened because it must be clear to all thinking men that 'as society advances and intellect begins to develop itself', the resulting diffusion of knowledge and education was bound to wake up the mass of the people in Europe to political opinions, interests, and sentiments.[1] In this last and inevitable stage of the advance of civilization—'commercial and enlightened times'—there must always be some channel by which the sense of the people might be let in to act upon the administrators of their government. The French Revolution was the result of a lack of some proper contrivance for ascertaining and bringing to bear the sentiments of the actual strength of the nation. If in France there had been some provision in the structure of the government by which the increasing power of the 'lower orders' could have made itself distinctly felt, the Revolution would have been averted.[2] The lesson for England was clear: 'If the people have risen into greater consequence, let them have greater power.'[3]

As a loyal Whig who prided himself on 'a spice of aristocracy in my own nature'[4] Jeffrey had not the slightest desire to end the predominance of the power of landed property or to institute democracy. He was simply frightened of what would happen if the governmental structure did not yield to popular pressure in order to preserve a society otherwise (he thought) threatened with complete subversion. In that sense the Radical criticism of the Edinburgh Review, by men like Leigh Hunt and William Cobbett, was certainly correct. For Jeffrey, no less than Lords Grey and Grenville, thought that the Whigs should have their cake and eat it as well. Yet, in 1809, he was (as Professor Roberts points out) the only important Whig to see the Reform agitation in its true light, linking it with the economic distress

[1] Jeffrey, *ER*, XXXIV (February, 1811), *1*, 281–282.
[2] Jeffrey, *ER*, XL (November, 1812), *4*, 331–332.
[3] Jeffrey, *ER*, XXXIV (February, 1811), *1*, 288.
[4] Jeffrey to Horner, July 20, 1810, Cockburn, *Life of Jeffrey*, II, 129.

that lay in back of it.[1] And though he continued, in the *Review*, to talk in eighteenth-century terms, he also showed an awareness of the fact that the old Whiggery was dead. It was left to Brougham and the Radicals to build the new—but the *Edinburgh Review*, by placing the process in its historical setting, may well have helped to ease the shock of the transition.

[1] 'For Jeffrey, from the Olympus of Calton Hill, has a sudden flash of super-natural vision.' Roberts, *Whig Party*, 257.

Classical Economics and the Middling Classes

The *Edinburgh Review* has been called, 'for its day and generation, a "Reader's Digest" of economic literature', and its influence on economic thought and economic policy in Britain in the Napoleonic period and the years following 'far greater than economists have recognized'.[1] From its very first issue, which contained no fewer than four economic articles, three of them by Horner, current economic controversies, practical and theoretical, constituted one of its principal subjects.

To what extent did the politics of the *Edinburgh Review* influence its views on economic matters? This is not an easy question to answer, since in the period under consideration there existed no clear-cut relation between class structure and political alignment. It would indeed be convenient if one could call the Tories the party of commerce and free trade, and the Whigs the party of agriculture and protection—and it would certainly be more reasonable than to look for the precursors of Cobden and Bright among the Whig aristocrats of the early nineteenth century. After all, it was Pitt, and not Fox, who gloried in his discipleship to Adam Smith, and who was not at all miscast in the role of patron saint of the *nouveaux riches*. Nevertheless, the political and economic situation during this period was far too fluid and complex to lend itself to any such generalization.

For one thing, farmers and landlords, forming on the whole one solid body of opinion, were not averse to free trade while

---

[1] Frank Whitson Fetter, 'The Authorship of Economic Articles in the *Edinburgh Review*, 1802–1847', *The Journal of Political Economy*, LXI, No. 3 (June, 1953), 234.

Classical Economics and the Middling Classes

the prosperity of the war years lasted.[1] For another, the Government's policy of Orders in Council, designed as a counter-move to Napoleon's attempted blockade, ended the hitherto fairly solid alliance between the Tories and the commercial interests. Brougham and the *Edinburgh Review* vehemently opposed the Orders in Council, and the significance of this opposition is underlined by Halévy's conclusion that it was Brougham's large (though not victorious) vote in the Liverpool election of 1812 which first demonstrated that the business world had swung over to the Opposition on the question of commercial freedom.[2] Can one then safely assume that after 1812 the Whigs replaced the Tories as the party of commerce? Hardly, for both parties were split over questions of economic policy—and one need only mention the names of Canning and Huskisson to forestall any rash and premature identification of Whiggism and economic liberalism.

It might seem that if there were one area in which interaction between party politics and economics could be rather closely discerned in the pages of the *Review*, it would be that of financial policy. For in 1804 Brougham, still trying to ingratiate himself with Pitt, wrote a slashing review of Lauderdale's economic principles, in which he not only dismissed the Scottish Whig leader's fruitful distinction between individual riches and national wealth, but defended Pitt's sinking-fund scheme against Lauderdale's attacks. He followed this review with another denying that the suspension of specie payments by the Bank of England (1797) and the consequent inundation of the country with paper money had had any adverse effects.[3]

Sub specie aeternitatis (so to speak) Brougham appears to have been wrong in his strictures on Lauderdale's opposition to parsimony as a desirable economic virtue, and right in his defence of Pitt's war financing.[4] Yet, regardless of the eternal verities,

[1] Elie Halévy, *England in 1815* (2nd rev. ed., London, 1949), 223.
[2] *Ibid.*, 320.
[3] Brougham, *ER*, VIII (July, 1804), 8, 343–377; especially 374–376; Brougham, *ER*, IX (October, 1804), 8, 107–113.
[4] Cf. Lord Keynes's praise of Malthus's opposition to excessive saving in his essay on 'Robert Malthus'. (John Maynard Keynes, *Essays in Biography* [new ed., London, 1951], 118–123.) And, for a defence of British war financing, 1793–1815, see Norman J. Silberling, 'Financial and Monetary Policy of Great Britain during the Napoleonic Wars', *Quarterly Journal of Economics*, XXXVIII (1923–1924), 214–233, 397–439.

125

one might be tempted (knowing Brougham's editorial influence) to see a connection between his definite alignment with the Whigs and the *Review*'s subsequently consistent attack on sinking funds and the suspension of specie, and its advocacy of a return to cash payments.

But the leading reviews on the monetary question in 1802–1803 had come from Horner's pen, and their message was a warning against monetary expansion—the same message proclaimed some years later in articles written by Malthus to some degree under Horner's influence.[1] Thus it is doubtful whether Brougham was instrumental in shaping the attitude of the *Review* on the monetary issue, however much he may have had to do with other aspects of its economic policy such as its opposition to the Orders in Council.[2]

There was nothing peculiarly Whiggish about the advocacy of a return to cash payments. It is true that Horner was Chairman of the Bullion Committee of 1810 which recommended this course, and that the Government opposed this Committee's Report from September, 1810, on. But Huskisson and Canning sat on the Committee, and they (as well as the *Quarterly*) supported the main theme of the Report, that the Bank of England was issuing too much money; though some of the members of the Committee seem to have been less enthusiastic than Horner about the proposal to resume specie payments within the space of two years.[3]

After Waterloo, the *Review* combined its generally pacific

[1] Horner, *ER*, I (October, 1802), *25*, 172–201; Horner, *ER*, IV (July, 1803), *11*, 402–421; Malthus, *ER*, XXXIV (February, 1811), *5*, 340–372; Malthus, *ER*, XXXVI (August, 1811), *10*, 448–470.

[2] On this latter point I am grateful to Professor Frank W. Fetter for calling my attention to a letter by James Stephen dated May 23, 1808, among some Spencer Perceval papers in private hands. Stephen particularly criticizes (Brougham), *ER*, XXIII (April, 1808), *13*, 225–246, a vigorous attack against the Orders in Council whose author Stephen probably surmised correctly. In any event, going beyond this specific article, he blames Brougham's general direction of *Edinburgh* policy on this subject.

[3] On this point see Frank Whitson Fetter, 'The Bullion Report Reexamined', *Quarterly Journal of Economics*, LVI (1941–1942), 655–665. For the *Review*'s attacks on Pittite financial policy, cf. *ER*, XIX (April, 1807), *5*, 84–85; *ER*, XXXIV (February, 1811), *5*, 340–371; and *ER*, XLVIII (February, 1815), *2*, 294–319.

inclinations with financial advice, in pointing out that had there been no war, 'we might have had good French wines for eighteen pence or two shillings a bottle; porter at less than twopence a pot; and a post-chaise at sevenpence or eightpence a mile'; and in proclaiming that Britons now had a right to be exempted from every penny of their burden not absolutely necessary.[1] But its opposition to the income tax, vigorously stated in the same article, represented the views held by business and agricultural interests regardless of party.[2]

And there was little if any party politics in the *Review's* championing of Adam Smith and his doctrines. The Whigs were divided on the question of free trade, with the Grenvillites (schooled under Pitt) far more enthusiastic than Grey and the Foxites. But the *Edinburgh* reviewers, banished to a desert island with only the proverbial favourite volume, would undoubtedly have chosen *The Wealth of Nations*, certainly in preference to either Testament. The *Review* extolled 'the master-principle of individual interest—the power which connects and maintains the whole system, as gravitation regulates the movements of the heavenly bodies'.[3] The general principles of exchange, following from the master-principle, 'appear to us to have been already very satisfactorily elucidated', wrote the reviewer, 'so that, in our apprehension, nothing further remained to be done by succeeding writers than to point out, from a wider survey of the facts, the invariable coincidence which exists on this subject between the sound conclusions of principle, and the results of experience'.[4]

This being so, the *Review* saw its function primarily in the

---

[1] *ER*, L (October, 1815), *13*, 545. The reviewer could bring himself to write that Britain ought to be more cautious of again 'plunging into war'.

[2] Cf. Halévy, *England in 1815*, 375.

[3] Brougham, *ER*, IX (October, 1804), *1*, 16.

[4] *ER*, XVII (October, 1806), *8*, 111–112. Horner, in private correspondence, struck a more cynical note. He declared himself reluctant to expose Smith's errors before his work had operated to full effect. 'We owe much at present to the superstitious worship of Smith's name; and we must not impair that feeling, till the victory is more complete. There are few practical errors in the *Wealth of Nations*, at least of any great consequence; and, until we can give a correct and precise theory of the nature and origin of wealth, his popular and plausible and loose hypothesis is as good for the vulgar as any other.' Horner to Thomas Thomson, August 15, 1803, Leonard Horner, ed., *Memoirs and Correspondence of Francis Horner, M.P.* (London, 1843), I, 229.

realm of pedagogy, for it appeared that there were still some benighted souls who, though familiar with the ideas of the Master, did not carry them into practice. Thus Brougham reprimanded those 'sound, solid practical men' who were always condemning general principles, who talked about 'the celebrated Dr. Adam Smith' and 'his immortal work', but were quite willing to see the contents of that work frittered down to absolutely nothing in the application.[1] Another reviewer admitted that the fundamental doctrines of political economy were far better known in Britain than anywhere else. Nevertheless, there was probably not one man in a hundred who really saw that individual interest was 'the grand, and all-sufficient spring, both of intelligence and of activity in the entire field of human industry'.[2]

'It is really provoking to find', commented the *Review* in exasperation, 'how very slowly truth and sound reason make their way, even among the reading classes of the community.'[3] It was reprimanding William Spence for his 'absurd statement' that agriculture creates wealth, whereas a reading of Dr. Smith would have shown Spence that a nation grows rich as much from improvement in industry as from its progress in agriculture.[4] At the same time it conjured up the vision of a variety of nations joined together in one great mercantile confederacy, 'ministering to each other's enjoyments by a free and liberal intercourse'.[5] For the *Edinburgh Review*, the advantages of free trade had been axiomatic from the start. Horner, in the second number, had called the doctrine one of those great and

---

[1] Brougham, *ER*, XVIII (January, 1807), 5, 337.

[2] *ER*, XXVII (April, 1809), 2, 22.

[3] (Buchanan and Jeffrey), *ER*, XXVII (April, 1809), 4, 50–51.

[4] *Ibid.*, 55. The review was of William Spence's pamphlet *Agriculture the Source of the Wealth of Britain: A Reply to the Objections urged by Mr. Mill, the Edinburgh Reviewers, and Others* (London, 1808). The *Review* had previously attacked the notion of agriculture as the sole source of wealth in *ER*, IX (October, 1804), 5–15. This was one instance where Dugald Stewart disagreed with Adam Smith whose teachings he expounded. Stewart thought that Smith's definition of national wealth as the annual produce of land and labour was not as just as that of the French Economists who measured it by 'rude produce', excluding completely the results of manufacturing industry. Dugald Stewart, 'Lectures on Political Economy', Sif William Hamilton, ed., *The Collected Works of Dugald Stewart* (Edinburgh, 1854–1860), VIII, 252.

[5] (Buchanan and Jeffrey), *ER*, XXVII (April, 1809), 4, 55.

permanent discoveries which had succeeded in unfolding the operations of nature.[1] And Brougham once again broke a lance with Lauderdale in upbraiding the latter for opposing English loans to Ireland, out of fear that they would force cheap Irish produce into the English market, thus undermining English industry. If the goods we need can be furnished more cheaply from Ireland than from at home, he wrote, why not let Ireland furnish them?[2]

In the same spirit the *Review* fairly consistently opposed the trading monopoly of the East India Company.[3] This question was complicated by political considerations, in so far as putting an end to the Company's political powers meant that the Government could then take over the Company's immense patronage power. This is pointed out in an article written (not surprisingly) shortly after the fall of All the Talents. The writer of the article concludes that the Company should retain its patronage and political power, but that the Indian trade ought to be opened to all. He assumes that his readers are familiar with the observations of Dr. Smith on the subject of commercial monopolies, 'or, at least, that they will take instantaneous measures to verify our conjectures, by poring over every tittle of those observations, before they proceed with this humble commentary upon them'.[4] The problem of the Company's future became acute in 1812, when preliminary negotiations for a renewal of the Company's Charter got under way. The *Review* (in this case James Mill) stuck to its position that the trade should be opened to all merchants, and suggested the need for a general inquiry on the political future of India.[5] In 1815, when the Company's

[1] Horner, *ER*, II (January, 1803), *16*, 446.

[2] Brougham, *ER*, XII (July, 1805), *2*, 290.

[3] For its first attack on the Company's exclusive privileges, see *ER*, VIII (July, 1804), *5*, 308–309, where the Indian monopoly is called 'singularly mischievous'.

[4] *ER*, XX (July, 1807), *7*, 339. For recommendations on the political and commercial future of the Company, see 364–367.

[5] *ER*, XL (November, 1812), *13*, 471–493. This is in line with previous attacks on the East India monopoly, e.g. *ER*, XXXI (April, 1810), *6*, 129–137, and *ER*, XXXVII (November, 1811), *10*, 230–245, especially 233–234; and does not contradict the *Review*'s endorsement of the Directors' governmental policies in India, *ER*, XXXIX (July, 1812), *3*, 38–54. However, on one occasion a reviewer defended the Company's trade monopoly on the ground that it was in the public interest to raise exports and imports to the highest level possible, and that the

commercial monopoly had been abolished, a reviewer praised its retention of political patronage, since its officers were sufficiently connected with the 'more respectable classes of the community' to exempt their patronage power from the direct influence of the Crown.[1]

If the *Review* followed Adam Smith in regard to free trade and monopoly, it was only to be expected that it would take the anti-protectionist line on the question of corn bounties and corn import restrictions. During the war years the agricultural interests were generally favourable to free trade, since it did not materially affect their prosperity. But the demand for corn export bounties never abated completely, and when prices fell at the end of the war, the whole question of the advisability of restrictive Corn Laws became acute once again. The *Review* did not waver in its *laissez-faire* attitude on this matter, whether this meant defending the engrossing of corn on the part of the farmer[2] or (more frequently) attacking the proposed stimulation of corn exports through bounties.[3] In 1808 a reviewer admitted that bounties would probably have the effect of giving the farmer a higher price for his corn without raising the cost of labour, and would thus be beneficial for agriculture. 'But', he continued, 'we doubt the propriety of making the community pay a higher price for corn in order to encourage agriculture.'[4] And in the same vein, when Malthus came out in support of corn import restrictions in 1815—on the ground (authorized by Adam Smith) that Britain needed an independent subsistence above all—the *Review* opposed him because it did not think that the great mass of the community should be taxed for the benefit of landed

---

Company was able to fulfil this function more efficiently than private traders could. (*ER*, XXX [January, 1810,] *1*, 269–270.) In the event, Parliament, in 1813, did not renew the Company's trade monopoly, but permitted it to retain its political functions. On the Whig line-up in regard to this question (Tierney for the Company, Grey lukewarm, the Grenvilles opposed) see Cyril H. Philips, *The East India Company, 1784–1834* (Manchester, 1940), 187–192; *Historical Manuscripts Commission, Report on the Manuscripts of J. B. Fortescue, Esq., preserved at Dropmore* (London, 1927), X, 323–329.

[1] *ER*, L (October, 1815), 7, 441.

[2] Smith, *ER*, I (October, 1802), *20*, 129.

[3] Cf. Horner, *ER*, IX (October, 1804), *15*, 190–208; *ER*, XXV (October, 1808), *13*, 207–214.

[4] *ER*, XXV (October, 1808), *13*, 214.

proprietors or farmers, or even for the encouragement of agriculture.[1]

It is perhaps worth noting that in this less than charitable view of the welfare of landlord and farmer, the *Review* took its texts from Smith, without taking over his basically pro-agricultural orientation. For anyone interested in studying the resurgence of the Whigs as the party of commerce and industry, the *Edinburgh Review*'s attitude on this question becomes of some significance. Twenty-five years after the death of Adam Smith and twenty-five years before the founding of the Anti-Corn Law League, it seems to breathe the spirit of the latter rather than the former. It held the *Wealth of Nations* sacrosanct, but applied some of its principles in a new context, shaping eighteenth-century ideas to fit nineteenth-century needs.

If one can find foreshadowings of the Anti-Corn Law League in the *Review*, can one also find foreshadowings of the Poor Law Amendment Act? The question is relevant, for the abolition of outdoor relief to the poor with a view to their greater self-reliance was to be just as characteristic of the new economic liberalism as its support of free trade. If the opposition to the old principles of poor relief had a philosopher, it was Malthus. And the *Review* from the beginning supported Malthusian doctrine.[2] Malthus himself became a contributor in 1808, warning that any attempt to alter the natural results arising from the increased supply of labour in Ireland (in relation to the funds available to support it) would be a vain effort 'to reverse the laws of nature'.[3] Two years later a reviewer eloquently defended Malthus against his adversaries and, in tones that were soon to become the hallmark of a new Whiggism, announced that it was the nation's

[1] *ER*, XLVIII (February, 1815), *13*, 504. Horner and Jeffrey disagreed on this question, with the latter supporting Malthus but (interestingly enough) not to the point of insisting that his views be endorsed in the *Review*. Cf. Jeffrey to Malthus, May 12, 1814, Henry Thomas Cockburn, Lord Cockburn, *Life of Lord Jeffrey, with a Selection from his Correspondence* (Edinburgh, 1852), II, 146 ('Horner is much more Smithish'); and Horner to Malthus, February 12, 1815, *Horner Memoirs*, II, 232: 'It is this audacious and presumptuous spirit of regulating, by the wisdom of country squires, the whole economy and partition of national industry and wealth, that makes me more keenly averse to this corn bill of theirs than I should have been in earlier days of our time, when the principles of rational government were more widely understood, and were maintained by stronger hands at the head of affairs.'

[2] Cf. Smith, *ER*, I (October, 1802), *3*, 26.   [3] *ER*, XXIV (July, 1808), *4*, 348.

great business to discourage the helpless and improvident habits of the lower classes of society, and to raise them to the condition of beings who 'look before and after'.[1] In analysing the success of Utilitarian doctrines in an evangelical environment, Halévy sees asceticism as one of the characteristics common to both.[2] His thesis finds confirmation in the *Edinburgh Review* which, in endorsing Malthus on population, points out that, *this state* being one of discipline and preparation for another, why not accept a doctrine which submits the passions to reason and religion? For is not the Malthusian law one of those natural laws discovered by human experience which may be merged with considerable force with arguments in favour of revealed religion?[3]

The *Review* supported Malthus in his opposition to the existing Poor Laws, and proposed the complete exclusion of able-bodied labourers from parochial relief, with the proviso that some aid (possibly voluntary charity) still be given to the sick and the young or to those who personally exerted themselves. But, the reviewer continued, it was much safer to fall short than to exceed in relieving distress.[4] Six years later a reviewer pointed out that the poor rates kept down the wages of labour by permitting masters to reduce them to a minimum in the expectation that the parish would pay a supplement. The 'beneficent system' of poor relief only served as an engine in the hands of the masters to keep wages as low as would suffice for maintenance. He could suggest no remedy for a situation which thus degraded 'three quarters of mankind'.[5] And a subsequent article on the subject, without making any more positive suggestion than that of instituting savings banks, simply stated it as a fact that the warmest admirers of the poor laws were now candid enough to admit that the certainty of bounties had the sole effect of increasing the natural improvidence and thriftlessness of the labouring classes, and, moreover, corrupted them into the bargain.[6]

For the reviewers, who considered themselves the guardians

---

[1] *ER*, XXXII (August, 1810), *11*, 471. For other defences of Malthus, see *ER*, XLV (April, 1814), *2*, 51, and *ER*, XLIX (June, 1815), *6*, 142.
[2] Halévy, *England in 1815*, 585–586.
[3] *ER*, XXXII (August, 1810), *11*, 472–474.
[4] *ER*, XXI (October, 1807), 7, 115.
[5] *ER*, XLIII (October, 1813), *11*, 197–198.
[6] *ER*, XLIX (June, 1815), *6*, 142.

of universal truth, the laws of classical economics had the advantage of lending themselves to unequivocal exposition as 'that class of important truths which have only to be explained in order to command our immediate assent'.[1] But what of the readers of the *Review*? To what classes did the periodical appeal when it preached the gospel of Smith and Malthus? How many people were influenced by these teachings? No doubt 'the pages of the *Edinburgh* provided for the gentry a shortened version of the economic classics, of the brochures of controversy, and of the parliamentary reports'.[2] But it is difficult to answer these questions definitively. However, two lines of inquiry may be fruitfully pursued: one is to establish the numerical circulation of the *Review* during this period; the other, to examine its treatment of different social groups in order to gain some clues concerning the direction of its appeal.

Unfortunately, no 'official' statistics regarding the circulation of the *Edinburgh Review* are now available. But it is possible to construct, from various sources, a fairly complete set of figures for the period from 1802 to 1815. The whole matter is complicated by the fact that issues of the *Review* were constantly being reprinted months or even years after they had originally appeared. Thus the first edition of the first number (seven hundred and fifty copies) was followed in November, 1802, by a second edition of equal size, and within another year 2,150 copies of this number had been sold.[3] The next circulation figure emerges in a letter from Jeffrey to Lockhart Muirhead, dated March, 1803, in which he announces that No. III (April, 1803) is to be issued in an edition of 1,750.[4] A letter from Constable to Longmans dated November, 1804, contains the information that Nos. I, II, III, and IV are still being reprinted (in editions of 1,000 each) and that the initial printing of No. X (January, 1805) is to be 4,000 copies.[5] By the beginning of 1807 the Lon-

[1] A reviewer on Malthus, *ER*, XXI (October, 1807), 7, 102.

[2] Fetter, 'Authorship of Economic Articles', 234.

[3] Cf. *ante*, p. 30.

[4] Jeffrey to Muirhead, March, 1803, Boulton and Watt Collection, Birmingham Reference Library. Quoted by Leroy H. Buckingham, 'The Authorship of the First Twenty-five Numbers of the *Edinburgh Review*', Yale Doctoral Dissertation (1938), 303.

[5] Constable to Longmans, November 27, 1804, Constable Correspondence, National Library of Scotland, MS. 324.

don circulation is reported to be 3,500, while towards the end of that year the same source puts it at 5,000 out of 7,000 printed in Edinburgh.[1] In July, 1808, Archibald Constable writes that 'when in London, I saw 5,000 copies of the last number of the Edinburgh Review bought and paid for on the same day'.[2] Three months later Scott tells Gifford that 'from eight to nine thousand copies of that review [the *Edinburgh*] are quarterly dispersed'.[3] By June, 1809, Horner, in asking Jeffrey to take special pains with an article on parliamentary reform, tells him that he ought 'to consider what it is, to send out eleven thousand prints of your doctrine of that subject'.[4]

Jeffrey apparently calculated that each copy of the *Review* was seen by at least three readers. In a review (1810) of Scott's *Lady of the Lake* in which he had previously stated the fact that nearly 30,000 copies of the *Lay of the Last Minstrel* had been sold, and that the demand for the new poem was reported to be even greater, he commented that it was superfluous to present an analysis of a work 'which is probably, by this time, in the hands of as many persons as are likely to see our account of it'.[5] Shortly thereafter, in December, 1810, Archibald Constable set the circulation figure of the *Review* at 12,000.[6] And in September, 1814, Jeffrey wrote to Thomas Moore that 'it is something to think that at least fifty thousand people will read what you write in less than a month. We print now nearly 13,000 copies and may reckon, I suppose, modestly on three or four readers of the popular articles.'[7] The last available figure comes

[1] Samuel Smiles, *A Publisher and his Friends: Memoir and Correspondence of the late John Murray* (London, 1891), I, 80.

[2] Archibald Constable to Alexander Murray, July 17, 1808, *Archibald Constable and his Literary Correspondents*, ed. Thomas Constable (Edinburgh, 1873), I, 269.

[3] Scott to Gifford, October 25, 1808, *The Letters of Sir Walter Scott*, ed. Herbert J. C. Grierson (London, 1932–1937), II, 107. A week later he put the figure at 9,000. (Scott to George Ellis, November 2, 1808, *ibid.*, 121.) Early the next year, Jeffrey put the circulation 'very near' ten thousand. Jeffrey to James Watt, February 17, 1809, Boulton and Watt Collection, Birmingham Reference Library.

[4] Horner to Jeffrey, June 12, 1809, *Horner Memoirs*, I, 464.

[5] Jeffrey, *ER*, XXXII (August, 1810), *I*, 263, 274.

[6] Archibald Constable to Alexander Murray, December 2, 1810, *Constable and his Correspondents*, I, 288.

[7] Jeffrey to Thomas Moore, September 14, 1814, Lord John Russell, ed., *Memoirs, Journal, and Correspondence of Thomas Moore* (London, 1853–1856), II, 40. A maximum sale of 13,500 was reached in 1818. Harold Cox, 'The House of Longman', *ER*, CCCCXC (October, 1924), 221.

Classical Economics and the Middling Classes

from an entry in the letter book of the firm of Constable noting that 7,500 copies of No. XLVII (November, 1814) had been shipped to London.[1]

What is the significance of these statistics? The most obvious and, at the same time, the most striking fact they reveal is that in a period of twelve years the current circulation of the *Edinburgh Review* (i.e. the first printing) increased nearly twenty-fold, from seven hundred and fifty to 13,000 copies. To put this figure in perspective, it may be recalled that the circulation of *The Times* in 1816 was only 8,000 copies daily. But, the phenomenal popularity of the *Review* once acknowledged, it still remains to ask by whom it was read. 'No genteel family *can* pretend to be without it', wrote Scott in 1808, 'because, independent of its politics, it gives the only valuable literary criticism which can be met with.'[2] This was no longer true after the founding of the rival Tory *Quarterly* in 1809, but it may be assumed that—except for those who, like the Earl of Buchan, were mortally offended by the 'Cevallos' article—most of the readers of the *Edinburgh* continued to buy it.

Needless to say, they had to be able to afford to do so. The price, originally five shillings, was raised in 1809 to six shillings, 'owing to the greatly increased expenses of paper and printing, since the first establishment of the *Edinburgh Review*'.[3] A little more than a year before this 'Advertisement', the *Review* itself had reported the average price of labour in English cotton manufacture as being two shillings per day.[4] Thus, quite apart from questions of literacy and cultural interest, those who purchased the periodical—some may have read it in libraries—had to be fairly comfortably off.

[1] Constable to Longmans, December 21, 1814, Constable Letter Book, MS. 789, National Library of Scotland. Earlier in 1814 Longmans had repurchased (for £4,500) the London rights to the *Edinburgh Review* from Constable, having sold them in 1807 for £1,000. Longmans took over sole control in 1826. The account ledger books of Longmans show that the firm continued to take 7,500 copies of Nos. XLVIII through L (February, 1815, to October, 1815). The books show that under a half and half arrangement (with Constable), Jeffrey was paid £1,050 by Longmans for editing Nos. XLVII through XLIX and that the firm's profit on these three numbers amounted to £463 0s. 6d. Longman's Ledger 'C 2', 1814–1819, folio 260.

[2] Scott to George Ellis, November 2, 1808, *Scott Letters*, II, 121.

[3] 'Advertisement', *ER*, XXVII (April, 1809), [i].

[4] *ER*, XXII (January, 1808), *11*, 433.

Perhaps it suffices to say that the bulk of the *Review*'s readers belonged to the upper and middle classes—'one begins to catch the echo of its fame from country squires, rusticated peers, and provincial doctors', wrote Horner to Jeffrey in 1804.[1] It would certainly be difficult to be much more exact. But it might not be altogether uninstructive to examine the attitude of the reviewers towards various different social groups. Such an examination will not necessarily throw any light on the question: Who read the *Review*? But at the very least it may be possible to discover what the reviewers, always aware of their pedagogical function, wanted their *readers* to think about various social groups and— last not least—what they themselves thought about them.

First of all, let it not be said that the reviewers did not have a high regard for the general knowledge of their public to whose thirst for more knowledge they catered by learned articles on scholarly and scientific subjects.[2] A contemporary critic recently regretted the passing of *l'homme moyen intellectuel*, the reader to whom everything did not always have to be explained. The *Edinburgh Review* must receive its share of credit for helping to form this now seemingly extinct species. For it simply expected a certain amount of general knowledge, and presumably shamed those who did not possess it into acquiring it. Not that the reviewers always accepted the full implications of Sydney Smith's blithe announcement that 'to almost every Englishman up to the age of three or four-and-twenty, classical learning has been the great object of existence'.[3] But they assumed that it would be 'ridiculous' to suppose that any of their readers were ignorant of the beautiful though desultory illustrations of relations between Franks and Gauls in the last four books of the *Esprit des Lois*;[4] that Huygens, Gronovius, and Voet had been more than faintly heard of 'by every man of ordinary inform-

---

[1] Horner to Jeffrey, November 29, 1804, Horner Correspondence, L.S.E., II, 81.

[2] This in spite of the fact that in 1803 Brougham had told Horner that he agreed with most of his remarks on 'the dryness of scientific articles, to the bulk of readers'. Brougham to Horner, October 24, 1803, Horner Correspondence, L.S.E., II, 24.

[3] Smith, *ER*, XXIX (October, 1809), 3, 43. Sydney Smith went on to point out the need for utilitarian as well as classical learning. Young men, he felt, should learn the principles of legislation, economics, trade, etc. *Ibid.*, 49–52.

[4] *ER*, XI (April, 1805), 17, 218.

ation';[1] and that the only people not acquainted with the relative position, distance, comparative size and advantages, cities, mountains, rivers, natural productions, and principal articles of manufacture and commerce of most of the nations of Europe were those 'in the lowest ranks of society'.[2]

These ranks were not to remain plunged in darkness. Jeffrey approvingly cited one author's demand for the instruction and illumination of the lower orders whom the division of labour had reduced to unthinking machines.[3] He was quite aware of the deleterious human effects of the industrial revolution, though he tended to accept them as inevitable and, on the whole, irremediable. The 'bustle of active industry', presenting such a cheerful spectacle to so many men, was in fact connected with unceasing labour, poverty, and misery. 'That there must be in all countries, where the population and the arts of civilized life have reached a certain point', he continued, 'a class of men who pass their days in labour for a pittance barely adequate to their subsistence, and who, of course, must be continually liable to want and misery, from accidents, and the follies and vices incident to human nature, is a position which we are afraid cannot be denied.'[4] The great discovery of the subdivision of labour on which national prosperity rested had exerted a sad effect on the lower orders and had degraded the bulk of the population.[5] But this was the unavoidable corollary of the present state of commercial civilization. 'The comforts of a labourer in the lowest ranks of society', Jeffrey had pointed out in the first number,

[1] *ER*, XX (July, 1807), *2*, 274.

[2] *ER*, V (October, 1803), *6*, 67. In its heavy concentration on reviews of travel books—with lengthy extracts—the *Edinburgh Review* certainly saw to it that this information reached its readers. Brougham's encyclopaedic tendencies were probably to some extent behind this policy. In justifying editorial partiality for books of travel he wrote with missionary fervour of how even in the poorest books of fact, there were some things deserving of notice. Brougham, *ER*, XXIII (April, 1808), *12*, 213.

[3] Jeffrey, *ER*, V (October, 1803), *13*, 175. An interesting parallel is to be found in Dugald Stewart's lectures. Stewart, after singing the praises of the division of labour principle, notes its 'displeasing' effect on those 'who are doomed to be the instruments of all those blessings to their fellow-citizens'. ('Lectures on Political Economy', *Works*, VIII, 329.)

[4] Jeffrey, *ER*, XXII (January, 1808), *7*, 379–380.

[5] Jeffrey, *ER*, XXXVI (August, 1811), *12*, 485. See also *ER*, XXXIV (February, 1811), *10*, 417; and Jeffrey, *ER*, XLI (February, 1813), *1*, 23.

'are scarcely superior, in most civilized societies, to the ordinary life of a savage.'[1]

Yet the *Review* 'cheerfully subscribe[d]' to the axiom that the distribution of comforts among the inferior orders was the best security for their virtues and regular conduct.[2] In most countries the lowest class of people was in the situation of the ass in the fable, who did not care who his master was since he must always carry his load. But if the load became too heavy, and if a new master offered to lighten the burden, it might no longer be possible to rely on the neutrality of the ass.[3] Sydney Smith combined humanitarian and political motives in warning of the evil effects resulting from that contempt of men's feelings, that passion for insulting multitudes 'which is so congenial to our present Government at home, and which passes now so currently for wisdom and courage'.[4]

The *Review*, though fatalistic about the effects of the division of labour, felt that the 'lower orders' should be treated with sympathy rather than condescension. 'We would rather', it stated editorially, 'leave out the most taking article in our Number to make room for the most homely directions for increasing the comforts of the labourers and peasantry of our country.'[5] One reviewer declared himself annoyed with the fact that terms like 'virtuous', 'hardy', 'spirited', and 'freeborn' were so regularly attached to the peasantry that it was sometimes forgotten that they might apply to other classes.[6] Jeffrey himself criticized an 'improving novel' for encouraging a feeling of too great servility in the lower ranks, a censure which (he added) also applied to Hannah More's productions. The poor, especially in Scotland, were quite apt enough already to pay at least due homage to wealth and station, and there was no particular need to inculcate 'vassal feelings'.[7] Yet Jeffrey's own

[1] Jeffrey, *ER*, I (October, 1802), 22, 147.
[2] *ER*, XI (April, 1805), 10, 115.
[3] *ER*, XIX (April, 1807), 3, 59.
[4] Smith, *ER*, XXXII (August, 1810), 7, 412–413.
[5] *ER*, XLIX (June, 1815), 6, 135. See also Jeffrey, *ER*, XVII (October, 1806), 3, 33, where he puts the communication of useful intelligence, in this case information about vaccination, above the amusement of readers or the formation of their taste.
[6] *ER*, IX (October, 1804), 1, 10.
[7] Jeffrey, *ER*, XXIV (July, 1808), 8, 410.

conception of society had its hierarchical side. After praising Scotland's excellent scheme of parochial education he added that 'it is comfortable to think that so great a proportion of the people is able to appretiate [sic] the advantages of its condition and fit to be relied on in all emergencies where steadiness and intelligence may be required'.[1] The reference here was to the peasantry rather than to industrial labourers. Jeffrey realized that the condition of the latter had few 'advantages' and that, unlike the Scottish cotters, their English counterparts might not always be relied on, since their misery was too great. But as their state was the concomitant of a particular stage of civilization, all that could be done in mitigation was instruction, illumination, and a more dignified treatment of the lower by the higher orders.

What of these 'higher orders'? How did *they* fare in the pages of the *Edinburgh Review*? In so far as they were country gentlemen, they did not have an easy time of it. In his *Memoirs* Lord Holland refers with contempt to the judgement of the gentry who 'always foster the narrow-minded maxims of past times'.[2] And this was pretty much the attitude of the reviewers. In the very first number Sydney Smith gravely announced that 'it is of some importance, too, that grown-up country-gentlemen should be habituated to read books'.[3] In a similar vein Horner had them speaking out 'with that explicit plainness from which they seldom deviate, even when they most mislead the public councils';[4] while Smith, in support of his view that female education was not a ludicrous project, adduced this happy illustration:

'A century ago, who would have believed that country gentlemen could be brought to read and spell with the ease and accuracy

[1] Jeffrey, *ER*, XXVI (January, 1809), *1*, 276. Brougham, too, ridiculed the idea that education would mean the end of subordination. 'As long as servility is necessary to some men's livelihood,' he wrote, 'they will obey others who can support them.' Brougham, *ER*, XXXIII (November, 1810), *3*, 62. The *Edinburgh Review* consistently supported the education of the poor, especially by the Lancaster method. See e.g. Smith, *ER*, XXI (October, 1807), *4*, 61–73; *ER*, XLI (February, 1813), *9*, 207–219.
[2] Henry Richard Vassall Fox, 3rd Baron Holland, *Memoirs of the Whig Party during My Time*, ed. Henry Edward Lord Holland (London, 1852–1854), I, 167.
[3] Smith, *ER*, I (October, 1802), *18*, 122.
[4] Horner, *ER*, IX (October, 1804), *15*, 208.

which we now so frequently remark,—or supposed that they could be carried up even to the elements of antient [*sic*] and modern history?'[1]

Having finished one of his 'Smithish' Corn Law articles, Horner had warned Jeffrey that it would 'probably spoil your sale in the county of Norfolk, and Jeffrey's health will not be toasted at Holk[h]am sheep-shearing'.[2] Jeffrey himself, perhaps remembering this, on one occasion managed to strike a kindly note of sympathy with those country gentlemen 'worn down by luxury and taxation, superseded by the activity of office, and eclipsed by the opulence of trade'.[3] But it may safely be presumed that those of the *Review*'s readers who belonged to that class turned with relief (as of 1809) to their *Quarterlies*, where they would be sure to find no such scurvy treatment accorded them.

The country gentry was criticized for its ignorance and backwardness; the aristocracy for its idleness and lack of moral fibre. It is true that the *Review* 'heartily join[ed]' in one author's compliment to English men of rank, bestowed in recognition of their respect for classical education;[4] and that Jeffrey, reviewing Lord Holland's *Lope de Vega*, was pleased to note that persons of his rank and political importance were dedicating a part of their leisure to the cultivation of learned studies.[5] But this was not the usual tone of the *Review*. Brougham's taunt at Byron's *Hours of Idleness* is far more typical:

'What right have we poor devils to be nice? We are well off to have got so much from a man of his Lord's station, who does not live in a garret, but "has the sway" of Newstead Abbey.'[6]

The *Review*'s anti-aristocratic tendency becomes more pronounced in 1808, the year of 'Don Cevallos', possibly because of Brougham's growing dissatisfaction with the Whig country houses. The 'Cevallos' number carried another, hardly less

---

[1] Smith, *ER*, XXX (January, 1810), *3*, 301. For other derogatory remarks regarding the country gentry, cf. *ER*, X (January, 1805), *3*, 302; *ER*, XVIII (January, 1807), *9*, 393; and *ER*, XXII (January, 1808), *11*, 434.
[2] Horner to Jeffrey, October 1, 1804, Horner Correspondence, L.S.E., II, 74.
[3] Jeffrey, *ER*, XXV (October, 1808), *1*, 2.
[4] *ER*, VI (January, 1804), *8*, 351.
[5] Jeffrey, *ER*, XVII (October, 1806), *16*, 240.
[6] Brougham, *ER*, XXII (January, 1808), *2*, 289.

explosive review stating that there was not a single instance in the history of mankind in which the power of the aristocracy did not exceed its proper limits—and that this was the 'grand disturbing cause in the movements of the social machine'.[1] Shortly thereafter, the privileged orders outside France were invited to examine the salutary example of the instability of human affairs exhibited by 'decayed gentlemen' in that country.[2]

What was the great crime of persons of rank in England? The members of four out of five families in that class, exempted from the necessity of daily industry, spent their time in the great and laborious pursuit of being thought fashionable.[3] These fashionable pursuits were not only deleterious for those who *pretended* to fashion, but in equal measure for its very leaders.[4] The reformation of morals in the upper ranks of society had not kept pace with the extraordinary increase in charitable exertions.[5] In short, the aristocracy, unlike the rest of the country, was giving itself to opulence and idleness.

What of those who neither belonged to the upper or lower strata? Merchants, traders in government securities, loan contractors, and insurance brokers were characterized in 1807 as a class of men who could contemplate the complete degradation of mankind over the great part of Europe as well as the downfall of foreign empires with composure; who submitted with exemplary resignation to the sufferings of the poor; and bore up nobly under the hardships of soldiers and sailors.[6] Brougham, already the great champion of commercial freedom, still talked in 1809 of 'the established prejudices of the mercantile mob'.[7] Later that year the *Review* pointed out that the mercantile classes would do anything to elude the tax collectors.[8] After

[1] *ER*, XXV (October, 1808), *12*, 197.
[2] *ER*, XXVI (January, 1809), *9*, 441.
[3] Jeffrey, *ER*, XXVIII (July, 1809), *7*, 378.
[4] Jeffrey, *ER*, XXXIX (July, 1812), *7*, 102.
[5] *ER*, XLV (April, 1814), *2*, 46.
[6] *ER*, XVIII (January, 1807), *13*, 461.
[7] Brougham, *ER*, XXVI (January, 1809), *7*, 413. In 1804 he had referred contemptuously to 'attorneys and pettifoggers', with the whole tribe of money-dealers', whom all good citizens wished to see reduced in number and importance. Brougham, *ER*, VI (January, 1804), *19*, 477.
[8] *ER*, XXIX (October, 1809), *14*, 235.

1810 its attacks on the merchants ceased, but although the *Edinburgh*, through its opposition to the Orders in Council and the American war, put the mercantile interests in its debt, it never went so far as to bestow praise on the class as a whole. Perhaps it did not consider it part of 'that great proportion of our readers which must necessarily belong to the middling or humbler classes of the community'.[1] It was for this group that the *Review* reserved its greatest encomia. There were reservations. Yet the increasing numbers and improving character of the middling class were considered to be the sole countervailing forces against the despotic tendencies of the upper classes.[2]

Jeffrey was not above chiding the 'diligent readers of poetry in this country' who consisted chiefly of 'young, half-educated women, sickly tradesmen, and enamoured apprentices'.[3] True, he contrasted these, 'the millinery misses and aspiring apprentices of our country towns' with the 'great and respectable multitude of English tradesmen, yeomen, and manufacturers in that most important part of our population which consists of the well-educated in the lower and middling orders of the people'. But he did this in the course of recommending a work written 'to make them proud of their independence, and cheerful in their submission, and to point out the happiness which is placed in the reach of all who are industrious and affectionate'.[4] The *Review* generally retained a paternalistic strain in its attitude towards 'the honest shopkeepers, and industrious tradesmen',[5] even while admitting, in 1812, that 'though we are not absolutely nor altogether a nation of shopkeepers, we are very much afraid that more than nine-tenths of the middling and better sort of people among ourselves belong to this reprobated class of traders and dealers, and have very much the same manners with their brethren in America'.[6]

The good father is proud of his children, even though he is not afraid to scold them. Thus the *Review* praised the true

---

[1] Jeffrey, *ER*, XL (November, 1812), *2*, 279.

[2] *ER*, XXXIV (February, 1811), *10*, 417–418.

[3] Jeffrey, *ER*, XVIII (January, 1807), *6*, 348.

[4] Jeffrey, *ER*, VIII (July, 1804), *6*, 330–331. The book reviewed was by Maria Edgeworth.

[5] *ER*, XVII (October, 1806), *14*, 204.

[6] *ER*, XL (November, 1812), *11*, 461.

happiness that could be achieved only by those in the middle classes of life who were above fear of want, yet had sufficient motive for the exertion of their faculties;[1] condemned those who thought it mere romance for people in the middling conditions of life to fight for political privileges, or for the choice of their rulers;[2] and celebrated 'the sound and disinterested part of the community—those who have to pay the taxes, and the contractor and the minister'.[3] It had special words of kindness for those living on income from stock, who suffered through the depreciation so vehemently decried by the reviewers. One of the few explicitly self-revealing passages to appear in the *Review* during this period is an ironical editorial comment in an article ascribed to Malthus. It occurs just after the statement that *rentiers*, unlike merchants and landholders, would suffer from the increased circulation of paper money:

'It seldom falls to the lot of a fraternity of reviewers to possess money in the stocks; but it is well known that we are richer than many of our brethren; and the report of our having accumulated above a hundred pounds in the three per cents (though we did not mean to boast of it) is really true.'[4]

Jeffrey, to my knowledge, only once defined what he understood by 'the middling classes'. The definition may be found in a footnote to his statement, written in 1812, that there were probably not less than two hundred thousand persons reading for amusement and instruction among the middling classes of society.[5] 'By the middling classes', the footnote runs, 'we mean almost all those who are below the sphere of what is called fashionable or public life, and who do not aim at distinctions or

[1] Jeffrey, *ER*, XVII (October, 1806), *9*, 148.
[2] Jeffrey, *ER*, XIX (April, 1807), *1*, 3.
[3] (Brougham) *ER*, XLVIII (February, 1815), *12*, 264.
[4] *ER*, XXXVI (August, 1811), *10*, 467. It is worth noting that a few years later the *Review* upbraided Malthus for his lack of consideration for public annuitants. (*ER*, XLVIII (February, 1815), *13*, 504.)
[5] In significant contrast, cf. his statement, eight years earlier, that 'there are in these kingdoms at least *eighty thousand* readers'. Jeffrey, *ER*, VIII (July, 1804), *6*, 329. The phenomenally increasing circulation of the *Review* probably contributed to his higher estimate of the reading public. That public itself, of course, *did* increase in the course of this eight-year period. It is also possible that Jeffrey had originally excluded from his estimate of eighty thousand the perhaps more than one hundred thousand readers he thought could be found among tradesmen and artificers. See Jeffrey, *ER*, XVI (July, 1806), *7*, 341.

notoriety beyond the circle of their equals in fortune and situation.'[1] Perhaps the most interesting aspect of this definition is the fact that it is really concerned with status rather than class in any economic sense, and that it is so largely negative. Is the implication: don't ape your betters and you, too, may belong to the middle class? If so, Jeffrey might well be called the Hannah More of the bourgeoisie.

There is no denying a certain snobbishness in his reprobation of the good tradesman spoiled by his unlucky ambition for literary and political glory,[2] or in his scathing attack on the pretensions of provincial intellectuals not sufficiently humbled by the constant presence of the more permanent aristocracies of wealth, office, and rank.[3] Moreover, in both these instances the authors under fire were Radicals (Thelwall in the first, Priestley in the second) for whom Jeffrey was particularly willing to suspend his belief in the career open to talents. He was not altogether pleased with the vertical mobility of class and status so characteristic of English society: 'A trader, who has bought his borough but yesterday, will not give his influence to any set of noblemen or ministers, who will not receive him and his family into their society, and treat them as their equals.'[4] Through the operation of this principle the community was mingled in private life, 'it must be owned with some little discomfort', by the ultimate action of the same system which combined it, to its 'incalculable benefit', in public life.[5]

Yet the middle classes were really not the losers in not aiming at distinctions or notoriety beyond the circle of their equals. For the world of fashion was also that world from which corruption could spread through the whole body of the people.[6] The fact that there were as yet no people of fashion in America simply meant that 'those who are rich and idle have not yet existed so long, or in such numbers, as to have brought to full perfection that system of ingenious trifling and elegant disspation, by means of which it has been discovered that wealth and

---

[1] Jeffrey, *ER*, XL (November, 1812), *2*, 280.
[2] Jeffrey, *ER*, III (April, 1803), *21*, 200.
[3] Jeffrey, *ER*, XVII (October, 1806), *9*, 147.
[4] Jeffrey, *ER*, XXX (January, 1810), *13*, 462.
[5] *Idem.*
[6] Jeffrey, *ER*, XVI (July, 1806), *18*, 460.

leisure may be agreeably disposed of'.[1] Miss Edgeworth was wasting her time in trying to render service to the happiness and respectability of the higher classes, 'persons who scarcely deserved to be cured, and were scarcely capable of being corrected'. For the middle classes disputed and thought about didactic books and were impressed by their lessons. But this was not true of fashionable persons.[2] The trouble with eighteenth-century French society was that with all its glittering accomplishments it was not very moral, and that its most distinguished members were not very happy.[3] The trouble with English public-school education was that it disdained the cultivation of those 'middling talents' of which the great mass of human beings was possessed, and thus had a tendency to lead to premature debauchery.[4] In short, virtue was on the side of the middle classes. And virtue could conquer even fashion. 'Our fashionable readers', Jeffrey wrote with perhaps less irony than he intended, 'may detect the extreme rigour of our Calvinistic education.'[5]

Culture, virtue, and industry—these are the *Review*'s yardsticks for social approbation. Country squires, lacking the first, fail to gain it; as do merchants and stockjobbers, lacking the first and the second. As for the lower orders, those given to idleness must learn to fend for themselves. The others, hardworking and virtuous, are either helpless victims of the division of labour —and thus of the same principle to which civilization owed its present advanced state—or small peasants attempting to combine a measure of culture and independence with their poverty. There are also the 'industrious poor'. They, like the rest of the lower orders, deserve sympathy and illumination rather than condescension. In the attitude of the *Review* towards the aristocracy and the middle class, one finds a curious ambivalence: on the one hand, respect for the culture and learning of the higher ranks and disdain for the vulgarity and *gaucherie* of the bourgeois; on the other, a feeling, not, one may venture to suppose, unconnected with the *Review*'s place of origin, that idle opulence and widespread profligacy among the upper classes stand in

[1] *ER*, XL (November, 1812), *11*, 461.
[2] Jeffrey, *ER*, XXVIII (July, 1809), 7, 376.
[3] Jeffrey, *ER*, XXX (January, 1810), *13*, 478.
[4] Smith, *ER*, XXXII (August, 1810), *3*, 331–333.
[5] Jeffrey, *ER*, XVI (July, 1806), *18*, 460.

detrimental contrast to the virtuous industry of those below them. Can this ambivalence be explained in part by the class situation of the principal reviewers themselves?

It may be recalled that Jeffrey, on one occasion, called Lords Grey and Grenville too aristocratic and therefore likely to be inefficient.[1] As early as 1800 he had written to his brother:

'I have associated, too, a good deal of late with men of high rank, prospects, and pretensions, and feel myself quite upon a level with them, in everything intrinsic and material.'[2]

And yet this equality of achievement was not matched either by equality of status or political influence. 'The actual government of the country', he wrote to Horner in 1806, 'is carried on by something less, I take it, than two hundred individuals, who are rather inclined to believe that they may do anything they please, so long as the more stirring part of the community can be seduced by patronage, and the more contemplative by their love of ease and their dread of violence and innovation.'[3] This was one side of the coin. The other emerges in an account of a dinner at Holland House, that Mecca of aristocratic culture in its most flourishing state:

'The old Duke of Norfolk, almost as big and as fond of wine as Lord Newton, but with the air and tone and conversation of an old baron bidding defiance to his sovereign. Lords Say and Seele, Harrington, Besborough [*sic*], Cowper, Dundas, and c., with Dudley North, a wit and patriot of the old Fox school, breaking out every now and then into little bursts of natural humour. Ladies Besborough, Cowper, Caroline Lamb, and c. A most magnificent repast, and Lady Holland in great gentleness and softness; sat between D. North and the Duke, and had a good deal of talk with both.'[4]

---

[1] Cf. *ante*, p. 115.

[2] Francis to John Jeffrey, March 2, 1800, Cockburn, *Life of Jeffrey*, I, 105. It is interesting to note that an American visitor to Edinburgh some years later ascribed Jeffrey's excessively destructive proclivities to social insecurity: 'His foible is an unceasing effort to act the high finished gentleman, consequently he is blessed with such an immaculate degree of taste as to contemn every thing in the whole world both moral and physical.' Henry Brevoort to Washington Irving, March 11, 1813, G. S. Hellman, ed., *Letters of Henry Brevoort to Washington Irving* (New York, 1916), I, 84.

[3] Jeffrey to Horner, September 18, 1806, Cockburn, *Life of Jeffrey*, II, 110–111.

[4] Jeffrey to Mrs. Morehead, May 13, 1811, *ibid.*, II, 137. See also Horner's complaint to Murray, in 1811, that he had scarcely seen anything of Jeffrey in

The inefficiency of the aristocracy did not make it any the less entertaining.

What of Horner? On January 9, 1804, he made the following entry in his journal:

'Form a connection with the Whig aristocracy of England. Upon what footing do I join? Upon what footing am I at present received or invited? As lawyer to be—as having already studied political philosophy;—preserve this independent character. Early part of Burke's life—Lord Somers's—Romilly's. Transfer examples and maxims from Plutarch and Livy to England.'[1]

He, too, referred to the Grenvilles with some bitterness as 'the unbending, grasping aristocracy',[2] though he was not quite so proud in his dealings with them as Brougham who 'seemed, from his first introduction to men of the highest birth and the most distinguished position, to feel himself on an entire equality with them, and without any approach to vulgarity or impertinence . . . treated them with the utmost familiarity'.[3] The Whigs continued to treat Brougham as a 'new man', all the same. Even Horner, annoyed by Brougham's excessive ambition, expressed the hope that 'we are not in our day to be governed by adventurers, whether they force themselves upon the crown by their talents, or wriggle into its favour by servility. New men are a most useful and necessary race, like projectors in trade; but we have no hold on them.'[4] But here Horner spoke as a voice from the past.

The social position of the reviewers, no less than the social class attitudes of the *Review*, is the index of an age of transition. Thirty years after 'Don Cevallos', Brougham sat in the House of Lords, Jeffrey had become a Scottish Law Lord, and many

London, since Smith was taking him to all 'the dinners of foolish people that like to stare at eminent persons; and both of them seem to prefer that sort of high seasoned society to quieter and more homely fare'. Horner to Murray, May 4, 1811, Horner Correspondence, L.S.E., V, 17.

[1] Horner, 'Journal', January 9, 1804, *Horner Memoirs*, I, 340.

[2] Horner to Jeffrey, September 15, 1806, Horner Correspondence, L.S.E., III, 36. Omitted from published version, *Horner Memoirs*, I, 376.

[3] John Lord Campbell, *Lives of the Chancellors*, VIII, 251, quoted in Geoffrey T. Garratt, *Lord Brougham* (London, 1935), 29. Cf. Brougham's reference to the '*Idiotcracy*', Brougham to Horner, June 27, 1803, Horner Correspondence, L.S.E., II, 14. On his living 'too gaily' and snubbing Smith (1809). See *Smith Letters*, I, 163.

[4] Horner to Murray, October 25, 1804, Horner Correspondence, L.S.E., II, 76.

thought that the premiership had eluded Horner only through his premature death. Sydney Smith, alas, was not yet a Bishop; and perhaps this accounts for the special poignancy of an entry dated April 2, 1838, in George Ticknor's Journal.[1] The latter had breakfasted with Smith, Hallam, and Tytler:

'The conversation, at one time during the breakfast, was extraordinary. It fell on the influence of the aristocracy in England, on the social relations, and especially on the characters of men of letters. To my considerable surprise, both Hallam and Smith, who have been to a singular degree petted and sought by the aristocracy, pronounced its influence noxious. They even spoke with great force and almost bitterness on the point. Smith declared that he had found the influence of the aristocracy, in his own case, "oppressive", but added, "However, I never failed, I think, to speak my mind before any of them; I hardened myself early."'

That same evening Ticknor dined at Lansdowne House, where he found it odd to stumble at once upon Sydney Smith. 'When I saw Smith's free good-humour,' he noted, 'and the delight with which everybody listened to him, I thought there were but small traces of the aristocratic oppression of which he so much complained in the morning.'

There appears to be something familiar about the combination of classical economics and high seriousness with the praise of virtue, industry, and middle-class morality. For isn't this what we have always been taught to regard as the 'Victorian' ethos? Certainly these early numbers of the *Edinburgh Review* tend to reinforce the view that the Crystal Palace was not required for the crystallization of that ethos; that, in fact, it derives from the beginning rather than the middle of the century. Sydney Smith, to be sure, attacked the Society for the Suppression of Vice as 'a Society for suppressing the vices of persons whose income does not exceed £500 *per annum*'.[2] But Jeffrey, in the article that was to lead to his duel with Thomas Moore, saw it as axiomatic that the purity of the female

---

[1] This and the following quotation from *Life, Letters, and Journals of George Ticknor* (Boston and New York, 1909), II, 150–151.

[2] Smith, *ER*, XXVI (January, 1809), 4, 342.

character must always be guarded, especially at a time when polite society, increased in number by the greater diffusion of opulence, was necessarily becoming promiscuous and corruptible.[1] French writers of the previous seventy years were reproached for their shameful indelicacy; and the *Review* saw itself forced to censure the relationship between Lord Nelson and Lady Hamilton, with all due praise to Nelson's achievements at sea, since otherwise a bad example might be given to a public all too inclined towards imitation.[2]

The impulse behind this moralism was not primarily religious. Horner's private admission to Jeffrey that scepticism was his 'real sentiment' has already been noted, along with his recognition of the necessity to hide this scepticism in any *Review* articles.[3] Sydney Smith was a clergyman, without a doubt; but as a reviewer tended to confine his spiritual ministrations to attacks on Methodists and misguided missionaries, all part of a general conspiracy by fanatics against common sense and orthodoxy.[4] In fact, John Gibson Lockhart—no impartial observer, to be sure—noting after the publication of Jeffrey's *Letters* that they did not contain the remotest allusion either to the beliefs of Christianity or to its moral influence, adds this comment: 'I fancy the whole set were really most thorough infidels, and S. Smith at the top of them in that respect as in all others.'[5] This was a barb that might more appropriately have been launched at John Allen, whose scepticism was notorious, than at the Smith of Smiths who combined good humour with a sturdy religiosity. Jeffrey, in the *Review*, elaborately endorsed Paley's arguments from design, and dutifully quoted the author's devotional hymn to the epiglottis—'not two guests are choked

---

[1] Jeffrey, *ER*, XVI (July, 1806), *18*, 459.

[2] Jeffrey, *ER*, XLII (July, 1813), *1*, 284; *ER*, XLVI (September, 1814), 7, 404.

[3] Cf. *ante*, pp. 12–13

[4] See e.g. Smith, *ER*, XXII (January, 1808), *5*, 341–362; Smith, *ER*, XXIII (April, 1808), *9*, 169–180.

[5] Marion Lochhead, *John Gibson Lockhart* (London, 1954), 291. The evidence of an *Edinburgh* reviewer may also be cited here. Brougham, attending Henry Thornton's funeral, recalled that when he had first come to London he was accustomed to hearing Christian doctrines spoken of in a sceptical manner. It was only, he claimed, when he saw hard-headed men like Thornton and Zachary Macaulay devout Christians at the same time that it struck him there must be more in Christianity 'than the Edinburgh wits dreamt of'. Quoted in Viscountess Knutsford, *Life and Letters of Zachary Macaulay* (London, 1900), 482.

in a century'.[1] But the *Edinburgh*'s frequent defences of Hume against his detractors, clerical and otherwise, carry more conviction than occasional playful references to 'our Presbyterian pages'. Their native country supplied the reviewers with a two-fold heritage: Puritanism and Enlightenment. They retained the ethical postulates of the former along with the intellectual presuppositions of the latter.

Scottish Whigs disseminating this heritage to a public impelled to bid it welcome by the combined impact of French and industrial revolutions must take a place, however humble, beside the Evangelicals as progenitors of the nineteenth-century English middle-class ethic. There is a certain irony in this; for Evangelicals, along with Methodists, were more than once gleefully lambasted by the *Review* as fanatical children of darkness.

[1] Jeffrey, *ER*, II (January, 1803), 3, 297–298. For a comment on the offence given by the *Review*'s levity on sacred subjects see Brougham, *Life and Times*, I, 262–263.

[6]

The Little Gilded Closet

Your opinion of Jeffrey is just—he is a depraved coxcomb; the
greatest Dunce, I believe, in this Island, and assuredly the Man who
takes most pains to prove himself so.

Wordsworth to Gillies, February 14, 1815
MARKHAM L. PEACOCK, Jr., *The Critical Opinions of*
William Wordsworth (Baltimore, 1950), 286

*

I have been for a couple of days to Hatton where Jeffrey lives in a
great house, and writes his reviews in a little gilded closet.

Horner to his sister, September 9, 1812
LEONARD HORNER, ed., *Memoirs and Correspondence of*
Francis Horner, M.P. (London, 1843), II, 123

The *Edinburgh Review*'s attitude towards the romantic
poets has been repeatedly and exhaustively treated, most
fully by Jeffrey's first biographer since Lord Cockburn.[1]
There is little point in traversing once more the well-trodden
ground of this controversy. There is even less in indulging in
the weary quest for a new definition of romanticism, or in questioning the weary quest itself. Professor Wellek maintains that
by applying the criteria of creative imagination, organic nature,
and the 'prophetic' use of myth and symbol, it becomes possible
to define a coherent and European-wide romantic movement.
Professor Lovejoy had previously warned that nothing but confusion and error could result from a search for the intrinsic
nature of a 'hypostatized essence' called romanticism.[2] But a

[1] James A. Greig, *Francis Jeffrey of the Edinburgh Review* (Edinburgh and
London, 1948).
[2] René Wellek, 'The Concept of "Romanticism" in Literary History', *Comparative Literature*, I (1949), 1–23, 147–172. Arthur O. Lovejoy, 'The Meaning
of Romanticism for the Historian of Ideas', *Journal of the History of Ideas*, II
(1941), 260.

151

refusal to define romanticism leaves one exposed to the charge of being 'romantic' oneself. For it has been said that to define everything as romanticism, but never romanticism as anything is to show the 'romantic' attitude of protecting the indefinable nature of the term.[1] The prospect seems bleak. Yet worse is to come.

The *Edinburgh Review* is often regarded as the voice of Whiggery, in literary criticism as well as in politics. It is easy to go on from this basic supposition as follows: Whigs, being perpetually of the eighteenth century, simply *cannot* be romantics; Jeffrey was a Whig, and we all know what he had to say about *The Excursion*; *ergo*, the *Edinburgh Review* must have opposed the sort of thing that we intuitively 'know' as romanticism: vague longings, mountains and waterfalls, long-haired ladies, and people like Edgar Allan Poe. But even assuming the correctness of these premises (and, of course, this assumption is entirely unwarranted), confusion is confounded when Mr. Eliot calls 'Whiggery' in literary criticism that approach which maintains that the great artist is an unconscious artist, unconsciously inscribing on his banner the words 'Muddle Through'[2]—the very opposite of the *Edinburgh Review*'s approach; and when we learn that Stendhal, declaring '*Je suis tout* Edinburgh Review in (1818), considered the *Review* as the bulwark of English romanticism.[3] Perhaps the *Edinburgh* could flatter itself that Stendhal's own definition—'the romantic is the interesting, the classical the boring'—accounted for this judgement. The term 'counter-romanticist' has been used to describe those who, like Stendhal, preferred cosmopolitanism to nationalism, rationalism to mysticism, irony to sentiment; and who combined somewhat advanced views in politics with somewhat old-fashioned views in literary taste.[4] Was Jeffrey, then, a counter-romantic?

To trace his own varied use of the term 'romantic' does not help much and merely serves to illustrate the sundry current meanings of the word. Writing to his brother in 1794 he described the approach of spring which had helped awaken his spirits by the rustling of the western gales, by the appearance

[1] Carl Schmitt, *Politische Romantik* (2nd ed., Munich and Berlin, 1925), 10–11.
[2] T. S. Eliot, *The Use of Poetry and the Use of Criticism* (London, 1933), 30.
[3] Frederick C. Green, *Stendhal* (Cambridge, 1939), 119.
[4] Harry Levin, *Toward Stendhal* (Murray, Utah, 1945), 33.

of buds, sun, and showers. 'Every day I see greater reason for believing', he added, 'that this romantic temper will never depart from me now.' Two years later he reported to a friend that he had spent 'tranquil, romantic days' in the country.[1] Using the word in the *Review* he seemed sometimes to consider it a synonym for 'strange' or 'foolish'—'is there anyone so romantic as to believe'[2]—sometimes as a synonym for 'extraordinary'—'we surely cannot be accused of any very romantic flight of morality'[3]—and sometimes as a synonym for 'sentimental'— 'there is a good deal of this affectionate, romantic style of writing throughout the book'.[4]

As an historical term denoting a literary movement the word 'romantic' did not become current until much later in the nineteenth century; though Mackintosh, in his review of Madame de Staël's *De l'Allemagne*, introduced her distinction between 'classical' and 'romantic' literature to readers of the *Edinburgh Review*.[5] Thus the chase after definitions of 'romanticism', whether they be those of contemporary observers, later commentators, or indeed Jeffrey's own, is likely to lead to complication rather than clarification. The aim of this chapter is primarily to present a brief survey of recent scholarly views concerning the problem of Jeffrey's hostility towards the Lake School, and to isolate some of the elements in the poetry of that school which led him to campaign against its disciples.

The first and still very prevalent school of thought on Jeffrey as a literary critic saw him as a neo-classic survival of the eighteenth century, naturally hostile to currents of thought he could not hope to understand. Thus Bagehot:

[1] Francis to John Jeffrey, March 2, 1794, Henry Thomas Cockburn, Lord Cockburn, *Life of Lord Jeffrey, with a Selection from his Correspondence* (Edinburgh, 1852), I, 62; Jeffrey to George J. Bell, October 7, 1796, Cockburn, *Life of Jeffrey*, II, 25.

[2] Jeffrey, *ER*, XLV (April, 1814), *1*, 30.

[3] Jeffrey, *ER*, XXI (October, 1807), 8, 117.

[4] Jeffrey, *ER*, XXV (October, 1808), *1*, 12. For other uses of 'romantic' in the *Edinburgh Review* cf. Jeffrey, *ER*, XXV (October, 1808), *4*, 69; Jeffrey, *ER*, XXXV (May, 1811), *1*, 14–15; Brougham, *ER*, XXXVII (November, 1811), *5*, 143; *ER*, XLII (July, 1813), *11*, 463; *ER*, XLVI (September, 1814), *11*, 470; Jeffrey, *ER*, XLVII (November, 1814), *11*, 208; *ER*, XLVII (November, 1814), *12*, 243; *ER*, XLVIII (February, 1815), *11*, 453; and *ER*, L (October, 1815), 8, 447.

[5] *ER*, XLIII (October, 1813), 205–206.

'Nature ingeniously prepared a shrill artificial voice, which spoke in season and out of season, enough and more than enough, what will ever be the idea of the cities of the plain concerning those who live alone among the mountains; of the frivolous concerning the grave; of the gregarious concerning the recluse; of those who laugh concerning those who laugh not; of the common concerning the uncommon; of those who lend on usury concerning those who lend not; the notion of the world of those whom it will not reckon among the righteous—it said, "This won't do!"' [1]

Leslie Stephen, in a similar vein, pitied 'poor Jeffrey [who] blundered into grievous misapprehensions, and has survived chiefly by his worst errors'. [2] 'Who now reads Jeffrey?' asked another critic at the turn of the century. And answered, in a melancholy vein: 'Only those, it may be feared, who are intent on some scholarly purpose or victims of sharp necessity.' [3] Jeffrey, he concluded, was unable to read and interpret the age in which he lived. Some years later the historian of English periodical literature reiterated this traditional view, describing Jeffrey as defending his pseudo-classical citadel, long after the battalions of romantics had conquered the field. [4] And still more recently a critic in *Scrutiny* called for a return to Leslie Stephen's position that Jeffrey, in his general habits of mind, belonged to the eighteenth century. [5]

A second school consists of those who refuse to content themselves with the simple view of Jeffrey as an eighteenth-century survival and who therefore assign other, special labels to him. One contrasts him with Addison, Pope, and Dryden as being more concerned with exposing faults than with expounding beauties, and ascribes his power to his broad and convincing subjectivism; [6] another sees the real explanation of his critical

[1] Walter Bagehot, 'The First Edinburgh Reviewers', *Literary Studies* (Everyman ed., London, 1911), I, 24–25.

[2] Leslie Stephen, 'The First Edinburgh Reviewers', *Hours in a Library* (new ed., London, 1907), III, 112.

[3] Lewis E. Gates, 'Francis Jeffrey', *Three Studies in Literature* (New York, 1899), 1.

[4] Walter Graham, *English Literary Periodicals* (New York, 1930), 235.

[5] R. G. Cox, 'Homage to Common Sense', *Scrutiny*, XVI (1949), 171.

[6] Richard Elsner, *Francis Jeffrey, der Hauptbegründer der Edinburgh Review, und seine kritischen Prinzipien* (Berlin, 1908), 23, 85.

position in the fact that he was an 'intellectualist';[1] a third sees all his strength as well as all his weaknesses arising from his ethical approach which makes him the Platonist *par excellence* of nineteenth-century criticism;[2] while a fourth, allowing him a degree of sensibility in judging Wordsworth's poetry, takes him to task for applying Aristotelian canons of heroic dignity to poetical criticism.[3]

The third school of thought may be referred to as 'the moderates'. Its adherents, without feeling the need for the use of special labels, simply see Jeffrey (and thus the *Edinburgh*) as transitional, not altogether friendly to new literary currents, but far from hostile. They attack the standard view of the two great quarterlies as carrying on the eighteenth-century critical tradition, though they see the *Edinburgh* as only rather timidly following the lead of the *Quarterly* in consistently and vigorously opposing the imposition of a classical code.[4] Another 'moderate', author of a dissertation on Jeffrey as a literary critic, finds few Augustan elements in Jeffrey's thought, regarding him rather as the proponent of a relaxed and liberalized neo-classicism.[5] In another place this same author expresses the view that the concessions made by Jeffrey to the romantic spirit were made with too many reservations to permit his identification with that spirit.[6]

The fourth school, drawing not a little of its sustenance from Professor Irving Babbitt, counts among its supporters those who are not so much concerned with showing what Jeffrey was as with showing that he was always right. Its watchword might be said to be: 'Any enemy of Wordsworth's is a friend of ours'; and its leading representative at present is Mr. James A. Greig

[1] D. Nichol Smith, ed., *Jeffrey's Literary Criticism* (London, 1928), xxi.

[2] Merritt Y. Hughes, 'The Humanism of Francis Jeffrey', *Modern Language Review*, XVI (1921), 243–251.

[3] Herbert Read, *Wordsworth* (London, 1930), 248.

[4] John J. Welker, 'The Position of the Quarterlies on some Classical Dogmas', *Studies in Philology*, XXXVII (1940), 548, 562. Cf. Crane Brinton, *The Political Ideas of the English Romanticists* (Oxford, 1926), 209–211.

[5] J. Raymond Derby, 'Francis Jeffrey as a Literary Critic', Harvard Doctoral Dissertation (1929), 238, 276. For the moderate point of view, see also Joseph M. Beatty, Jr., 'Lord Jeffrey and Wordsworth', *Publications of the Modern Language Association*, XXXVIII, No. 2 (June, 1923), 221–235.

[6] J. Raymond Derby, 'The Paradox of Francis Jeffrey: Reason versus Sensibility', *Modern Language Quarterly*, VII (1946), 500.

who entitles his chapter on early nineteenth-century romanticism 'The Menace', compares Wordsworth to Hitler, and sings
one long hymn of praise to Jeffrey's prescience in seeing that the
path to romanticism could lead only 'downwards'.[1]

The fifth school is in many ways the most interesting. For its
adherents regard Jeffrey less as literary critic than as persecu-
tor, a man willing to go to almost any lengths of duplicity in
order to wage his campaign against Wordsworth and the Lake
poets. And why? Because this persecution helped increase the
sales of the *Edinburgh Review*! This view, first stated by Mr.
Russell Noyes,[2] was put forward in even stronger terms in an
article appearing in the course of the following year (1942) in
the *Sewanee Review*. Its author, Mr. Robert Daniel, begins with
the premise that as a result of the 'rehabilitation' of Jeffrey
which, he feels, has taken place during recent years, we now find
it hard to see him as what he really was—a representative literary man of the romantic movement. 'He was not a belated neo-
classicist, he was not interested in literature to the exclusion of
everything else, and he was not above being swayed in his
judgments by personal and other ulterior motives.'[3] The *Review* carried slashing articles against the Lake poets because
these articles were a guarantee of good sales and would therefore help to propagate its political ideas. Not only was Jeffrey
out to persecute Wordsworth—he did so against his convictions, since his real sentiments, personally expressed, were far
different from those which appeared in the *Review*. Since his
reviews were thus 'insincere', it has become 'pointless' to
examine them as specimens of literary criticism.[4]

If one accepts this last thesis, the problem of Jeffrey's view of
the romantics is both insoluble and not worth discussing. For
how does one know whether on any given occasion he really
meant what he said? There are, of course, his own statements
on this point. 'When I take up my reviewing pen,' he told Mrs.
Grant, 'I consider myself as entering the temple of truth, and

[1] Greig, *Jeffrey*. See especially 262–288, 301–305.

[2] Russell Noyes, *Wordsworth and Jeffrey in Controversy* (Bloomington, Indiana, 1941), especially 47–48.

[3] Robert Daniel, 'Jeffrey and Wordsworth: The Shape of Persecution', *Sewanee Review*, L (1942), 196.

[4] *Ibid.*, 201–212.

bound to say what I think.'[1] And, writing to Scott two years later, he admitted asperities in his review of *Marmion*, but at the same time declared himself unable to regret having told the truth according to his oath of office.[2] What, then, is one to make of Scott's description of Jeffrey: I'[ve] seen him weep warm tears over Wordsworth's poetry and you know how he treats the poor Balladmaker when he is mounted into the Scorner's chair'?[3] What of Jeffrey's assuring Coleridge that he was a great admirer of Wordsworth, whose *Lyrical Ballads* were always on his table? What of Coleridge's statement that 'I give you my honour that Jeffrey himself told me that *he* was himself an enthusiastic admirer of Wordsworth's poetry, but it was necessary that a Review should have a character'?[4] And, perhaps most damning of all, what of this entry in Henry Crabb Robinson's diary? (He is quoting Tillbrook, an admirer of Wordsworth):

'He says that Wilson the poet assured him that Jeffrey, the *Edinburgh* reviewer, declared to him that he is a great admirer of Wordsworth, and that he had attacked him in the way he has done, not because he himself thinks lowly of him, but because the public think lowly of him. I had heard a similar tale before, but never on such good authority.'[5]

[1] Mrs. Anne Grant to Mrs. Hook, *Memoir and Correspondence of Mrs. [Anne] Grant of Laggan*, ed. J. P. Grant (London, 1845), I, 285–286.

[2] Jeffrey to Scott, August 11, 1810, *The Private Letter-Book of Sir Walter Scott*, ed. Wilfred Partington (London, 1930), 16.

[3] Scott to George Ellis, July 6, 1810, *The Letters of Sir Walter Scott*, ed. Herbert J. C. Grierson (London, 1932–1937), XII, 324.

[4] 'Conversations with Henry Crabb Robinson', 1810, *Coleridge's Miscellaneous Criticism* (London, 1936), 385. In 1799 Jeffrey had written to his cousin: 'Then I have been enchanted with a little volume of poems, lately published, called "Lyrical Ballads", and without any author's name.' And furthermore, had guessed the author as Coleridge! Francis Jeffrey to Robert Morehead, March 21, 1799, *Memorials of the Life and Writings of the Rev. Robert Morehead, D.D.*, ed. Charles Morehead (Edinburgh, 1875), 102; Coleridge to Daniel Stuart, July 9, 1825, *The Letters of Samuel Taylor Coleridge*, ed. Ernest Hartley Coleridge (London, 1895), II, 742. Note Crabb Robinson's description of a dinner at Rolfe's, April 5, 1835. Jeffrey was present. 'His treatment of Wordsworth would not allow me to like him, had he been greater by far than he was, and therefore when he said "I was always an admirer of Wordsworth" I could not repress the unseemly remark "You had a singular way of showing your admiration"'. Edith J. Morley, ed., *Henry Crabb Robinson on Books and their Writers* (London, 1938), II, 461.

[5] *Robinson on Books and Writers*, I, 151, October 25, 1814. Also see Willard L. Sperry, *Wordsworth's Anti-Climax* (Cambridge, Mass., 1935), 107, for the comment that 'having scored an initial hit, Jeffrey was committed to following up the attack as occasion offered'.

The Little Gilded Closet

The last quotation indicates that Mr. Daniel may have some truth on his side when he accuses Jeffrey of insincerity. And statements like 'When will Wordsworth and Southey come forth? I shall try to give you a little pointed criticism then'[1] seem to provide additional confirmation for the persecution thesis. However, a letter of Jeffrey's (hitherto unpublished), written several months before the *Edinburgh Review* was founded, and thus certainly exempt from the charge of being influenced by any extraneous considerations, appears to offer grounds for hesitation before too lightly charging Jeffrey with duplicity. This letter was written by Jeffrey in response to a request by his friend James Grahame[2] who had submitted to him for criticism a play on the subject of Mary, Queen of Scotland. Jeffrey's letter, dated April 8, 1801, is devoted to a lengthy analysis of this play, in the course of which he lays down certain critical principles.[3] It is the statement of these principles at this early date which lends particular interest to the document.

After praising various aspects of the play, Jeffrey offers some negative criticism: there is too much bombast and extravagance; though in these excesses there is vigour and originality reminiscent of Shakespeare—'but still it is Shakspere in a frenzy however fine'. What is really unpardonable, however, is the author's device of writing occasionally with 'a sort of infantine simplicity'.

'It is a style indeed that has much beauty in it and very frequently a great deal of tenderness—but it is not fit for the profane ears of the multitude—it is liable to ridicule and will often appear silly to those whose minds are familiarized with grosser interests or have been little accustomed to the unambitious playfulness of affection.—Every man that appears before the public appears before a company to whom he owes respect and on whose sympathies he ought not to reckon too securely and with whom he should not be too familiar. . . . We never think of entertaining a drawing room full of strangers with the prattle of our children nor think of giving way in their presence to any

[1] Jeffrey to Horner, August 5, 1804, *Memoirs and Correspondence of Francis Horner, M.P.*, ed. Leonard Horner (London, 1843), I, 257.

[2] Later author of *The Sabbath*. Byron's 'Sepulchral Grahame'.

[3] Jeffrey to James Grahame, April 8, 1801, National Library of Scotland, MS. 3519, folios 3–6.

of those simple emotions which constitute the charm of our domestic society.'

Jeffrey here adumbrates a double standard which offers a more satisfactory explanation for his contradictory attitude towards Wordsworth than the *thèse de complot* of Messrs. Noyes and Daniel. For there can be no question that he is here expressing his personal opinion—and that opinion specifically makes allowance for the possibility that the same poetry may be criticized in different ways from the personal and the public standpoint.

This same principle, in a somewhat different guise, lies at the heart of Archibald Alison's book on *The Nature and Principles of Taste* (1811) which Jeffrey considered to be the best and most pleasing work yet produced on the subject of taste and beauty.[1] Alison and Jeffrey both adhered to the associationist school of aesthetics: objects were not beautiful in themselves, but only in so far as they suggested certain associations (usually human) to the mind. This led on the one hand to a completely relativistic view, since each individual could have different associations suggested to him by the same object. Yet, though Jeffrey admitted that this was so, it did not follow for him either that all tastes were equally good or desirable, or that no standards of judgement could be established.[2]

For to creative artists fell the special responsibility of employing only such objects in their art as were natural signs and inseparable concomitants of emotions to which the greater part of mankind were susceptible. Ideally those who addressed themselves to the public were to possess two tastes: 'One to enjoy, and one to work by,—one founded upon universal associations, according to which they challenged universal praise,—and another guided by all casual and individual associations, through

---

[1] Jeffrey, *ER*, XXXV (May, 1811), *1*, 1. See Byron Guyer, 'Francis Jeffrey's *Essay on Beauty*', *Huntington Library Quarterly*, XIII (1949–1950), 71–85, and the same author's 'The Philosophy of Francis Jeffrey', *Modern Language Quarterly*, XI, No. 1 (March, 1950), 17–26, for an approach to Jeffrey's critical criteria based on close analysis of his essay on Alison. René Wellek, *A History of Modern Criticism* (New Haven, 1955), II, 110–120—which appeared after the present manuscript was completed—also dwells with much justice on the importance of Alison in any consideration of Jeffrey. It appears to me to be by far the best treatment of the subject in print.

[2] *Ibid.*, 43–45.

which they looked fondly upon nature, and upon the objects of their secret admiration.'[1] It was the task of the critic to judge poetry by its successful appeal to universal associations, but there was no reason at all why the critic himself should not follow his individual bent in his personal tastes. Thus there was no real contradiction in Jeffrey's shedding tears over Wordsworth's poems, and at the same time condemning and ridiculing him in the *Review*.

It is interesting to observe how Jeffrey returned to this theme of 'private virtues, public vices' thirteen years after he had expounded it to Grahame in the letter quoted above. The occasion was his most (in)famous review—the one of Wordsworth's *Excursion* beginning 'This will never do'. 'An habitual and general knowledge of the few settled and permanent maxims, which form the canon of general taste in all large and polished societies,' he writes, 'a certain tact, which informs us at once that many things, which we still love and are moved by in secret, must necessarily be despised as childish, or derided as absurd, in all such societies—though it will not stand in the place of genius, seems necessary to the success of its exertions.'[2] What is particularly striking about this passage is its implication that the particular stage of civilization—that of large and polished societies—demands certain aesthetic criteria; and that these criteria are not necessarily in accord with the most sensitive minds in those societies.

The previous chapter has given evidence of the *Review*'s great concern with fostering admiration for the seriousness and high moral purpose of the middle classes. Jeffrey seems to feel that it is almost his highest duty to preserve society from childishness. Many things, even beautiful things, *must necessarily* be despised as childish. And under this rubric comes Wordsworth's 'mass of childishness and insipidity'[3] as well as Southey's 'childish affection' and 'babyisms'.[4] For childishness, though it may engage

---

[1] *Ibid.*, 46.
[2] Jeffrey, *ER*, XLVII (November, 1814), *1*, 3. Cf. also Jeffrey, *ER*, XXVII (April, 1809), *1*, 3–4, where he points out that a picturesque stanza may be well enough relished while the reader is getting his hair combed, but that certain scenes of tenderness and emotion will not do for the corner of a crowded drawing-room.   [3] Jeffrey, *ER*, XXI (October, 1807), *14*, 231.
[4] Jeffrey, *ER*, XXXIV (February, 1811), *11*, 429, 452.

the sympathies of the sophisticate in the privacy of his chambers, must not be allowed to corrupt 'that great proportion of our readers which must necessarily belong to the middling or humbler classes of the community'.[1]

Not only are these persons 'in middling life' naturally most touched with the emotions that belong to their condition, but 'these emotions are in themselves the most powerful, and consequently the best fitted for poetical and pathetic representation'.[2] Jeffrey made this statement in reviewing Crabbe's *Tales*. Crabbe was one of his favourite poets, because, unlike Wordsworth and the Lake School, he represented the emotions of the middling and humbler classes of the community as they really were or, rather, as what they ought to have been in their particular situation. For what infuriated Jeffrey about Wordsworth's 'hysterical schoolmasters', 'sententious leechgatherers', and philosophical pedlars was not so much their lowly condition, but their presumption in speaking out of turn. 'A man who went about selling flannel and pocket-handkerchiefs in this lofty diction', he remarked about the pedlar in the *Excursion*, 'would soon frighten away all his customers.'[3] Coleridge, curiously enough, made the very same point: 'Is there one word for instance, attributed to the pedlar in THE EXCURSION, characteristic of a *Pedlar*?'[4]

But Coleridge objected because he felt that Wordsworth could have made *The Excursion* a more successful poem had he told of a poet in the character of a poet. Jeffrey objected principally

---

[1] The phrase is used in Jeffrey, *ER*, XL (November, 1812), 2, 279. For an amusing example of this double standard as applied by Jeffrey himself, see his sonnet entitled '28 March, 1837' which contains the lines

> *And violets blue are springing at their feet,*
> *But wintry blasts their gentle wooing meet*
> *And unthawed hailstones in each shady nook*
> *Dance to their music.*

This by the man who had commented on Wordsworth's 'stuff about dancing daffodils'. Strang Lawson, 'Jeffrey's Dancing Hailstones', *Notes and Queries*, CXCVI, No. 1 (January 6, 1951), 16.

[2] Jeffrey, *ER*, XL (November, 1812), 2, 281.

[3] Jeffrey, *ER*, XLVII (November, 1814), *1*, 30.

[4] George Sampson, ed., *Coleridge, Biographia Literaria, Chapters I–IV, XIV–XXII. Wordsworth, Prefaces and Essays on Poetry, 1800–1815* (Cambridge, 1920), 138.

to the *idea* of a pedlar stepping out of his appointed place in the social order and presuming to deliver himself of moral teachings. Crabbe, on the other hand, by depicting ordinary men and women *as they really were*, could arouse sympathy rather than ridicule from his readers.[1] Jeffrey's attitude in this matter is consistent with his generally paternalistic view of the middle and lower classes. He liked the 'authentic rustics' of Burns's *Cotter's Saturday Night* because they did not assume the garb of philosophers.[2] The lesson of virtue and goodness they had to teach arose from their situation rather than from what they had to say.

It is not surprising that Jeffrey could never really get over Wordsworth's 'preface' to the second edition of *Lyrical Ballads*. For it was there that the Lake School actually flaunted its departure from those standards which poetry, like religion, was given long ago 'by certain inspired writers whose authority it is no longer lawful to call in question';[3] there that public announcement was made of the 'charitable endeavours of Messrs. Wirdsworth and Co. [sic] to accommodate [the common people] with an appropriate vein of poetry';[4] and there that Wordsworth struck directly at the heart of Jeffrey's own critical convictions by warning his readers not to listen to that mode of criticism, 'so destructive of all sound unadulterated judgment', which fostered statements such as: 'I myself do not object to this style

[1] Cf. Jeffrey, *ER*, XXIII (April, 1808), *8*, 133–136; Jeffrey, *ER*, XXXI (April, 1810), *2*, 31–38.

[2] See article on Burns: Jeffrey, *ER*, XXVI (January, 1809), *1*, especially 276. In similar fashion Sydney Smith defends himself against allegations of having attacked the poor by attacking the Methodists. 'But are we to respect the poor, when they wish to step out of their province, and to become the teachers of the land?' Smith, *ER*, XXVIII (July, 1809), *3*, 42.

[3] Jeffrey, *ER*, I (October, 1802), *8*, 63.

[4] Jeffrey, *ER*, VIII (July, 1804), *6*, 330. Horner reacted to this review by telling Jeffrey that he could not forgive him the expression 'Wordsworth and Co.' For 'he merits criticism, but surely not contempt; to class him with his imitators is the greatest of all contempt'. Horner then reported that [Charles Kirkpatrick] Sharpe had gone to the other extreme: 'He has been living at the lakes with these crazed poets, Wordsworth sent him some thousand lines, and he repeated to me a few of these one day which I would not worship as he wished me.' Horner to Jeffrey, August 13, 1804, Horner Correspondence, L.S.E., II, 67. To which Jeffrey replied that he was almost as great an admirer as Sharpe, and that he had meant no contempt to Wordsworth by putting him at the head of the poetical firm. Jeffrey to Horner, September 3, 1804, Cockburn, *Life of Jeffrey*, II, 91.

of composition, or this or that expression, but, to such and such classes of people it will appear mean or ludicrous!'[1]

Jeffrey considered himself a guardian of the public taste and was completely out of sympathy with Wordsworth's dictum that the poet must himself create a taste for his productions. It could certainly happen that mistakes were occasionally made by those who addressed themselves to the public. But the public could not be expected to show indulgence when Southey showed himself obstinate enough to persist in 'errors of which he received very early warning',[2] or when Wordsworth came before it, 'after all the admonitions he has received', with a whole quarto of poetry written as if he had never been reprimanded.[3] The *Edinburgh Review*, speaking on behalf of the public, expected its advice to be followed. Those who feel that the recent history of public taste is dominated by 'the revolt of the masses' can certainly find some early ammunition in a critical review which pointed out that the fact that during a given period there appeared more than ten editions of Bloomfield's *Farmer's Boy* and five or six of Montgomery's *Wanderer of Switzerland*, as against three of Southey's *Joan of Arc*, two of his *Thalaba*, and one of *Madoc* was pretty strong testimony against Southey's taste![4] In all fairness it must, of course, be added that all five works are now dead as doornails.

At the same time that Jeffrey delicately announced that he would not offend Wordsworth by hinting at the 'prosperity' of Scott, Campbell, or Crabbe, he made this concession:

'We do not want Mr. Wordsworth to write like Pope or Prior, nor to dedicate his muse to subjects which he does not himself think interesting.'[5]

It is only proper to note the fact that Jeffrey did not completely confine his praise of Wordsworth to statements made in private. His duty as a critic, he thought, consisted in censuring 'childish language, mean incidents, and incongruous images'. But in his review of Alison's aesthetics he quoted 'from memory' and with

---

[1] Wordsworth, 'Preface to Lyrical Ballads', Sampson, ed., *Coleridge and Wordsworth*, 200.

[2] Jeffrey, *ER*, XXXIV (February, 1811), *11*, 432.

[3] Jeffrey, *ER*, XLVII (November, 1814), *1*, 2.

[4] Jeffrey, *ER*, XXXIV (February, 1811), *11*, 431.

[5] Jeffrey, *ER*, XXXVIII (February, 1812), *6*, 375.

great admiration Wordsworth's lines on the associations brought
to mind by a distant column of smoke rising into the sky;[1] and,
shortly afterwards, went so far as to comment on Wordsworth,
Southey, and Coleridge in the following encomiastic vein:

'... there is a fertility and a force, a warmth of feeling and an
exaltation of imagination about them, which classes them, in our
estimation, with a much higher order of poets than the followers
of Dryden and Addison; and justifies an anxiety for their fame,
in all the admirers of Milton and Shakespeare.'[2]

Confronted with passages like this, it is hard not to agree
with Professor Brinton's judgement that 'the *Edinburgh* on
Wordsworth goes far to prove the hold romanticism had on the
English people long before the Reform Bill'.[3]

Was Jeffrey, then, a romantic rather than an anti-romantic or
a counter-romantic? We shall remain obstinate in not offering
a new definition of the term. But the following distinctions may
fairly be made: in so far as the romantic movement represented a
breaking-away from formalism to feeling Jeffrey was completely
in sympathy with it. 'No flow from the heart', 'no softness',
'no enthusiasm', ran his comment on a collection of female
epistles.[4] The present state of society, he felt, demanded something more natural and impassioned than the protracted and
monotonous form of epic poetry.[5] The true characteristic of
this age of the world was a growing appetite for strong and
natural emotions, its corollary a demand for poetry devoted to
the stronger and deeper passions.[6] Jeffrey certainly aligned himself with those protests against artificiality and over-refinement
and that search for the 'natural' which represented one major
aspect of the English romantic movement. However, in so far as
romanticism meant that pedlars and leechgatherers were of a
sudden endowed with the tongues of philosophers, in so far as
it could see a world in the grains of wisdom dispensed by 'the

[1] Jeffrey, *ER*, XXXV (May, 1811), *1*, 29.
[2] Jeffrey, *ER*, XXXVI (August, 1811), *1*, 283. Cf. also Jeffrey, *ER*, XLVII
(November, 1814), *1*, 29.
[3] Brinton, *Political Ideas of English Romanticists*, 210. For a similar judgement,
see R. C. Bald, 'Francis Jeffrey as a Literary Critic', *The Nineteenth Century and
After*, XCVII, No. 576 (February, 1925), 201–205.
[4] Jeffrey, *ER*, XXIX (October, 1809), *5*, 76–77.
[5] Jeffrey, *ER*, XXIX (October, 1809), *2*, 40.
[6] Jeffrey, *ER*, XLV (April, 1814), *9*, 201.

idiot mother of an idiot boy', it had to be condemned as childish and absurd. For then it played havoc with accepted social gradations and with the high seriousness of the emotions and the morality of the middle class, which Jeffrey had made it his task to foster and confirm.

Walter Scott, in a marvellous phrase, pointed out that Jeffrey's literary criticism lacked 'that enthusiastic feeling which like sun-shine upon a landscape lights up every beauty and palliates if it cannot hide every defect'.[1] Jeffrey would probably have been quite frank in admitting to this lack. As he looked back on his critical career he declared himself proudest of 'having constantly endeavoured to combine Ethical precepts with Literary Criticism, and earnestly sought to impress my readers with a sense, both of the close connection between sound Intellectual attainments and the higher elements of Duty and Enjoyment; and of the just and ultimate subordination of the former to the latter'.[2] Thus, by his own admission, he was really more of a moralist than a critic, though his reputation need not rest entirely on his ethical precepts. There will always be Jeffreyans whose tolerance for lyricism is temperamentally somewhat limited. It would be rash to conclude on this note—for did we not observe Jeffrey shedding tears over *Lyrical Ballads*? Suffice it to say that when he came to write his reviews, he found it desirable to retire to his little gilded closet, actual at Hatton, elsewhere of the spirit.

[1] Scott to Joanna Baillie, October 31, 1808, *Scott Letters*, II, 116.
[2] Francis Jeffrey, *Contributions to the Edinburgh Review* (2nd ed., London, 1846), xii.

[7]

'Rude and Refined'

In one of his early reviews Jeffrey made a special point of criticizing a bad example of that sort of composition very fashionable among Scottish writers, in which the history of political institutions was deduced metaphysically from a supposed era of extreme barbarism, through successive stages of improvement.[1] 'Conjectural history' of this kind, usually concerned with the progressive development of societies from 'rudeness' to 'politeness', had indeed been a favourite preoccupation of writers like Ferguson, Robertson, Kames, and Millar who, though often led into misjudgements by their insistence that the starting-point for historical study was psychology from which logical deductions about man's progress could always be drawn, nevertheless blazed a trail for modern historians and sociologists through their interest in comparing the customs of different peoples and their stress on the importance of social and economic factors in history.[2]

While Jeffrey showed an occasional awareness of the pitfalls to which this approach was liable to lead, this did not prevent the *Edinburgh Review* from adopting it, sometimes from motives of practical reform. Thus one finds one reviewer conceding that an existing regulation forbidding certain witnesses to testify in a court of law might be suitable for a very rude period of society,

[1] Jeffrey, *ER*, III (April, 1803), 23, 206–207.
[2] For an excellent appreciation and critique of these writers, see Gladys Bryson, *Man and Society: The Scottish Inquiry of the Eighteenth Century* (Princeton, 1945); see also Roy Pascal, 'Property and Society: The Scottish Historical School of the 18th Century', *Modern Quarterly*, I (1938), 167–179, the same author's 'Herder and the Scottish Historical School', *English Goethe Society Publications*, New Series, XIV (1938–1939), 23–42, and Ronald L. Meek, 'The Scottish Contribution to Marxist Sociology', John Saville, ed., *Democracy and the Labour Movement* (London, 1954), 84–102.

but not 'in a state of the human mind to which it is altogether alien'.[1] The preceding chapters have shown that both class structure and standards of literary taste were regarded as natural concomitants of a certain stage of society. In order fully to understand the attitude of the *Edinburgh* reviewers towards the problems of their day—political, social, and aesthetic—it is essential to take a closer look at the manner in which their outlook of this particular stage meshed into their view of the past and their vision of the future.

To see the history of mankind in terms of a great movement from a rude, primitive state to one of increasing opulence and refinement does not necessarily imply approval of the process. But Sydney Smith, related to the Savoyard Vicar only through his clerical collar, revelled in the sight of villages, churches, and farms rising from the wilderness; condemned the exaltation of nature as an 'absurd paradox'; and, in his best categorical manner, told readers of the *Review* that the most deplorable savage knew that civilization brought the means of ameliorating famine and disease.[2] Another reviewer asserted with no less confidence that 'the visions of primeval innocence melt away before the touch of inquiry. The true savage is a cold, cruel, sullen, suspicious, and designing animal. Man grows generous exactly in proportion as he becomes civilized.'[3] Such a complacent view of the virtues of civilization—in effect, the commercial civilization of Western Europe—informed many of the articles concerned with such well-known semi-savage societies as China, India, Lapland, and the United States of America.

One of the more remarkable aspects of the *Edinburgh*'s many travel reviews in this period is that while these demonstrate intense curiosity about the geography, customs, and arts of distant nations and peoples, they show little of the benevolently cosmopolitan attitude of their eighteenth-century predecessors. Thus reviews of Chinese travel books seem often to be intended chiefly as antidotes against *chinoiserie*. The reviewers were seldom able to forgo the somewhat malicious pleasure of pricking fashionable balloons with factual darts. To learn that they were

[1] *ER*, XXXIII (November, 1810), *4*, 112.
[2] Smith, *ER*, III (April, 1803), *2*, 30–31, 42.
[3] *ER*, XXXI (April, 1810), *10*, 253.

never in great doubt about their facts should not occasion undue surprise. 'We have always been disposed', writes Jeffrey (no less suspicious of a philosophizing Chinaman than of a metaphysically inclined leechgatherer), 'to consider this celebrated people [i.e. the Chinese] as a mean and semi-barbarous race, distinguished by fewer virtues or accomplishments than most of their neighbours, and remarkable only for their numbers, and their patience and dexterity in the practice of certain mechanical professions.'[1] And this disposition is fully shared by a reviewer who, in recommending a book on China as the most valuable which European good sense and intelligence—'there really seems to be no other'—had produced, assigns a certain amount of merit to Chinese gardening and pottery while pointing out that many a British peasant is better lodged than the Emperor of China.[2]

India does not fare much better. Having at one point decided that Indian civilization had been asserted rather than proved, the *Review* resumes the subject a few months later, sick of the dull morality of the Hindus and weary of their toilsome and abortive attempts at poetry.[3] The ancient Egyptians could plead some mitigating circumstances; for, in the midst of the grossest ignorance, bigotry, depravity, and superstition they had been able to make some advances in the sciences.[4] Not so the Laplanders who were 'filthy, lazy, ignorant, superstitious, and knavish'.[5]

The case of America was more complex. For while China or India could be said to have advanced little beyond the infancy of a fixed or agricultural society, this was certainly not true of a kindred people constantly extending the limits of civilization and 'destined to carry our language, our arts, and our interests too, over regions more vast than ever acknowledged the sway of the Caesars of Rome'.[6] How, then, could one account for the

[1] Jeffrey, X (January, 1805), *1*, 262. See also *ER*, XXVI (January, 1809), *2*, 284; and Jeffrey, *ER*, XXXII (August, 1810), *12*, 476–499. 'I had always a profound contempt for the Chineses'; Jeffrey to Horner, Sept. 3, 1804, Cockburn, *Life of Jeffrey*, 2, 93.

[2] *ER*, XXVIII (July, 1809), *9*, 413, 424–426.

[3] *ER*, XXIX (October, 1809), *12*, 175–176; *ER*, XXXV (May, 1811), 7, 209–210.

[4] (Sir William Drummond and Brougham), *ER*, XXXVI (August, 1811), *9*, 436.

[5] *ER*, XXXVIII (February, 1812), *3*, 338.

[6] *ER*, XXX (January, 1810), *11*, 444.

low estate of literature and fine arts in the United States? For the *Review* took it as axiomatic that in the realm of culture and intellect nothing better than the mediocre could, for the time being, emerge from America. If all of American learning (with the exception of Benjamin Franklin's works) were lost, nothing useful or agreeable would disappear. And the destruction of the whole of American literature (with no exceptions at all) would occasion less regret than the loss of a few leaves from an ancient classic.[1] The reason for this state of affairs lay in the current American economic situation and class structure. Refinement in literature—and literature, readers of the *Review* were told, was justly regarded as the most infallible criterion of the point of civilization at which any people had arrived[2]—was dependent on a state of opulence which the United States had not yet attained. Opulence meant a great accumulation of wealth as well as the operation of the principle of the division of labour. It meant a society broken into distinct classes, including a leisure class with inherited wealth, willing and able to appreciate poetry and to create an effective demand for good literature.

As things stood, because of the great demand for labour, the American working classes were not dependent on the patronage or employment of the upper classes. The natural influence of wealth and intelligence (essential for literary productions of the first rank) would only be exerted when, through an increased population and a lessening demand for labour, a nominal democracy became a virtual aristocracy of property, talents, and reputation.[3] At present, however, Americans were still far removed from 'that advanced state of society, where there are numerous classes who either do not labour at all or are occupied only with the liberal arts. Their generals distil brandy; their colonels keep taverns; and their statesmen feed pigs.'[4]

---

[1] *Ibid.*, 446. For other derogatory comments see Brougham, *ER*, IV (July, 1803), *15*, 447; Horner, *ER*, IX (October, 1804), *14*, 181; *ER*, XXV (October, 1808), *10*, 169.

[2] *ER*, XLV (April, 1814), *10*, 230.

[3] For various statements of this theory, see Brougham, *ER*, IV (July, 1803), *15*, 447; Horner, *ER*, IX (October, 1804), *14*, 185; *ER*, XXV (October, 1808), *10*, 169; Jeffrey, XXIX (October, 1809), *2*, 24; *ER*, XXX (January, 1810), *11*, 442–446; *ER*, XLVII (November, 1814), *12*, 246, 263.

[4] *ER*, XIII (October, 1805), *11*, 162–163. In connection with Jeffrey's own attitude towards American culture, here is a letter from a visiting (and non-savage)

'Rude and Refined'

These comments on the state of culture in other continents are of interest not only as the statement of a sociological theory of literature remarkable for its emphasis on class structure as the primary dynamic factor.[1] They also reveal a self-satisfied pride in the achievements of modern European commercial civilization. For in sneering at the rather limited accomplishments of the Chinese and the Americans—limited perforce, in view of the particular economic phase reached by the two societies—the *Edinburgh* reviewers appear to be surveying less advanced stages of development from a pinnacle of politeness and refinement to which they had themselves been catapulted by those beneficent twin powers, accumulated wealth and division of labour. Did they really believe that the society of the early nineteenth century in Britain and Western Europe had reached its highest stage, and that the only comfort for those less advanced in the cycle lay in pleasing reflections like that of Sydney Smith, to the effect that 'at the distance of half the globe, a Hindoo gains his support by groping at the bottom of the sea, for the morbid concretion of a shell-fish, to decorate the throat of a London alderman's wife'?[2]

Aldermen's wives in search of self-congratulation could certainly find grounds for such in the *Edinburgh Review*. In contrast to the despotic governments of the East (including that of Russia) Europe, 'light of the world' and 'ark of knowledge', could consider herself fortunate indeed.[3] Here, the activity of the

American, written from Edinburgh: 'His [i.e. Jeffrey's] opinion of the Society in New York and Philadelphia is singularly ludicrous, I marvel that the polished Town of Wapping was not coupled with Glasgow and Manchester, as rivalling in elegance. The chief sources of [Jeffrey's] American intelligence is [*sic*] a brother who resided a number of years in Boston, moving in a sphere which I should judge authorizes his humble opinions of American civilization.' Henry Brevoort to Washington Irving, December 9, 1812, G. S. Hellman, ed., *Letters of Henry Brevoort to Washington Irving* (New York, 1916), I, 66.

[1] It was based, to large extent, on the writings of Hume, Millar, and Robertson. See e.g. David Hume, 'Of the Rise and Progress of the Arts and Sciences' and 'Of Refinement in the Arts', T. H. Green and T. H. Grose, ed., *The Philosophical Works of David Hume* (London, 1898), III, 177–195, 300–306; John Millar, *An Historical View of the English Government from the Settlement of the Saxons in Britain to the Revolution in 1688* (London, 1803), IV, 139–160; William Robertson, *The History of the Reign of the Emperor Charles the Fifth, with an Account of the Emperor's Life after his Abdication by William H. Prescott* (new ed., London, 1887), 35–40.

[2] Smith, *ER*, III (April, 1803), *14*, 144.   [3] Smith, *ER*, III (April, 1803), *4*, 64.

human mind, long since thoroughly roused, was increasing in velocity. 'Industry is become a passion; and even pleasure mimics labour in her amusements and relaxations.'[1] To this could be added the reassuring thought that 'who ever has had an opportunity of comparing the people of England with those of the Continent, must have remarked, that, with a sense of honour equally acute, the former possess far more rigid notions of morality and justice'.[2] And why not, since 'perhaps the ecclesiastic, like the civil polity of England, possesses a racy flavour of its native soil, which, by nations of different temperament and prejudices, may rather be admired than imitated'.[3] The condition of the English people was certainly superior to that of all other nations.[4]

These sanguine sentiments found reinforcement in reflections on the present age as unique in terms of the great events to which it stood witness. Just the ten years between 1790 and 1800 supplied the abridged experience of as many centuries.[5] And the defeat of Napoleon was one of those events probably destined to determine the fortune of succeeding ages.[6] Indeed, for those 'who have beheld the tremendous convulsions, and gigantic revolutions which late years have brought forth', to look to the petty squabbles of Popes and Cardinals in the age of the Renaissance was something that could only be done with feelings of indifference, mingled perhaps with contempt. This held true in realms of quality as well as quantity. Washington (along with Franklin, another favoured American) and Burke were certainly more edifying than Lorenzo or Poggio;[7] while it was a vain endeavour to look in the past for three such outstanding historians as Hume, Robertson, and Gibbon, 'historians whom no age but such a one as the present could produce'.[8]

---

[1] Smith, *ER*, V (October, 1803), *12*, 150.

[2] *ER*, XXVI (January, 1809), *13*, 493.   [3] *ER*, XVI (July, 1806), *6*, 314.

[4] *ER*, XLVIII (February, 1815), *14*, 519.   [5] *ER*, XXVII (April, 1809), *15*, 213.

[6] Jeffrey, *ER*, XLV (April, 1814), *1*, 1. See also *ER*, XXVIII (July, 1809), *6*, 360, where the unparalleled interest of the present crisis is said to sink all past history into comparative insignificance.

[7] *ER*, III (April, 1803), *3*, 43–44, 53. See also Jeffrey's comment that society had never been characterized by a more sober, level, and equable tone than in present times. Jeffrey, *ER*, XLVIII (February, 1815), *8*, 398.

[8] Jeffrey, *ER*, XXIX (October, 1809), *1*, 23. His reference to the eighteenth century as 'the present age' is noteworthy.

Yet in classifying the reviewers as apostles of progress, pure and simple, one would find oneself in error. It is true that Brougham, having noted in 1803 that all European governments had tended 'uniformly, and not very slowly' towards greater freedom and mildness, does not hesitate to assure his readers two years later that the proposition that no limit could be assigned to the extent or acceleration of the progress of mankind now deserved the name of a general fact rather than a plausible speculation.[1] It is also true that echoes of Horner's statement in the second number that it was more agreeable to believe in unchecked improvements in opulence and knowledge than to acquiesce in 'that mournful analogy which assimilates the political fortunes of a people to the progress of individual life' resound through the *Review* with a brave regularity.[2] Nevertheless, it was hardly to be expected, while Napoleon was overrunning all of Europe and threatening Britain herself, that even the most perfervid paean to progress should not contain some sour notes. Jeffrey might find some comfort in reflecting (several years before Clausewitz) that in the enlightened policy of modern times, war was 'only a more coarse sort of diplomacy', no longer the concern of individuals but of governments.[3] And, even when things looked blackest, could not disaster and turmoil somehow serve as a prelude, almost a necessary prelude, for better times to come?[4] For instance, did not even Napoleon's threatened mastery of Spain and Portugal hold out the hope that the Inquisition would cease 'to pollute the soil of Europe'?[5] But a whole cabinet of Whiggish nostrums of this sort did not always suffice to dispel the gloom of defeat and retreat.

In 1809 more than one reviewer wondered whether his generation would live to see the troubled waters subside and the

[1] Brougham, *ER*, II (January, 1803), *9*, 358; Brougham, *ER*, XII (July, 1805), *8*, 345.

[2] Horner, *ER*, II (January, 1803), *16*, 440; *ER*, XXVII (April, 1809), *2*, 21; *ER*, XXXII (August, 1810), *8*, 428; Brougham, *ER*, XLIX (June, 1815), *5*, 113.

[3] Jeffrey, *ER*, XV (April, 1806), *1*, 13; see also Jeffrey, XIX (April, 1807), *1*, 26, where he cautiously hopes that a series of hostile truces and breathing spells may perhaps be prolonged into habitual amity.

[4] See *ER*, XXVII (April, 1809), *15*, 243; *ER*, XXVIII (July, 1809), *6*, 360; and Jeffrey, *ER*, XLV (April, 1814), *1*, 2.

[5] *ER*, XXXII (August, 1810), *8*, 429.

ancient landmarks of the world reappear above the flood.[1] Two
years later another, by his own admission 'not the least sanguine
in anticipating the improvement of human affairs', reluctantly
confessed that the circumstances persuading him to dejection
were neither few nor of light account.[2] In the same number
Jeffrey, lamenting the death of Windham, held out the melancholy possibility that the age which had witnessed the eclipse of
the ancient splendour and independence of Europe 'seems also
to be that in which the Heroic Race of England is doomed to
become extinct and perish'.[3]

Thus the harsh pressure of external events served at times to
inhibit whatever optimistic propensities the reviewers possessed.
One of them, exclaiming 'Alas! it was *always* thus', saw no
change from Sesostris to Bonaparte and no hope for change in
the future; while another suggested that the polished kingdoms
of Europe were not to be a permanent part of civilized life, but
had merely taken the place of Egypt and Ionia for a limited
span of time.[4] But what was perhaps more important, the theory
of the gradual progress of civilization from rude beginnings to
ultimate refinement could not really supply complete consolation
in time of crisis. On occasion it conveniently lent itself for use
as a reservoir of complacency and hope. But it had its darker side.

It is this side which is brought out most clearly in Jeffrey's
review of Madame de Staël's *De la Littérature considérée dans
ses Rapports avec les Institutions Sociales*, where he takes issue
with her unshaken faith in the philosophical creed of perfecti-
bility.[5] He admits that in the past history of mankind there has
been an accumulation of useful knowledge which is likely to
increase. But he has grave doubts whether any similar increase
could be expected in the realms of reason, morality, and enjoyment. Actions producing misery are not generally performed in
ignorance of their consequences. Men seem to delight in wars,

[1] *ER*, XXVI (January, 1809), *13*, 499; see also *ER*, XXVI (January, 1809),
2, 279.
[2] *ER*, XXXIV (February, 1811), *10*, 415.
[3] Jeffrey, *ER*, XXXIV (February, 1811), *1*, 254.
[4] *ER*, XXXIII (November, 1810), *2*, 55; *ER*, XXI (October, 1807), *3*, 40.
External events, when they meant good news, could, of course, exert an opposite
effect. See, e.g., Jeffrey on the deliverance of Europe from Napoleon, *ER*, XLV
(April, 1814), *1*, 1–4.
[5] Jeffrey, *ER*, XLI (February, 1813), *1*, 8–24.

which have become more constant and sanguinary in spite of European enlightenment and humanization. And there is no prospect of any reduction in the abuse of power and wealth. The very process of advancement towards polish and intelligence creates its own miseries and vices. For as soon as man is freed from the task of earning a living for himself and his family—it may here be recalled that a leisure class was held to be the essential prerequisite for superior cultural achievements—he generally falls into a state of considerable unhappiness. He finds it much harder to engage in pursuits that will interest him. In this situation the general diffusion of knowledge (and here Brougham must have writhed) actually operates 'as a bounty upon indolence and mental imbecility'. Encyclopaedists, geographical compilations, trashy biographies, and ravings about orthodoxy and Methodism have replaced such works as those of Bacon, Shakespeare, and Hooker.[1] This state of affairs results when the principle of the subdivision of labour—a vital factor in the growth of commercial civilization—is introduced into literature. Improvements in the mechanical and domestic arts, 'better methods of working metal, and preparing cloth; and commodious vehicles, and more efficient implements of war', will continue. But as far as a general enlargement of the understanding and an increase of good judgement are concerned, nothing save decline is to be expected, 'till some new deluge shall restore the vigour of the glebe by a temporary destruction of all its generation'.

The 'lower orders' have still less to hope for. With increasing ingenuity and refinement come factories owned by men whose interest demands their keeping population in excess in order to depress wages—an interesting anticipation of Marx's doctrine of the reserve army of labour. Thus the general progress of commercial civilization aggravates rather than relieves the condition of the labouring classes. Education and habits of foresight, self-control, and rigid economy may alleviate their tendencies towards waste and profligacy. But their situation

[1] For exactly similar sentiments on this point, see Jeffrey, *ER*, XXXIII (November, 1810), *9*, 169. To study the influence of these and related ideas on Macaulay who, by his own admission, owed so much to Jeffrey's articles in the *Edinburgh Review*, would be a rewarding project. See for instance his essay on 'Milton', and his remarks there on poetry and society.

cannot in the nature of things fundamentally change for the better.

Luxury and refinement, by inculcating sensuality and selfishness, exert a no less deleterious effect on political life. Patriotism and unselfishness come to be increasingly at a discount. Eventually a luxurious, patronizing, and vicious monarchy, firmly established, will receive the adulation of a corrupt nation.[1]

Here, then, is the paradox of the *Review*'s attitude towards civilization and progress. On the one hand, refinement and politeness are desirable, for their attainment implies superiority over rude and barbarous nations and without them no distinguished achievements in the arts are possible. For proof one need do no more than look at the United States of America. On the other hand, there can be no progress towards refinement without commercial wealth and division of labour. This progress has certainly taken place in Britain and Western Europe. But it has exacted its price in dissipation for the upper, misery for the lower classes, and in a general lowering of standards. While material conditions may continue to improve, no comparable amelioration—in fact, rather the reverse—is to be expected in the spiritual and moral realms. It was nice to have one's cake, but alas, one could not eat it as well.

Such was the general pattern of the concurrent growth and decline of civilization presented to the readers of the *Edinburgh Review*. The process, when not 'arrested', as in China, was inevitable. And, as shown in previous chapters, its concomitants ranged from class structure to literature. It was useless to do much more than to try slightly to alleviate the condition of the labouring classes, since the present stage of refined, commercial civilization demanded their depressed condition, just as it demanded poetry devoted to the stronger and deeper passions. As in the old round, its cry was 'Follow me!'

Had history followed? Was the same lesson of inevitability, writ large in terms of the passage from rudeness to refinement,

[1] See also Jeffrey, *ER*, XXXVI (August, 1811), *12*, 484–488; Jeffrey, *ER*, V (October, 1803), *13*, 174–175; *ER*, XXXIV (February, 1811), *10*, 414–417, for a presentation of the same pattern. And see Jeffrey, *ER*, XVI (July, 1806), *15*, 439, and Jeffrey, *ER*, XVI (July, 1806), 7, 329, for doubts about the benefits of refined civilization and its educational influences.

to be deduced in detail from the European past since the Middle
Ages? Or was history in these specific terms an altogether different compartment? To the *Edinburgh Review* history was
almost as 'new' as it would one day reveal itself to certain
professors at Columbia University. No man had the right, the
Review asserted, to fill three quarto volumes with the history of
the House of Austria, or with that of any house whatsoever.
Clio's concern must be with nations rather than families, subjects rather than sovereigns.[1] Unlike their ancient predecessors
modern historians were engaged in 'measuring the mutual and
ever-varying action of laws, arts, and manners; of national circumstances, fortunes, and character; and combining particular
details with that tacit, but constant and learned reference to
general truths, which converts a local narrative into a chapter
in the natural history of the species'.[2] To make history a school
of experience, a register of the past pregnant with instruction
for the future, the historian must go beyond mere tales of wars
and political events to relate above all what guided nations
toward their real interest, or what led them astray from it.[3]

The study of history in this sense could not but be useful to
those who devoted themselves to it. For one thing, since great
bodies of people acted from passion, prejudice, and misguided
zeal rather than from reason, future events, unlike the general
cycle of civilization, could not be predicted except upon the em-
pirical basis of what had previously occurred.[4] For another, historical investigation was bound to throw light on the moral
character of nations in different stages of society, light which
could well serve to illuminate the problems and condition of the
present age.[5] 'In history, as in the real scenes of many-coloured
life,' postulates one reviewer with a certainty worthy of an
Acton, 'there is always room for a variety of moral remarks; and
the historian ought unquestionably to provide himself with a

[1] *ER*, XXIII (April, 1808), *10*, 185. See also Jeffrey, *ER*, XXIV (July, 1808),
1, 283.

[2] *ER*, XVIII (January, 1807), *9*, 394.

[3] *ER*, XLV (April, 1814), *10*, 233.

[4] Jeffrey, *ER*, XXI (October, 1807), *8*, 134; also see Jeffrey, *ER*, XIX (April,
1807), *1*, 26.

[5] *ER*, XXIII (April, 1808), *10*, 184; on the use of history see Brougham, *ER*,
III (April, 1803), *26*, 240; *ER*, II (January, 1803), *11*, 396; *ER*, XXX (January,
1810), 7, 377; and *ER*, XLIX (June, 1815), *3*, 63–64.

considerable assortment upon the supposition that the reader cannot moralize for himself.'[1]

How fortunate the readers of the *Edinburgh* who, aided by the reviewers, could reap such an abundant moral harvest! They could sympathize with Dante whose polish and elegance 'might have done honour to a more advanced period'; welcome the age of Sir Thomas More when the human mind, sunk in torpor, received an impulse which had carried it forward 'in the career of improvement' ever since; celebrate the Reformation, for 'that must be, indeed, a very young reader, who does not soon see that the Reformation was well worth the struggle which it cost, and who does not admit the advantages which have accrued from it to this kingdom'; pay their respects to the period from the middle of Elizabeth's reign to the Restoration, a period greater than the ages of Pericles, Augustus, Leo X, and Louis XIV; endorse 'the unanimity which seems to prevail as to the merits of the Revolution in 1688'; and rejoice greatly over the eighteenth century—'the proudest aera in the annals of the species; the period most distinguished for learning, and skill, and industry; for the milder virtues, and for common sense'.[2] Above all, they could ponder the moral of that momentous event which put an end to this proudest of eras—the French Revolution, an object lesson to rulers as well as subjects in its demonstration of what was liable to happen when the main body of a people was excluded from political power.[3]

Where was one to look for the causes of major historical changes like those manifested by the French Revolution and its sequel? Writing in the very first number of the *Review*, Jeffrey, in dismissing the *thèse de complot*, avers that events of this kind are never due to 'extraordinary and mysterious agents', but must be regarded as produced by the co-operation of a complicated set of causes.[4] The more the subject is meditated, the more

[1] *ER*, IX (October, 1804), *12*, 153.

[2] *ER*, II (January, 1803), *5*, 309; *ER*, XXVIII (July, 1809), *6*, 360; *ER*, XIII (October, 1805), *5*, 94; Jeffrey, *ER*, XXXVI (August, 1811), *1*, 276; Jeffrey, *ER*, V (October, 1803), *13*, 170; Brougham, *ER*, II (January, 1803), *9*, 348.

[3] Jeffrey, *ER*, I (October, 1802), *1*, 17; *ER*, XXVII (April, 1809), *15*, 217–219; Jeffrey, *ER*, XIX (April, 1807), *1*, 10; Jeffrey, *ER*, XXI (October, 1807), *8*, 125–126.

[4] Jeffrey, *ER*, I (October, 1802), *1*, 13–14.

M   177

certain will it appear that all permanent and important changes occurring in the internal body of a country are the result of changes in the general character of its population. To understand the causes influencing the character of a people, one must look not to political events, but to manners, education, prevailing assumptions, religion, taste, and, above all, to the state of prejudice and opinions.[1] And changes in national character are generally the result of 'causes laid deep and wide in the structure and condition of society . . . which necessarily *produce* those combinations of individuals, who seem to be the authors of the revolution when it happens to be ultimately brought about by their instrumentality'.[2]

What of these deep-laid causes? When faced with this question the reviewers frequently found refuge in phrases like 'the spirit of the age', or 'the state of the human mind'. But when they went beyond these to ask about the fundamental force in the shaping of national character, their answer was likely to be 'the state of government'. Thus the ancient historians invited criticism because they were said to have ignored this all-important factor; and the deleterious influence of Christianity on literature during the Dark Ages was held to be due not to its tenets, but to 'that vitiated state of the human mind, of which the vices of government were the great and primary cause'.[3] In an early stage of society climate may have played an important role as a determinant of national character. But it was the glory of an enlightened government to have been able to counteract its debasing influence.[4] Why was there such a difference between the ancient Romans and the modern Italians, in spite of the fact that the Italian climate had been relatively constant? And why were Englishmen much closer to the Romans, in spite of obvious

[1] Jeffrey, *ER*, XXIV (July, 1808), *1*, 282–284. And see Brougham, *ER*, II (January, 1803), *22*, 494, on manners and customs as the real security for the endurance of laws.

[2] Jeffrey, *ER*, XLII (July, 1813), *1*, 282. This is almost a restatement of Millar's formulation in his *Historical View of the English Government*. In 1803 Jeffrey declared himself mildly critical of its categorical infallibility. See Jeffrey, *ER*, V (October, 1803), *13*, 157.

[3] *ER*, XLV (April, 1814), *10*, 233, 238. See also *ER*, XXVI (January, 1809), *2*, 281, where the state of government is cited as a principal cause for the low moral and intellectual habits of the people of South America.

[4] *ER*, XVI (July, 1806), *5*, 301.

climatic differences? The answer was that the possession of
liberty and laws, and above all, the superiority a man derived
from having a share in the system of government, had produced
a greater resemblance of character than climate and situation
could ever have done.[1] History, observation, and reflection con-
curred in pointing out the state of her government as the true
cause of Ireland's unprecedented miseries. For government had
the power to modify almost all the circumstances in which a
people happened to be placed, in such a way as fully to account
for all variations of character and enjoyment.[2] It was not, for
example, a matter for surprise that the inhabitants of some
French provinces had opposed the arbitrary measures of the
revolutionary government more vigorously than others. They
were those which possessed at least a shadow of free government.[3]

It was in this way that the reviewers linked their view of civilization and history to the politics of the present day and their
own political role, just as they had linked it to their attitude
towards the contemporary social and literary situation. The concept of a 'free government', and its corollary, the terrible danger
of despotism, achieved an importance far beyond that which it
occupied as a mere *sine qua non* of Whiggery. In earlier stages
of society, when the lowest orders passed their time partly in
idleness, partly in strenuous and hazardous sports, they were
always ready for that sort of action to which leaders in open
resistance to oppression incited them. In the present, 'refined'
stage, these same classes, enured to habits of incessant industry,
were less easily incited, more easily subdued. The only countervailing force against despotism had come to reside in the increasing numbers of the 'middling classes', themselves creatures of
refined civilization. It was chiefly through the power of the
press, through the diffusion of just opinions, that these classes
could be raised to a state of importance in which they would be
able to counterbalance the despotic tendencies engendered in
other classes by the progress of improvement.[4]

[1] *ER*, XXI (October, 1807), *12*, 194.
[2] *ER*, XLII (July, 1813), *5*, 344. See also *ER*, XXVII (April, 1809), *8*, 105:
'Any country, however small, which enjoys liberty, will speedily find itself in the
career of improvement.'   [3] *ER*, VII (April, 1804), 7, 103.
[4] *ER*, XXXIV (February, 1811), *10*, 417–418. On the press as the 'palladium
of civilized society' see also Brougham, *ER*, XLIX (June, 1815), *5*, 112–113.

'Rude and Refined'

In Britain, since the French Revolution, the habit of presuming in favour of authority and against popular discontent and commotion had become dangerously prevalent. Together with the 'monstrous patronage' of the Crown—dispensed by the Tory governments—it constituted a grave threat to the beneficent effects of middle-class influence.[1] At this critical juncture in the history of civilized society, was it not providential indeed that Britons possessed in the *Edinburgh Review* a staunch opponent of Tory despotism, an unfailing repository of just opinions liberally dispensed, and a rod and staff ever ready to comfort and sustain their great and only hope, the middling classes?

[1] Jeffrey, *ER*, XXIV (July, 1808), *1*, 275; on the danger of despotism arising from the increased influence of the Crown, see also Jeffrey, *ER*, XXXIV (February, 1811), *1*, 276–278.

Epilogue

'What do you mean by public opinion?' said Tancred. 'The opinion of the reflecting majority,' said Vavasour. 'Those who don't read your poems,' said Coningsby.

DISRAELI, *Tancred*

It would be both logical and satisfying to end with an accurate estimate of the effect of the *Edinburgh Review* on public opinion and thus on the course of events. It is certain that the reviewers were confident of their power and influence. In the very first article ever published in the *Review*, Jeffrey defended the thesis that the dissemination of 'enlightened' ideas had a great deal to do with the causes of the French Revolution. And he would not have been in disagreement with the anonymous correspondent who wrote in 1818:

'A man who has been observant of the change which has taken place in the tone and character of public opinion within these last twenty years cannot but perceive how infinite a portion of this change is *demonstrably* chargeable upon the influence of *two* publications only, the Edinburgh Review and the Morning Chronicle.'[1]

We know that the *Review* had 'much reputation with all the Eton boys, the gentlemen Commoners of Oxford, and Ladies who mark their progress in a book with a bit of fine pink ribbon';[2] and that it pleased less fashionable ladies by exalting 'the reign of the domestic affections, and quiet home-born felicities of life above all that dazzles and captivates the children of

---

[1] J.H. (?) to an unknown correspondent (about 1818?), *The Letters of George IV*, ed. Arthur Aspinall (Cambridge, 1930), III, 495.

[2] Charles Kirkpatrick Sharpe to Walter Scott, March 5, 1809, *The Private Letter-Books of Sir Walter Scott*, ed. Wilfred Partington (London, 1930), 13.

this world, distinctively so termed'.[1] But is it possible to be more specific in singling out measures that would not have been passed but for its intervention, thoughts that would not have been thought had not their thinkers perused it?

The problem is difficult, if not insoluble. If anything, what has gone before has shown the complexity of the process of the dissemination of ideas, and the importance of the role played in it by the fortuitous. If a few young Whig lawyers in Edinburgh had been able to keep their time fully occupied with their legal work, if Sydney Smith had not brought his pupil to the unfragrant city of his delight, there might well have been no *Edinburgh Review*. Ultimately, it is true, the reason why young Michael Hicks-Beach went to Edinburgh rather than to Weimar —the Napoleonic wars—may be linked with that 'anti-Jacobin' atmosphere which provided Jeffrey with some extra hours of leisure; just as 'the Sid's' second choice of Edinburgh after Weimar was in the last resort due less to accident than to the accomplishments of the age of Hume and Smith, which had endowed the Athens of the North with its glittering reputation. So the determinists may have their day.

The problem of cause and effect becomes even more difficult where it concerns the evaluation of ideas. There is a pattern in the *Review*, to be sure, the pattern of a particular stage in the cycle of civilization moving from rudeness to refinement. It is a pattern that comprehends the social and economic realm where the division of labour, sure sign of 'polish', not only creates the leisured class so essential for the highest cultural achievements, but also dooms the lower classes to a state of sullen subsistence only slightly tempered by hopes of education; it comprehends the realm of literary taste and production which can be saved from desiccation due to over-refinement only by renewed emphasis on the natural passions; and it comprehends the realm of politics where the virtuous middling classes alone (assisted, of course, by the Whig party and the *Edinburgh* reviewers) can attempt to prevent the encroachments of a new despotism—and of the latest *Quarterly*.

But as one tries to define the pattern more closely, as one

[1] Mrs. Anne Grant to Mrs. Gorman, July 16, 1815, *Memoir and Correspondence of Mrs. [Anne] Grant of Laggan*, ed. J. P. Grant (London, 1845), II, 77.

sharpens its outlines and is about to elaborate on its beauties and perfections, the shadow falls. Jeffrey's natural pessimism reinforced by his personal tribulations, Brougham's 'bolting out of the course', Smith's making up his mind between his second and third cups of tea, Horner's concealed scepticism, the simple need for filling and selling each number of the *Review*, the particular foreign and domestic political situation at the time of writing, the exigencies of Whiggishness and waggishness, the reviewers' own complex and far from secure social position—these are but a few of the warnings against concluding too readily in terms of schema and system.

Again, as one comes to estimate the 'influence' of the *Review*, one soon enters the realm of the conjectural. There can be no doubt of its immense popularity—the growing circulation figures attest to that; nor of its ability to keep itself in the public eye—the great number of pamphlets written against it attest to that. Yet the question remains: how many people did it convert to its doctrine, to what extent did it help to form opinions? Hazlitt was convinced that the public read the *Edinburgh* and the *Quarterly* and believed both, 'or if there is a doubt, malice turns the scale'.[1] Smith wrote to Jeffrey that 'every man takes up a Review with a lazy spirit, and wishes to get wise at a cheap rate';[2] while Macaulay, admitting the great effect produced by the first perusal of an article, added that few people read such an article more than once.[3]

There are occasional striking instances providing dramatic illustrations for the theme: 'Ideas have Consequences!' 'I remember Sackville, Lord Thanet,' writes Brougham, 'saying he waited to see the quarterly pamphlets before he made up his mind on such and such a matter; for the rival journal pursued the same plan.'[4] And Smith, congratulating Jeffrey on one of his articles on the Catholic question, tells this story:

[1] Hazlitt, 'On Living to One's Self', *Table Talk* (Everyman ed., London and New York, 1942), 99.

[2] Smith to Jeffrey, January, 1812, Nowell C. Smith, ed., *The Letters of Sydney Smith* (Oxford, 1953), I, 220.

[3] Macaulay to Napier, July 20, 1838 *Selection from the Correspondence of the late Macvey Napier*, ed. Macvey Napier (London, 1879), 262.

[4] Henry Brougham, 1st Baron Brougham and Vaux, *The Life and Times of Henry Lord Brougham, Written by Himself* (Edinburgh and London, 1871), I, 261.

Epilogue

'The duke of —'s agent in Ireland is an Orangeman; and in spite of all the remonstrances of the Duke, who is too indolent or too good-natured to turn him off, he has acted like an Orangeman. What the Duke could not effect, you have done by your review, and the man is now entirely converted to the interests of the Catholics, merely by what you have written upon the subject. This fact Lord Ponsonby told me yesterday.'[1]

But the *Review* itself admitted (with regard to Byron) that 'our alleged severity upon a youthful production has not prevented the noble author from becoming the first poet of his time; and the panegyrics upon more than one female writer, with which we have been upbraided, have not relaxed their meritorious exertions to add to the instruction and amusement of their age'.[2] Even if one cannot agree completely with James Mill's dictum that periodical literature, since it must succeed immediately, is almost certain to profess and inculcate the opinions already held by the public to which it addresses itself,[3] one must be wary of blithely chronicling persuasion and conversion.

Suffice it to conclude that during its early years the *Edinburgh Review* played a significant part in the transition to a more popular Whiggism; that it fought against abuses; that it met the needs of a new public anxious for enlightenment and moral guidance; and that perhaps its most important service was to instil in its readers respect for the power of their own opinions, in other words, to exalt the *idea* of public opinion in the eyes of the public. But to ask how many minds were swayed one way or the other by the *Review* is to ask the impossible. It is clear that its readers took it seriously, and that within a few years it succeeded in establishing itself as a vital part of nineteenth-century cultural scenery. There is something curiously moving and appropriate about Creevey's description of the Dowager Marchioness of Salisbury, an old lady in her seventies, reading

---

[1] Smith to Jeffrey, February 16, 1808, *Smith Letters*, I, 132.

[2] *ER*, XLIV (January, 1814), *10*, 416. Crabbe's son's reminiscence could be cited on the other side: 'I believe that within two days after the appearance of Mr. Jeffrey's admirable and generous article, Mr. Hatchard sold off the whole of the first edition of these poems.' *The Life of George Crabbe—by His Son* (World's Classics ed., London, 1932), 177.

[3] *The Autobiography of John Stuart Mill* (first complete ed., New York, 1924), 65.

Epilogue

the *Edinburgh Review* on a summer's day in 1828, Jeffrey's last year as editor:

'I wish you just saw her as I do now. She thinks she is alone, and I am writing at the end of the adjoining room, the folding doors being open. She is reclining on a sofa, reading the *Edinbro' Review*, without spectacles or glass of any kind. Her dress is white muslin, properly loaded with garniture, and she has just put off a very large bonnet, profusely gifted with bright lilac ribbons, leaving on her head a very nice lace cap, not less adorned with the brightest yellow ribbon.'[1]

A passage like this may serve as a reminder that once upon a time the *Edinburgh Review* was actually read for pleasure.

[1] Thomas Creevey to Miss Orr, August 20, 1828, *The Creevey Papers*, ed. Sir Herbert Maxwell (New York, 1904), 508–509.

Appendix:

The Founding of the *Edinburgh Review*

People say the review was planned in a garret, but this is incredible. Merely to take such a work into a garret would be inconsistent with propriety; and the tale that the original conception, the pure idea to which each number is a quarterly aspiration, ever was in a garret is the evident fiction of reminiscent age—striving and failing to remember.

WALTER BAGEHOT[1]

It was surely most inconsiderate of its projectors to leave the exact story of the *Review*'s origin to the realm of conjecture. Our reward is to savour the ironical consequences which have saddled a publication whose principal message may be summed up in the words 'There are no mysteries!' with a mysterious beginning; our punishment, to disentangle the twisted threads woven by Bagehot's 'reminiscent age—striving and failing to remember'.

The first aged person to step into the witness box is the Reverend Sydney Smith who, thirty-seven years after the event (in 1839), provided the classical account of the *Review*'s origin in the preface to his collected *Works*:

'Among the first persons with whom I became acquainted [in Edinburgh] were, Lord Jeffrey, Lord Murray (late Lord Advocate for Scotland), and Lord Brougham; all of them maintaining opinions upon political subjects a little too liberal for the dynasty of Dundas, then exercising supreme power over the northern division of the island.

'One day we happened to meet in the eighth or ninth story or flat in Buccleuch-place, the elevated residence of the then Mr.

[1] 'The First Edinburgh Reviewers', *Literary Studies* (Everyman ed., London, 1911), I, 1.

Appendix: The Founding of the 'Edinburgh Review'

Jeffrey. I proposed that we should set up a Review; this was acceded to with acclamation. I was appointed Editor, and remained long enough in Edinburgh to edit the first number of the Edinburgh Review. The motto I proposed for the Review was

"Tenui musam meditamur avena"
"We cultivate literature upon a little oatmeal".

But this was too near the truth to be admitted, and so we took our present grave motto [judex damnatur cum nocens absolvitur] from Publius Syrus, of whom none of us had, I am sure, ever read a single line; and so began what has since turned out to be a very important and able journal.'[1]

Nearly thirty years later Brougham, then eighty-nine years old and near the end of his seemingly interminable career, commented that nothing could be more imaginary than almost the whole of Smith's account.[2] First of all, wrote Brougham, there never was a house eight or nine stories high in Buccleuch Place, or in any of that portion of the New Town of Edinburgh. This criticism was legitimate in so far as Jeffrey's house (No. 18 Buccleuch Place) had only three stories—a fact that may be verified at first hand today[3]—illegitimate in so far as Buccleuch Place is not in the New Town, but on the south-west side of the Old Town.[4] Furthermore—and perhaps more important— Brougham denies that Smith was *appointed* editor (while admitting that he may be said to have edited the first number), and adds that the motto finally adopted was suggested by Horner who didn't appreciate Smith's 'oatmeal' joke.[5]

He then gives his account of the meeting in Jeffrey's house, an

[1] *The Works of the Rev. Sydney Smith* (Boston, 1854), 3.

[2] Henry Brougham, 1st Baron Brougham and Vaux, *The Life and Times of Henry Lord Brougham, Written by Himself* (Edinburgh and London, 1871), I, 246.

[3] Also see illustration in Stuart J. Reid, *A Sketch of the Life and Times of the Rev. Sydney Smith* (New York, 1885), 59.

[4] On this point cf. *Notes and Queries*, Fourth Series, III (May 29, 1869), 499, where Smith's reference to the eighth or ninth story is interpreted as a joke. To go along with this interpretation requires risibilities beyond this writer's ken. It is conceivable that, had Smith made the statement in conversation or written it in a letter, he might have had some humorous connotation in mind—harking back to the uncommon height of many houses in old Edinburgh. But since he was writing his account (so to speak) for posterity, this seems to me highly unlikely.

[5] Brougham, *Life and Times*, I, 246–248.

account much more specific than that of Smith. According to
Brougham only he himself, Smith, and Jeffrey were present at
this meeting which did *not* mark the occasion of Smith's first
proposing the establishment of a review. For, writes Brougham,
Smith had already mentioned the idea to Jeffrey and Horner. But
it was at the meeting at Jeffrey's house that Smith first announced the project to Brougham, and that (one can almost read
'now that I was informed' between the lines) the project was
for the first time seriously discussed:

'I at first entered warmly into Smith's scheme. Jeffrey, by
nature always rather timid, was full of doubts and fears. It
required all Smith's overpowering vivacity to argue and laugh
Jeffrey out of his difficulties. There would, he said, be no lack
of contributions. There was himself, ready to write any number
of articles, and to edit the whole, there was Jeffrey, *facile
princeps* in all kinds of literature; there was myself, full of
mathematics, and everything relating to colonies, there was
Horner for political economy, Murray for general subjects;
besides, might we not, from our great and never-to-be doubted
success, fairly hope to receive help from such leviathans as
Playfair, Dugald Stewart, Robison, Thomas Brown, Thomson,
and others? All this was irresistible.'[1]

And, in spite of Jeffrey's hesitations, the project was carried
through.

Two other well-known accounts, those of Cockburn and
Jeffrey, appeared between 1839 and 1867, the dates, respectively,
of the Smith and the Brougham versions. Cockburn's (1852)
is interesting chiefly for its meteorological detail. He informs

[1] *Ibid.*, I, 251. *Sir James Archibald Murray, Lord Murray* (1779–1859), Scottish
judge. Friend of Horner, with whom he corresponded until the latter's death in
1817. Frequent contributor to the *Edinburgh Review.—John Playfair* (1748–1819),
mathematician and geologist. From 1785 to 1805 joint professor of mathematics
(with Adam Ferguson) at the University of Edinburgh. From 1805, Professor of
Natural Philosophy at the University of Edinburgh.—*Thomas Brown* (1788–1820),
metaphysician. Member of Academy of Physics. One of first *Edinburgh* reviewers;
author of an article on Kant in the second number which Leslie Stephen, in the
D.N.B., calls 'at least a proof of courage, as it is founded entirely upon Villiers's
French account of Kant'. Withdrew from *Edinburgh Review* because of some editorial interference in the third number.—*Thomas Thomson* (1768–1852), jurist and
legal antiquary. Occasional contributor to *Edinburgh Review*; sometimes in editorial charge during Jeffrey's absences.—*John Robison* (1739–1805), scientific
writer.

us that 'it happened to be a tempestuous evening and I have heard him [Jeffrey] say that they had some merriment at the greater storm they were about to raise'.[1] Brougham, as we have seen, manages to recall a 'stormy evening' and, in view of Scottish weather conditions in winter and early spring, there seems no particular reason for doubt in this matter, nor for rejecting too peremptorily Mr. Hesketh Pearson's vivid embellishments of rattling windows, shaking doors, and winds roaring in the chimney.[2] The other account, Jeffrey's own, given in 1846 to Robert Chambers for the latter's *Cyclopedia*, makes no mention of the weather and, what is far more significant, does not refer to a particular evening at all.

Jeffrey had previously (1843) made it clear beyond all controversy that Sydney Smith was 'the original projector of the Edinburgh Review'.[3] Three years later he no longer singles him out:

'I cannot say exactly where the project of the Edinburgh Review was first talked of among the projectors. But the first serious consultations about it—and which led to our application to a publisher—were held in a small house, where I then lived, in Buccleuch Place (I forget the number). They were attended by S. Smith, F. Horner, Dr. Thomas Brown, Lord Murray (John Archibald Murray, a Scottish advocate, and now one of the Scottish judges) and some of them also by Lord Webb Seymour, Dr. John Thomson, and Thomas Thomson.'[4]

Jeffrey goes on to say that Smith was 'by far the most timid

[1] Henry Thomas Cockburn, Lord Cockburn, *Life of Lord Jeffrey, with a Selection rom his Correspondence* (Edinburgh, 1852), I, 125.

[2] Hesketh Pearson, *The Smith of Smiths* (London, 1934), 44.

[3] In the dedication and preface, dated 1813, of his *Contributions to the Edinburgh Review* (1st ed., London, 1844). Note Jeffrey's letter to Napier, September 30, 1843: 'I am just about finishing my grand republication, which I have resolved to dedicate to *Sydney*, as the true founder of the *Review*, and the only survivor (except Murray, who never did anything) of the original *conspirators*. I should not wonder if Brougham should resent its not being to *him*. But I don't care. He did not come in till after the third Number, and our assured success.' *Selection from the Correspondence of the late Macvey Napier, Esq.* (London, 1879), 433. Note also Smith's letter to Jeffrey, November 13, 1804: '. . . Constable has omitted to send quarterly tributes of reviews to Horner and to me;—to me, the original proposer of the Review, and to Horner, the frumentarious philosopher! . . .' Nowell C. Smith, ed., *The Letters of Sydney Smith* (Oxford, 1953), 100.

[4] *Chambers's Cyclopedia of English Literature* (4th rev. ed., London and Edinburgh, 1893), II, 385.

of our confederacy', insisting on secret conferences and conspiratorial tactics, and that it was due to Smith's dread of Brougham's indiscretion and rashness that the latter was not admitted to the association until after the third number, i.e. April, 1803.

How reliable are these four accounts? In what do they agree? What problems do they leave unsolved? The first thing to be noted is the fact that they were all supplied many years after the event, the earliest thirty-seven, the latest sixty-five. The unreliability of Brougham's *Life and Times* as a source is notorious and well documented.[1] Brougham's reputation rests neither on exemplary veracity nor on his capacity to suppress his ego, and he was almost ninety at the time he wrote his version of the story. But though they might be considered more trustworthy, and though much less time separated them from the event, it would be too much to expect accurate recall even from the others. It is clear from these frequently quoted accounts that Sydney Smith suggested the idea; that there was some discussion about it in Jeffrey's (three-storied) house in Buccleuch Place; that one of the discussions took place on a stormy evening; and that Smith performed some sort of editorial function for the first number or numbers. But several rather important questions still remain unanswered, and conflicting testimony makes it difficult to answer them. First, what was the date of the famous meeting? Smith simply refers to 'one day'; Brougham says 'March, 1802'; and neither Cockburn nor Jeffrey particularizes. And, whatever the date, was the meeting itself decisive? Cockburn justly remarks on the discrepancy between Smith's account, which makes it appear that the decision to begin the *Review* was a sudden and unpremeditated one—the by-product of a convivial evening—and Jeffrey's emphatic distinction between the first mention of the project (whose locale he cannot recall) and the 'serious consultations' which took place at his house.[2] Brougham indicates that by the time *he* heard about the project (i.e. March, 1802) Smith had already mentioned it to Jeffrey

---

[1] See Arthur Aspinall, 'Brougham's *Life and Times*', *English Historical Review*, LIX (January, 1944), 87–112. And note Brougham's own warning against mistakes made by 'persons reflecting backward from one period to another'. *Life and Times*, I, 16.

[2] *Chambers's Cyclopedia*, II, 385.

and Horner. This seems to solve one problem by making the meeting at Jeffrey's house less decisive than Smith's version would seem to indicate, but raises two others, one minor and one major:

The minor problem is that of Horner's suggested motto. For Smith, in his account, has left the impression that his 'oatmeal' suggestion was rejected at what he recalls as the crucial meeting; while Brougham, agreeing with Smith in not listing him as among those present on the 'stormy night', singles out 'the painstaking and solemn Horner who [was] as incapable of understanding a joke as Smith was of writing the *Principia*' as the person who rejected Smith's motto and 'discovered' a new one in Publius Syrus. It is fairly easy to resolve this matter, without taking away credit for lack of humour from the 'Knight of the Shaggy Eye-brows' (Smith's name for Horner). For Smith is evidently telescoping events that extended over a period of several days, if not weeks, into one evening. It is probable that he suggested his motto that evening; that it was then thought to be funny, but 'too near the truth to be admitted'; that Horner was informed of this, was decidedly not amused, and looked for another motto which, to use Brougham's word, he finally 'discovered'.

The major problem is not so easily settled. It concerns Brougham. Smith notes Brougham's presence at what he remembers to have been the founding meeting. Brougham himself, while admitting that Jeffrey and Horner had been notified beforehand, recalls in detail his own presence at the same meeting. Yet Jeffrey not only omits to mention Brougham's name among those who attended the first 'serious consultations', but adds that he was not admitted to the association until after the third number. This would seem to be patently untrue, since Brougham according to all scholarly estimates (not to speak of his own) wrote at least three and more probably six and a half articles for the first number of the *Edinburgh Review*.[1] Moreover, Jeffrey

[1] Brougham claims six articles of his own and one jointly with Jeffrey. (*Life and Times*, I, 258.) Cockburn states that four articles were 'commonly ascribed' to Brougham. (*Life of Jeffrey*, I, 131.) W. A. Copinger, in his *On the Authorship of the First Hundred Numbers of the Edinburgh Review* (Manchester, 1895), 2, ascribes two to Brougham and one jointly to Brougham and Smith. Arthur Aspinall's list in his *Lord Brougham and the Whig Party* (Manchester, 1939), 256, which was sup-

himself had written as follows to Francis Horner in April of 1802:

'Brougham must have a sentence to himself; and I am afraid you will not think it a pleasant one. You remember how cheerfully he approved of our plan at first, and agreed to give us an article or two without hesitation. Three or four days ago I proposed two or three books that I thought would suit him; he answered, with perfect good humour, that he had changed his view of our plan a little, and rather thought now that he should decline to have any connection with it.'[1]

In Brougham's own version of this incident[2] he states that the reason for his temporary secession at that time was the lack of an adequate guarantee that the sole and undivided management of the *Review* was to be in Jeffrey's hands, and quotes Horner's letter to Jeffrey of September 1, 1802—'Brougham is now an efficient and zealous member of the party'[3]—to show that once this guarantee had been secured he resumed his connection with the *Review*.

Is Brougham's account accurate? If so, why did Jeffrey make the statement that Brougham was not 'admitted' until later? A little-known account of the founding of the *Review* given by Smith to George Ticknor just a year before the former wrote his fuller version may throw some light on this issue. Ticknor notes in his journal that he breakfasted with Sydney Smith on April 2, 1838, that Smith told him that the *Edinburgh Review* was begun by Jeffrey, Horner, and himself, that he [Smith] was the first editor, and that 'they' [presumably the three he mentioned] were originally unwilling to give Brougham any direct influence over the *Review*, 'because he was so violent and unmanageable'.[4] Implicit here is a dichotomy between those who

plied to him by Harold Cox, the last editor of the *Edinburgh Review*, assigns three articles to Brougham. The latest estimate, in Elisabeth Schneider, Irwin Griggs, and John D. Kern, 'Brougham's Early Contributions to the Edinburgh Review: A New List', *Modern Philology*, XLII (1945), 158–159, tentatively assigns six and a half to Brougham, thus confirming his own statement.

[1] Jeffrey to Horner, April 9, 1802, *Memoirs and Correspondence of Francis Horner, M.P.*, ed. Leonard Horner (London, 1843), I, 186.

[2] *Life and Times*, I, 249–250.

[3] Cf. *Horner Memoirs*, I, 201.

[4] George Ticknor, *Life, Letters and Journals* (Boston and New York, 1909), II, 150.

had 'direct influence' over the *Review* and those who merely contributed. Two letters of Brougham's tend to confirm this hypothesis. In January, 1803, he writes:

'My first tome was nearly ready when that d—d, blasted, b—g, brutal *Review* stopped it for a whole calendar month. . . . I had to contribute (Oh! Nefas) a hundred pages of print, *tho' I am not one of the editors* [italics mine]—they gave their tens and twenties and I had literally to *write*, I may say, the whole. And then, to crown all, a supply came from an unexpected quarter and I had only 70 pages printed.'[1]

The second letter, already quoted in a previous chapter,[2] is dated June 27, 1803, and contains Brougham's self-justification (to Horner) in the matter of his threatened second withdrawal from the *Review* in the face of Sydney Smith's alleged persecution of himself. Here Brougham decisively confirms the fact that he first heard of the *Review* in March, 1802;[3] and quite definitely implies the existence of two groups of 'original' associates. For he reports to Horner that Jeffrey had assured him that 'Smith should be told in plain terms that from the beginning to the end I had as much the management *as if I had been formally considered one of the set*' [italics mine]. If this is what Jeffrey meant when he recalled that Brougham was not one of the 'association' until after the third number, it was perfectly consistent for him not to list Brougham among those who were involved in the 'serious consultations'. For this still makes allowance for Brougham's initial enthusiasm for the project (before the *serious* consultations began), the temporary break (whose causes Brougham has undoubtedly painted in a light too favourable to himself), and the reconciliation which led to his return as a contributor, though not as an associate until after his protest to Jeffrey in June, 1803.

Were the associates tantamount to editors? Smith, as we have seen, claims that he was *appointed* editor, a claim denied by Brougham who admits, however, that Smith may be said to have edited the first number. Jeffrey, we know, did not receive

---

[1] Brougham to James Loch, January 28, 1803, *Brougham and his Early Friends*, ed. R. H. M. Buddle Atkinson and G. A. Jackson (London, 1908), II, 32.

[2] See *ante*, pp. 61–62, Brougham to Horner, June 27, 1803, Horner Correspondence, L.S.E., II, 14.

[3] 'I need not add that from the beginning (in March, 1802) I had perceived the existence of certain exceptions against myself', etc.

a definite offer of the editorship from Constable and Longmans until after the third number had made its appearance, though he had apparently declined to a more informal offer some time before March, 1802. He himself states that the job was then pressed upon him, that up to that point there had been no individual editor, and that as many as could (of the associates) met in 'a dingy room of Willison's printing office, in Craig's Close', where they read proofs of articles and accepted a few manuscripts offered by strangers.[1]

Can these accounts be harmonized? Dr. L. H. Buckingham who went into this problem very thoroughly has concluded that there is no doubt that Smith served as editor, 'after a fashion', for the first and third numbers, though Jeffrey agreed to correct and criticize the contributions.[2] It was certainly Smith who made the publishing arrangements with Constable and Longmans, and who persuaded Constable to offer generous financial terms to the permanent editor and the contributors.[3] But two pieces of evidence tend to show that Jeffrey played an important part in the actual editing of the first three numbers, one that went beyond correction and criticism.[4] In August, 1802, two months before the appearance of No. I, he sent a letter of instructions to Constable, telling him to print the first five articles in a certain order. At the same time he asked him to 'put as much into a page as possible and send me a specimen by-and-bye that I may be able to calculate our riches'.[5] In another letter to Constable

---

[1] *Chambers's Cyclopedia*, II, 385.

[2] Leroy H. Buckingham, 'The Authorship of the First Twenty-five Numbers of the *Edinburgh Review* (1802–1808),' Yale Doctoral Dissertation (1938), 369–372.

[3] Cf. letter from Smith to Constable (n.d.), Thomas Constable, *Archibald Constable and his Literary Correspondents* (Edinburgh, 1873), I, 52–53; and Brougham, *Life and Times*, I, 254, where Smith is called 'quasi-editor'.

[4] This thesis finds support in David Welsh, *Account of the Life and Writings of Thomas Brown, M.A.* (Edinburgh, 1825), 506, where Welsh states that Jeffrey 'superintended the work from the very beginning'. The less reliable Brougham confirms this (*Life and Times*, I, 250) in recalling that by the summer of 1802 ample security had been received that Jeffrey was to have sole charge. In this connection note Smith's letter to Jeffrey, dated 'August, 1802', which deals at length with various strictures Jeffrey had made on Smith's contributions to the first number. *Smith Letters*, I, 72–74.

[5] *Notes and Queries*, Fourth Series, V (March 12, 1870), 273. The indicated order of articles—Mounier, Parr, Godwin, Olivier, Rennel—was observed in No. I of the *Edinburgh Review*, though one review was interpolated between Godwin and Olivier, and three between Olivier and Rennel.

simply dated 'Edinburgh, 1802', but evidently written before the first number, Jeffrey commented on the printing, asked whether Constable 'could . . . not afford us a little blacker ink', and told him to take care that Mounier's name (Mounier was the author of the first book reviewed in No. I) was spelled correctly—since a blunder of that sort in the first article would create a bad impression.[1]

These two letters, taken together with another to Lockhart Muirhead just before the third number went to press, in which Jeffrey writes that 'I know almost as little of this coming No. of our review as a woman does of the sex of her child a fortnight before her delivery',[2] indicate that in this early period Jeffrey merits the title of quasi-editor as much as Sydney Smith. The associates—Thomas Brown, J. A. Murray, Webb Seymour, John Thomson, and Thomas Thomson—undoubtedly helped to plan the first number, as Jeffrey suggests.[3] After that it is likely that there was a committee of editors consisting at least of Jeffrey, Smith, and Horner,[4] until Jeffrey who had already assumed, to some extent, the position of chairman of the committee was appointed *the* editor. Then Smith, Horner, and (eventually) Brougham came to constitute an inner circle of associates, more intimate and certainly more influential than the rather large number of original associates.

Original? Here the final question presents itself—for Jeffrey, in his account, distinguished between the 'projectors' whose first meeting he had forgotten and the 'confederacy' that had engaged in serious consultations at his house. Now it is clear that the projectors were Sydney Smith (who suggested the idea), Jeffrey, and Horner. Brougham admits this in saying that Jeffrey and Horner had been informed before *he* was. And in the founding account closest to the actual event—that of Horner—it is unequivocally stated. 'This Review was concerted', he writes in his Journal on September 30, 1802, 'about the end of last

---

[1] Constable Correspondence, National Library of Scotland, MS. 672, folio 42.

[2] Jeffrey to Lockhart Muirhead, March, 1803. Letter in Boulton and Watt Collection, Birmingham Reference Library, quoted in Buckingham, 'Authorship of the First Twenty-five Numbers of the *Edinburgh Review*', 303.

[3] Cf. *ante*, p. 189.

[4] Note again Brougham's statement in January, 1803, that he was not one of 'the editors'. Cf. *ante*, p. 193.

winter between Jeffrey, Sydney Smith, and myself. The plan was immediately communicated to Murray, Allen, and Hamilton; Brown, Brougham, and the two Thomsons have gradually been made parties.'[1]

Is it possible to determine the occasion of the 'very first meeting' more precisely? I think so. For Sydney Smith has left us a third version of the founding—one that assumes some significance since he gave it in 1810, only eight years after the event. At a dinner party Smith 'told Lady Glenbervie and me [Lord Glenbervie] some curious particulars of the Edinburgh Review. He says the design for it was first suggested by himself, at a tea-party in a small lodging of Jeffrey's in Buccleuch Place. The original set were there talking of different literary projects, when he said "Let us write a review." The idea immediately caught and the plan and arrangements were formed that very evening.'[2] Now it is, of course, possible that this 'tea-party' corresponds to Smith's much later reminiscence regarding the 'one day we happened to meet'. But, keeping in mind Horner's almost contemporary account and the undoubted fact that the *Review* was first suggested by Smith to Jeffrey and Horner, I should like to propose the following hypothesis as equally (if not more) credible:

There were two significant gatherings at Jeffrey's house at Buccleuch Place—one, that of March, 1802, recalled by Brougham, at which the idea was first presented to a larger group; the other the tea-party recalled by Smith in 1810 attended by the 'original set' of himself, Jeffrey, and Horner. It was the latter gathering which saw the real origin of the *Edinburgh Review*— but because the former was so much more dramatic and memorable, the two meetings, with the passage of time, became inextricably intermingled in the mind of Smith. This hypothesis not only clears up a great many puzzling discrepancies between various versions of the founding; it also helps to eliminate the serious problem of the exact date.

The first published mention of the *Edinburgh Review* that I have been able to find occurs in a letter of Jeffrey's to his cousin,

---

[1] *Horner Memoirs*, I, 202.
[2] Entry for March 8, 1810, *The Diaries of Sylvester Douglas, Baron Glenbervie*, ed. Francis Bickley (London, 1928), II, 58.

dated March 6, 1802. 'In the meanwhile,' Jeffrey writes, 'I hope that our Review will do something. We still expect to bring out the first Number on the 25th June, though there is not one of us, I believe, who has a single word of it written.' He goes on to say that the plan for the *Review* 'is pretty generally known now', and that he himself, though urged to accept the management, had declined to do so, since 'it would detach me a good deal from the duties of my profession, and interfere still more essentially with the opinion of my attention to them'.[1] This makes it quite clear that by early March, 1802, the project of the *Review* had already advanced considerably. We have seen that Horner, in September of 1802, recalled its beginning 'at the end of last winter'. And when Benjamin Silliman, during his visit to Edinburgh in 1806, obtained the story of the *Review*'s origin through the 'kind offices of a friend', he was told that it had been projected 'towards the end of the year 1801'.[2]

To sum up: the available evidence leads to the supposition that Sydney Smith first proposed the idea of the *Edinburgh Review* to Jeffrey and Horner while the three of them were discussing various literary projects late in 1801 or early in 1802. Some time in March the suggestion was taken up by a larger group, and Jeffrey's hesitations overridden. The principal editorial work on the first three numbers was carried out by Smith and Jeffrey, though Horner, as one of the three founders, retained throughout certain special prerogatives. Since he was in London from late March to early May (1802), he had less concern than did the other two with the editing of the first number in which various other associates—soon to become simply contributors—participated. However, Brougham alone was admitted to the inner circle of founding editors, though not until June, 1803, and not until he had previously been readmitted, after a temporary break, as a mere contributor. Jeffrey was appointed sole editor some time after the appearance of the third number. Brougham, Smith, and Horner, though all of them left Edinburgh for London, remained his closest and most powerful advisers.

[1] Jeffrey to Robert Morehead, March 6, 1802, Charles Morehead, ed., *Memorials of the Life and Writings of the Rev. Robert Morehead, D.D.* (Edinburgh, 1875), 111.

[2] Benjamin Silliman, 'Reminiscences' (typescript), Rare Books Room, Yale Library.

Bibliography

I. CONTEMPORARY MATERIALS

(A) *The Edinburgh Review.*
The Edinburgh Review, or Critical Journal, I through L (October, 1802–October, 1815).

(B) Manuscripts
Additional Manuscripts (Miscellaneous). British Museum.
Boulton and Watt Collection. Birmingham Reference Library, Birmingham.
Correspondence of Jeffrey. National Library of Scotland.
Correspondence and letter books of the House of Constable. National Library of Scotland.
Horner Collection. British Library of Political and Economic Science, London School of Economics.
Ledgers. Longmans, Green and Company, Ltd., London.
Mackintosh Papers. Wedgwood Archives, Barlaston.
Silliman Papers. Yale University Library, Rare Books Room.

(C) Pamphlets
[An Anti-Reformist] *A Letter to Francis Jeffrey, Esq., Editor of the Edinburgh Review.* Edinburgh, 1811.
[Boswell, Sir Alexander], *Epistle to the Edinburgh Reviewers.* Edinburgh, 1803.
Copleston, Edward, *Advice to a Young Reviewer, with a Specimen of the Art.* Oxford, 1807.
——, *A Second Reply to the Edinburgh Review and the Calumnies of that Review against Oxford.* Oxford, 1810.

Bibliography

'An Englishman', *Advice to the Whigs: with Hints to the Democrats and Cautions to the Edinburgh Reviewers*. London, 1810.

Expostulatory Letter to the Editor of the Edinburgh Review. London, 1809.

Jeffrey, Francis, *Observations on Mr. Thelwall's Letter to the Editor of the Edinburgh Review*. Edinburgh, 1804.

[Jeffrey, Francis, and John Gordon], *The Craniad: or Spurzheim Illustrated*. Edinburgh, 1817.

[Johnston, Edward], *A View of the Edinburgh Review Pointing Out the Spirit and Tendency of that Paper*. Edinburgh, 1756.

'Mentor', *The Dangers of the Edinburgh Review; or A Brief Exposure of its Principles in Religion, Morals, and Politics*. London, 1809.

Reform Bill Handbills and Broadsides. Edinburgh, 1832.

Ring, John, *The Beauties of the Edinburgh Review, Alias the Stinkpot of Literature*. London, 1807.

'Scipio, Cornelius', *A Sketch of the Politics of the Edinburgh Reviewers as Exhibited in their First Three Numbers for the Year 1807*. London, 1807.

'Senex', *A Letter to the Young Gentlemen Who Write in the Edinburgh Review*. London, 1808.

A Vindication of the Character of the Late Rt. Honourable William Pitt, from the Calumnies against him, Contained in the Fifth Article of the Edinburgh Review for April, 1810. Edinburgh, 1810.

Wharton, R[ichard], *Remarks on the Jacobinical Tendency of the Edinburgh Review*. 2nd ed., London, 1809.

(D) Newspapers and Periodicals

Annual Register.
Courier.
Critical Review.
Edinburgh Annual Register.
Monthly Magazine.
Monthly Review.
Morning Chronicle.
Political Register.
Quarterly Review.

Bibliography

(E) Works, Memoirs, Correspondence, etc.

Arnot, Hugo, *The History of Edinburgh to 1780*. Edinburgh, 1816.

Atkinson, R. H. M. Buddle, and G. A. Jackson, *Brougham and his Early Friends*. 3 vols. London, 1908.

Bentham, Jeremy, *The Works of Jeremy Bentham* (ed. Bowring). 11 vols. Edinburgh, 1843.

Bower, Alexander, *The History of the University of Edinburgh*. 3 vols. Edinburgh, 1817.

Brevoort, Henry, *Letters of Henry Brevoort to Washington Irving* (ed. G. S. Hellman). 2 vols. New York, 1916.

Brougham, Henry, 1st Baron Brougham and Vaux, *The Life and Times of Henry Lord Brougham, Written by Himself*. 3 vols. Edinburgh and London, 1871.

Carlyle, Alexander, *Autobiography of Alexander Carlyle 1722–1805*. London and Edinburgh, 1910.

Carlyle, Thomas, *Reminiscences* (ed. J. A. Froude). New York, 1881.

Cockburn, Henry Thomas, Lord Cockburn, *Life of Lord Jeffrey, with a Selection from His Correspondence*. 2 vols. Edinburgh, 1852.

——, *Memorials of His Time*. New ed. with introd. by Harry A. Cockburn. Edinburgh and London, 1910.

Coleridge, Samuel Taylor, *Biographia Literaria, Chapters I–IV, XIV–XXII. Wordsworth, Prefaces and Essays on Poetry, 1800–1815* (ed. George Sampson). Cambridge, 1920.

——, *The Letters of Samuel Taylor Coleridge* (ed. Ernest Hartley Coleridge). 2 vols. Boston and New York, 1895.

——, *Coleridge's Miscellaneous Criticism* (ed. Thomas Middleton Raysor). London, 1936.

Constable, Thomas, *Archibald Constable and His Literary Correspondents*. 3 vols. Edinburgh, 1873.

Copleston, Edward, *Remains of Edward Copleston* (ed. Richard Whately). London, 1854.

Crabbe, George, *The Life of George Crabbe by His Son*. World's Classics ed. London, 1932.

Creech, William, *Edinburgh Fugitive Pieces*. Edinburgh, 1815.

Bibliography

Creevey, Thomas, *Creevey's Life and Times: A Further Selection from the Correspondence of Thomas Creevey* (ed. John Gore). London, 1934.

——, *The Creevey Papers: A Selection from the Correspondence and Diaries of the Late Thomas Creevey, M.P.* (ed. Sir Herbert Maxwell). New York, 1904.

Cross, Maurice, ed., *Selections from the Edinburgh Review*. 6 vols. Paris, 1835.

Festing, Gabrielle, *John Hookham Frere and His Friends*. London, 1899.

Fletcher, Mrs., *Autobiography of Mrs. Fletcher* (ed. Lady Mary Richardson). Boston, 1876.

George IV, *The Letters of George IV* (ed. Arthur Aspinall). 3 vols. Cambridge, 1930.

Glenbervie, Sylvester Douglas Baron, *The Diaries of Sylvester Douglas Baron Glenbervie* (ed. Francis Bickley). 2 vols. London, 1928.

Grant, Mrs. [Anne], *Memoir and Correspondence of Mrs. [Anne] Grant of Laggan* (ed. J. P. Grant). 3 vols. London, 1845.

Granville, Granville Leveson-Gower, 1st Earl, *Private Correspondence, 1781–1821* (ed. Countess Granville). 2 vols. London, 1916.

Hazlitt, William, *The Spirit of the Age, or Contemporary Portraits* (ed. W. Carew Hazlitt). 4th ed. London and New York, 1894.

——, *Table Talk*. Everyman ed. London and New York, 1942.

Heseltine, G. C., 'Five Letters of Sydney Smith', *London Mercury*, XXI (1930), 512–517.

Historical Manuscripts Commission, *MSS of J. B. Fortescue* (Dropmore). 10 vols. London, 1892–1927.

——, *MSS. of the Earl of Lonsdale*. London, 1893.

Holland, Henry Richard Vassall Fox, 3rd Baron, *Further Memoirs of the Whig Party, 1807–1821* (ed. Lord Stavordale). London, 1905.

——, *Memoirs of the Whig Party During my Time* (ed. Henry Edward Lord Holland). 2 vols. London, 1852–1854.

Horner, Francis, *Memoirs and Correspondence of Francis Horner, M.P.* (ed. Leonard Horner). 2 vols. London, 1843.

Bibliography

Hume, David, *The Philosophical Works of David Hume* (ed. T. H. Green and T. H. Grose). 4 vols. London, 1898.

Hunt, Leigh, *The Autobiography of Leigh Hunt* (ed. J. E. Morpurgo). London, 1949.

[Innes, Cosmo], *Memoir of Thomas Thomson, Advocate*. Edinburgh, 1854.

Jeffrey, Francis, *Contributions to the Edinburgh Review*. 1st ed. 4 vols. London, 1844.

——, *Contributions to the Edinburgh Review*. 2nd ed. 3 vols. London, 1846.

——, *The Letters of Francis Jeffrey to Ugo Foscolo* (ed. J. Purves). Edinburgh and London, 1934.

Mackintosh, Sir James, *Miscellaneous Works*. New York, 1866.

Mill, John Stuart, *The Autobiography of John Stuart Mill*. 1st complete ed. New York, 1924.

Millar, John, *An Historical View of the English Government, from the Settlement of the Saxons in Britain to the Revolution in 1688*. 4 vols. London, 1803.

Minto, Sir Gilbert Elliot-Murray-Kynynmound, 1st Earl of, *Life and Letters of Sir Gilbert Elliot, First Earl of Minto, 1751–1806* (ed. Countess Minto). 3 vols. London, 1874.

——, *Lord Minto in India; Life and Letters of Lord Minto from 1807 to 1814* (ed. Countess Minto). London, 1880.

Moore, Thomas, *Memoirs, Journal and Correspondence of Thomas Moore* (ed. Lord John Russell). 8 vols. London, 1853–1856.

Morehead, Robert, *Memorials of the Life and Writings of the Rev. Robert Morehead, D.D.* (ed. Charles Morehead). Edinburgh, 1875.

Napier, Macvey, *Selection from the Correspondence of the Late Macvey Napier* (ed. Macvey Napier). London, 1879.

Ramsay of Ochtertyre, John, *Scotland and Scotsmen in the Eighteenth Century* (ed. Alexander Allardyce). 2 vols. Edinburgh and London, 1888.

Robertson, William, *The History of the Reign of the Emperor Charles V*. New ed. London, 1887.

Robinson, Henry Crabb, *Henry Crabb Robinson on Books and their Writers* (ed. Edith Morley). 3 vols. London, 1938.

Bibliography

Romilly, Sir Samuel, *The Life of Sir Samuel Romilly Written by Himself*. 3rd ed. 2 vols. London, 1842.

Scott, Sir Walter, *The Letters of Sir Walter Scott* (ed. Sir Herbert J. C. Grierson). 12 vols. London, 1932–1937.

——, *The Private Letter-Books of Sir Walter Scott* (ed. Wilfred Partington). London, 1930.

Sharpe, Charles Kirkpatrick, *Letters From and To Charles Kirkpatrick Sharpe*. 2 vols. Edinburgh and London, 1888.

[Simond, Louis], *Journal of a Tour and Residence in Great Britain During the Years 1810 and 1811*. 2 vols. New York, 1815.

Smiles, Samuel, *A Publisher and His Friends: Memoir and Correspondence of the Late John Murray*. 2 vols. London, 1891.

Smith, Adam, *An Inquiry into the Nature and Causes of the Wealth of Nations*. Cannan ed., Modern Library. New York, 1937.

Smith, Sydney, *The Letters of Sydney Smith* (ed. Nowell C. Smith). Oxford, 1953.

——, *The Works of the Rev. Sydney Smith*. 3 vols. in one. Boston, 1854.

Stewart, Dugald, *The Collected Works of Dugald Stewart* (ed. Sir William Hamilton). 10 vols. Edinburgh, 1854–1860.

Taylor, William, *A Memoir of the Life and Writings of the late William Taylor of Norwich* (ed. J. W. Robberds). 2 vols. London, 1843.

Ticknor, George, *Life, Letters, and Journals of George Ticknor*. 2 vols. Boston and New York, 1909.

Tytler, Alexander, Lord Woodhouselee, *Memoirs of the Life and Writings of the Honourable Henry Home of Kames*. 2nd ed. 3 vols. Edinburgh, 1814.

Welsh, David, *Account of the Life and Writings of Thomas Brown, M.A.* Edinburgh, 1825.

Windham, William, *Life and Correspondence of William Windham 1750–1810*. 2 vols. Boston, 1913.

——, *Diary of the Rt. Hon. William Windham 1784–1810* (ed. Mrs. Henry Baring). London, 1866.

Wodrow, Robert, *Analecta*, Maitland Club Publications. 4 vols. Edinburgh, 1842–1843.

Bibliography

II. LATER MATERIALS

(A) Reference Works

Census of British Newspapers and Periodicals 1620–1800 (ed. Ronald S. Crane and Frederick B. Kaye). Chapel Hill, N.C., 1927.

Chambers's Cyclopedia of English Literature. 4th ed., revised by Robert Chambers. 2 vols. London and Edinburgh, 1893.

Dictionary of National Biography (ed. Stephen and Lee). 23 vols. Oxford, 1921–1922.

(B) Periodicals

Edinburgh Review.
English Historical Review.
New Statesman and Nation.
Notes and Queries.
Quarterly Review.
Times Literary Supplement.

(C) Secondary Works
1. Articles

Aspinall, Arthur, 'Lord Brougham's *Life and Times*', *English Historical Review*, LIX (1944), 87–112.

Auden, W. H., 'Portrait of a Whig', *English Miscellany*, III (1952), 142–158.

Bald, R. C., 'Francis Jeffrey as a Literary Critic, *The Nineteenth Century and After*, XCVII (1925), 201–205.

Beatty, Joseph M., Jr., 'Lord Jeffrey and Wordsworth', *Publications of the Modern Language Association*, XXXVIII (1923), 221–235.

Blagden, Cyprian, '*Edinburgh Review* Authors, 1830–1849', *The Library*, Fifth Series, VII (1952), 212–214.

Charvat, William, 'Francis Jeffrey in America', *New England Quarterly*, XIV (1941), 309–334.

Clive, John, 'The Earl of Buchan's Kick: A Footnote to the History of the *Edinburgh Review*', *Harvard Library Bulletin*, V (1951), 362–370.

Bibliography

——, 'The *Edinburgh Review*: 150 Years After', *History Today*, II (December, 1952), 844–850.

Clive, John, and Bernard Bailyn, 'England's Cultural Provinces: Scotland and America', *The William and Mary Quarterly*, Third Series, XI (April, 1954), 200–213.

Cox, R. G., 'Homage to Common Sense', *Scrutiny*, XVI (1949), 169–172.

Daniel, Robert, 'Jeffrey and Wordsworth: The Shape of Persecution', *Sewanee Review*, L (1942), 195–213.

Derby, J. Raymond, 'The Paradox of Francis Jeffrey: Reason Versus Sensibility', *Modern Language Quarterly*, VII (1946), 489–500.

Fetter, Frank W., 'The Authorship of Economic Articles in the *Edinburgh Review*, 1802–1847', *The Journal of Political Economy*, LXI (June, 1953), 232–259.

——, 'The Bullion Report Reexamined', *Quarterly Journal of Economics*, LVI (1941–1942), 655–665.

Griggs, Irwin, John D. Kern, and Elisabeth Schneider, 'Brougham's Early Contributions to the *Edinburgh Review*: A New List', *Modern Philology*, XLII (1945), 152–173.

——, 'Early Edinburgh Reviewers: A New List', *Modern Philology*, XLIII (1946), 192–210.

Guyer, Byron, 'Francis Jeffrey's *Essay on Beauty*', *Huntington Library Quarterly*, XII (1949–1950), 71–85.

——, 'The Philosophy of Francis Jeffrey', *Modern Language Quarterly*, XL (1950), 17–26.

Hughes, Merritt Y., 'The Humanism of Francis Jeffrey', *Modern Language Review*, XVI (1921), 243–251.

Lovejoy, Arthur O., 'The Meaning of Romanticism for the Historian of Ideas', *Journal of the History of Ideas*, II (1941), 257–278.

Pascal, Roy, 'Property and Society: The Scottish Historical School of the 18th Century', *Modern Quarterly*, I (1938), 167–179.

——, 'Herder and the Scottish Historical School', *English Goethe Society Publications*, New Series, XIV (1938–1939), 23–42.

Bibliography

Silberling, Norman J., 'Financial and Monetary Policy in Great Britain During the Napoleonic Wars', *Quarterly Journal of Economics*, XXXVIII (1924), 214–233, 397–439.

Welker, John J., 'The Position of the Quarterlies on Some Classical Dogmas', *Studies in Philology*, XXXVII (1940), 542–562.

Wellek, René, 'The Concept of "Romanticism" in Literary History', *Comparative Literature*, I (1949), 1–23, 147–172.

2. Historical Works

Adam, Sir Charles Elphinstone, *View of the Political State of Scotland in the Last Century*. Edinburgh, 1887.

Brown, Philip Anthony, *The French Revolution in English History*. London, 1923.

Bryant, Arthur, *Years of Victory (1802–1812)*. New York and London, 1945.

Craik, Sir Henry, *A Century of Scottish History*. 2 vols. Edinburgh and London, 1901.

Davis, Henry W. C., *The Age of Grey and Peel*. Oxford, 1929.

Feiling, Keith, *History of England*. London, 1950.

——, *The Second Tory Party, 1714–1832*. London, 1938.

Graham, Henry Grey, *The Social Life of Scotland in the Eighteenth Century*. 4th ed., London, 1937.

Guttridge, George H., *English Whiggism and the American Revolution*. Berkeley and Los Angeles, 1942.

Halévy, Elie, *England in 1815*. 2nd rev. ed. London, 1949.

Mackinnon, James, *The Social and Industrial History of Scotland*. London, 1921.

Mathieson, William Law, *The Awakening of Scotland, a History from 1747–1797*. Glasgow, 1910.

Meikle, Henry W., *Scotland and the French Revolution*. Glasgow, 1912.

Namier, Sir Lewis B., *England in the Age of the American Revolution*. London, 1930.

Philips, C. H., *The East India Company, 1784–1834*. Manchester, 1940.

Porritt, Edward, *The Unreformed House of Commons*. 2 vols. London, 1909.

Bibliography

Pryde, G. S., ed., *The Treaty of Union of Scotland and England.* London and Edinburgh, 1950.

Rait, Robert, and George S. Pryde, *Scotland.* London, 1934.

Roberts, Michael, *The Whig Party, 1807–1812.* London, 1939.

Smart, William, *Economic Annals of the Nineteenth Century, 1801–1820.* London, 1910.

Trevelyan, George M., *Lord Grey and the Reform Bill.* New York and London, 1920.

3. Biographies

Aspinall, Arthur, *Lord Brougham and the Whig Party.* Manchester, 1927.

Bain, Alexander, *James Mill.* London, 1882.

Bullett, Gerald, *Sydney Smith: A Biography and Selection.* London, 1951.

Burdett, Osbert, *The Rev. Sydney Smith.* London, 1934.

Elsner, Richard, *Francis Jeffrey, der Hauptbegründer der Edinburgh Review und seine kritischen Prinzipien.* Berlin, 1908.

Furber, Holden, *Henry Dundas, First Viscount Melville.* London, 1931.

Garratt, Geoffrey T., *Lord Brougham.* London, 1935.

Gibson, Andrew, *New Light on Allan Ramsay.* Edinburgh, 1927.

Greig, James A., *Francis Jeffrey of the Edinburgh Review.* Edinburgh and London, 1948.

Hecht, Hans, *Robert Burns: The Man and His Work.* 2nd rev. ed. Glasgow and Edinburgh, 1950.

Jones, Howard Mumford, *The Harp that Once. A Chronicle of the Life of Thomas Moore.* New York, 1937.

Keynes, John Maynard, *Essays in Biography.* New ed. London, 1951.

Knutsford, M. F. Holland Viscountess, *Life and Letters of Zachary Macaulay.* London, 1900.

Lochhead, Marion, *John Gibson Lockhart.* London, 1954.

Pearson, Hesketh, *The Smith of Smiths,* London, 1934.

Reid, Stuart J., *A Sketch of the Life and Times of the Rev. Sydney Smith.* New York, 1885.

Reith, John, *Life of Dr. John Leyden.* Galashiels, 1923.

Russell, G. W. E., *Sydney Smith*. English Men of Letters
    Series. London, 1905.
Scott, William Robert, *Francis Hutcheson*. Cambridge, 1900.
Taylor, James, *Lord Jeffrey and Craigcrook*. Edinburgh, 1892.

4. Dissertations

Buckingham, Leroy H., 'The Authorship of the First Twenty-
    five Numbers of the *Edinburgh Review*, 1802–1808',
    Yale Doctoral Dissertation, 1938.
Derby, J. Raymond, 'Francis Jeffrey as a Literary Critic',
    Harvard Doctoral Dissertation, 1929.

5. Other Works

Aspinall, Arthur, *Politics and the Press*. London, 1949.
Bagehot, Walter, *Literary Studies*. Everyman ed., 2 vols. Lon-
    don, 1911.
Bate, Walter Jackson, *From Classic to Romantic*. Cambridge,
    Mass., 1946.
Brinton, Crane, *English Political Thought in the Nineteenth Cen-
    tury*. New ed. Cambridge, Mass., 1949.
——, *The Political Ideas of the English Romanticists*. Oxford, 1926.
Bryson, Gladys, *Man and Society: The Scottish Inquiry of the
    Eighteenth Century*. Princeton, 1945.
Collins, Arthur S., *The Profession of Letters: A Study of the
    Relation of Author to Patron, Publisher and Public*.
    London, 1928.
Copinger, W. A., *On the Authorship of the First Hundred Num-
    bers of the Edinburgh Review*. Manchester, 1895.
Craig, Mary Elizabeth, *The Scottish Periodical Press, 1750–
    1789*. Edinburgh and London, 1931.
Dalzel, Andrew, *History of the University of Edinburgh from
    Its Foundation*. 2 vols. Edinburgh, 1862.
Dickson, William K., *The History of the Speculative Society,
    1764–1904*. Edinburgh, 1905.
Eliot, T. S., *The Use of Poetry and the Use of Criticism*. London,
    1933.
Gates, Lewis E., *Three Studies in Literature*. New York, 1899.
Graham, Henry Grey, *Scottish Men of Letters in the Eighteenth
    Century*. London, 1901.

Bibliography

Graham, Walter, *English Literary Periodicals*. New York, 1930.

——, *Tory Criticism in the Quarterly Review, 1809–1853*. New York, 1921.

Grant, Alexander, *The Story of the University of Edinburgh During Its First Three Hundred Years*. 2 vols. London, 1884.

Green, Frederick C., *Stendhal*. Cambridge, 1939.

Grierson, Sir Herbert J. C., *Sir Walter Scott, Bart*. London, 1938.

Gunnell, Doris, *Stendhal et l'Angleterre*. Paris, 1909.

Halévy, Elie, *The Growth of Philosophic Radicalism*. (Tr. Mary Morris.) London, 1934.

History of the Dialectic Society. Edinburgh, 1887.

Ilchester, Giles Stephen Fox-Strangways, 6th Earl of, *The Home of the Hollands, 1605–1820*. London, 1937.

Kay, John, *A Series of Original Portraits and Caricature Etchings . . . with Biographical Sketches and Illustrative Anecdotes*. 2 vols. Edinburgh, 1878.

Klingberg, Frank J., *The Anti-Slavery Movement in England*. Yale Historical Publications, Miscellany: XVII. New Haven, 1926.

Levin, Harry, *Toward Stendhal*, 'Pharos', No. 3. Murray, Utah, 1945.

Esbitt, George L., *Benthamite Reviewing: The First Twelve Years of the Westminster Review*. New York, 1934.

Noyes, Russell, *Wordsworth and Jeffrey in Controversy*. Indiana University Publications, Humanities Series No. 5. Bloomington, Indiana, 1941.

Peacock, Markham L., Jr., *The Critical Opinions of William Wordsworth*. Baltimore, 1950.

Read, Herbert, *Wordsworth*. London and Toronto, 1930.

Saintsbury, George, *Essays in English Literature, 1780–1860*. London, 1890.

——, *A History of Criticism and Literary Taste in Europe*. 4th ed. 3 vols. Edinburgh and London, 1923.

Saville, John, ed., *Democracy and the Labour Movement*. London, 1954.

Sperry, Willard L., *Wordsworth's Anti-Climax*. Cambridge, Mass., 1935.

Bibliography

Schmitt, Carl, *Politische Romantik*. 2nd ed. Munich and Berlin, 1925.

Smith, David Nichol, ed., *Jeffrey's Literary Criticism*. London, 1910.

Smith, Elsie, *An Estimate of Wordsworth by His Contemporaries, 1793–1822*. Oxford, 1932.

Stephen, Leslie, *English Literature and Society in the Eighteenth Century*. London, 1904.

——, *The English Utilitarians*. 3 vols. London, 1900.

——, *History of English Thought in the Eighteenth Century*. 3rd ed. 2 vols. New York, 1927.

——, *Hours in a Library*. New ed., with additions. 4 vols. London, 1907.

Wellek, René, *A History of Modern Criticism, 1750–1950*. 2 vols. published. New Haven, 1955.

Index

Abbreviations used: *ER* for *Edinburgh Review*; fn for footnote.
For topics dealt with by *ER* see under '*ER* on:'.

211

Index

Index

Easy Club (Edinburgh), 20

Edgeworth, Maria, 145

Edinburgh, 17, 18, 20, 23, 24, 84, 85, 96, 134, 182, 187

Edinburgh Review (1755–1756), 19

Edinburgh Review and Critical Journal:

History of: first appearance, 17, 30; founding, 21–2, 25–26, 186–97; motto, 26, 191; price, 30, 135; first sales, 30, 30 fn; effect of first appearance, 30, 40; anonymity of reviewers, 32, 34; remuneration rates, 33, 34; advertisement for first issue, 35; moderate political tone of first number, 37; novelty of reviewing technique, 37; form of articles, 53–4; educational function, 54–5; politics, 65–7; as seen by principal contributors, 86–7; political line, 93, 95, 109, 113, 120–3; influence on British economic thought and practice, 124; influence, 133, 181, 183–4; circulation, 133–135; Longmans sells London rights (1807), 135 fn; Longmans repurchases London rights (1814), 135 fn; class and status of readers, 136–50

ER on: Abolitionists, 66; annuitants, 143; anti-Jacobinism, 96; aristocracy, 140–1; army commissions, sale of, 92; balance of power, 102, 104; Catholic Emancipation, 58, 66, 90–1; Chinese civilization, 167–8; Christianity, 178; civilization, stages of, 137, 173–5, 179, 182; civilization, virtues of, 167; Coleridge, 164; common sense, 91, 149; Constitution, balance of, 119; Constitution, theory of, 104–6; corn bounties, 130; Crabbe, 161; Crown, influence of, 180; culture and class structure, 174–5; decline, 173–5; democracy, 110–11, 114; division of labour, 138, 169, 174, 175, 182; East India Company, 129–30; education, 136–7, 145, 174; Egyptian civilization, 168; eighteenth century, 177; England, superiority of, 171; financial policy, 126–7; flogging in British Army and Navy, 92; free trade, 128–9; French Enlightenment, 97–98; French military power, 100; French Revolution, 95–97, 98, 99, 104, 122, 177; gentry, 139–40; government as causative force in history, 178–9; history, causation in, 177–9; history, definition and study of, 176; history, moral judgments in, 176–7; House of Commons, 105–6; import restrictions, 130; Indian civilization, 168; Lapland, civilization of, 168; legal reform, 92, 93; literature and society, 164, 169, 174, 175, 178, 182; 'lower orders', 138–9; Malthusian doctrine, 131–2; merchants,

Index

141–2; Methodism, 90, 149; Middle Ages, 177, 178; middle class, 142–5, 160–1, 179, 180, 182; missionaries, 149; morality, 148–9; morality of lower classes, 139; morality of middle class, 143–5; morality of upper classes, 141; Napoleon, 99; Orders in Council, 103; parliamentary reform, 111, 114–15, 117, 118; peace with France, 99–102; peasantry, 138, 139; Peninsular War, 115; Pitt, 88; Pittite persecutions of Scottish reformers, 96; poor relief, 131–2; present age, 171; power of press, 179; prison reform, 92; progress, 170–2; public opinion, 104, 163, 179; Reformation, 177; Renaissance, 171, 177; Restoration (of Charles II), 177; Revolution of 1688, 177; Romanticism, 152, 153, 151–65 *passim*; Santo Domingo, independent negro republic of, 87; slave trade, 87–9; slavery, 88; Southey, 164; Spanish Revolt, 110–111, 118; Test and Corporation Acts, 92; Tory Party, 90, 180; Tudor England, 177; United States of America, 103, 168–9; Utilitarianism, 92–5; wealth, effects of diffusion of, 137, 141, 149, 169, 174, 175; Whig need for popular alliance, 116; Wordsworth, 160–1, 163–4; working class, 137, 174, 175,

182. *See also:* Brougham, views on; *Edinburgh* reviewers; Horner, views on; Jeffrey, views on; Smith, Sydney, views on
Edinburgh reviewers: popular at Holland House, 79 fn; want to reform existing evils, 87; function as seen by themselves, 89, 91, 184; method of argument, 90, 166–7; on French Revolution, 95–6; aware of pedagogical role, 121; and classical economics, 132–3; attitude towards various social classes, 145–6; social position, 146–8; moralism, 148–9; religious views, 149–50; vantage point, 170; on historical causation, 178–9; their ordered world view, 182; role played by chance in reviews, 183
Edinburgh University, 21, 36
Egypt, 173
Eldon, John Scott, first Earl of, 71, 87, 92
Eliot, Thomas Stearns, 152
Elizabeth (Queen), 177
Elliot, Hon. A. M., 44
Ellis, George, 113
England, 76, 103, 147, 171. *See also* Britain
English Bards and Scotch Reviewers (Byron), 49 fn
Erskine, Henry, 23, 24, 37, 84
Esprit des Lois (Montesquieu), 136
État de l' Europe (Gentz), 102
Eton (College of), 181
Europe, 99, 170, 172, 175
Evangelicalism, 132, 150. *See also* Methodism

215

Index

Index

Index

Index

Index

223